THE LANGUAGE OF MEN

Anthony D'Aries

HUDSON WHITMAN
EXCELSIOR COLLEGE PRESS
ALBANY • NEW YORK

Published in the United States by
Hudson Whitman/ Excelsior College Press
7 Columbia Circle, Albany, NY 12203
www.hudsonwhitman.com

———

The Language of Men draws on material from the following
previously published essays by Anthony D'Aries:

"Exhausted"
Motif, Volume 3: All the Livelong Day: An Anthology of
Writings about Work (Motes Books, 2011)

"The Language of Men"
The Literary Review, Spring 2011, Vol. 54 / No. 03

"Chalk"
Solstice: A Magazine of Diverse Voices, Fall/Winter 2010-11
(This essay also appeared in Tarnished: True Tales of Innocence Lost. Pinchback Press, 2011)

———

Lyrics from *Try A Little Tenderness*
Words & Music by Harry Woods, James Campbell & Reginald Connelly
© Copyright 1932 & 1960 Campbell Connelly & Company Limited.
All rights for the USA and Canada assigned to EMI Robbins Catalog, Inc.
All Rights Reserved. International Copyright Secured. Used by permission.

Lyrics from *Piece of My Heart*
Written By Jerry Ragovoy and Bert Russell.
Published by Sloopy II Music, Sony ATV Songs LLC and Unichappell Music Inc.
All Rights Reserved. Used by permission.

———

Book design by Melissa Mykal Batalin
Cover Design by Phil Pascuzzo

LIBRARY OF CONGRESS CATALOGING-IN-PUBLICATION DATA
D'Aries, Anthony, 1982-
The Language of Men: a memoir / Anthony D'Aries

LCCN: 2012936319
ISBN 978-0-9768813-2-2 (hardcover)
ISBN 978-0-9768813-3-9 (paperback)

1. D'Aries, Anthony, 1982- 2. D'Aries, Anthony - Memoir
3. D'Aries, Anthony - Father-son relationships 4. D'Aries, Anthony - Vietnam
5. D'Aries, Anthony - Gender and masculinity studies

FIRST EDITION

For Vanessa,
for us

"It's a life's work to see yourself
for what you really are and
even then you might be wrong."

— Cormac McCarthy,
No Country for Old Men

I

IN COUNTRY

Buddy of mine, this black dude, Waller. We were cool, but not always. Whole different time, boy. If we were alone, we were cool. But when he was with the brothas, doin' that hand jive shit, he looked the other way. Don't mean nothin' cuz I did the same.

One day we stole a case of dehydrated applesauce from the mess hall and took it down to Saigon. The road was blown to hell by then, moon-sized craters, like we were drivin' over Jackie Gleason's face. Dudes used to warn us about little Vietnamese kids on the roads. "They'll fill old soda cans with shit and throw 'em at ya." *But we didn't see any kids that day.*

'Bout an hour ride and I was bustin' Waller's balls about James Brown the whole way. He was all into The Godfather of Soul and I was yellin' how Brown's sweaty ass wasn't nothin' next to Otis Redding. Monterey Pop Festival. Can't beat it. But Waller was stubborn, man. I tell ya.

So we pulled into the center of Saigon, right outside the Hotel de Ville. Dropped the tailgate and slid out the applesauce. It came in these lil' silver cans, no labels. Some mama- and papasans started shufflin' over and once we held up the cans they were on us like giant moths.

"Ladies and gentlemen. Number one fish for sale. Only five dollars."

You could say whatever you wanted.

"Act now, zipperhead. These prices are INSANE!"

It didn't matter. We had it; they wanted it.

Saw one poor old bastard bangin' a can against the curb: "Hey, papasan. You break it, you bought it."

We didn't trust no one, but they were throwin' money at us, grab-bin' handfuls of these silver cans. Mostly our money, too. We sold out in double time and hopped back in the jeep. Took the scenic route home.

We didn't wanna stop cuz once you did, it felt like somebody dropped a hot washcloth over your mouth. So we kept drivin', and Waller was screamin' "I Feel Good," *but I sure wasn't. Told him I never felt good when he was singin' and then I started in on Redding's* "Mr. Pitiful" *and Waller said,* "You got dat right."

The Beatles had just come out with Let It Be. *You know the album. You or your brother got my copy stashed 'round here somewheres, I know. I took my cut of the applesauce money and bought that and a bunch of shit at the PX. Waller hated The Beatles, friggin' hated 'em, so I listened to the whole album over and over by myself, until my shift.*

I was the night baker, and that was the first time I ever made doughnuts. Mixed the dough up in this giant vat, rolled it out, cut the rings with an empty soup can, punched out the holes with a salt shaker and shoved 'em in the oven. This sergeant came over and asked me what the hell I was doin'.

"Making doughnuts." *Though I probably said,* "Making dough-nuts, sir," *or some shit like that. And he goes,* "You're supposed to fry 'em, you dumb spoon." *They were always callin' us "spoons."*

Hey, hold the phone. You steal my silver dollar, boy?

Wait, I got it. Sittin' on it. Had this since before Vietnam, went to Vietnam and came back with me. Feel how smooth the edges are. My old man used to do the same thing, 'cept his looked like a quarter by the time he died. Mine ain't that thin yet.

|

MY FATHER speaks his own language. A hillbilly twang of the Looney Tunes dialect—Foghorn Leghorn, Yosemite Sam—mixed with the African-American jive of the dirtiest comedians—Redd Foxx or Richard Pryor. His swearing is part of a well-oiled machine, except when a driver cuts him off—then higher-octane terms explode from his mouth. He cuts words in half, stresses whichever syllable he wants. Verbs become nouns and vice versa. He throws in song lyrics, movie quotes, even slogans from TV commercials. It all swirls together and all you can do is try to keep up.

I tried. Sometimes we could speak at his pace. Other times, he'd lose me on a *Sanford and Son* reference, and our dialogue became a one-man show.

"I don't know where he got that pig language from," my grandmother says. "None of the other boys talk like that."

He gave all of my mother's sisters and my female cousins flirty, construction-worker-on-a-coffee-break nicknames: baby, suga', sweets, momma, girl, honey. He calls my wife, Vanessa, "Van Halen," and when he met my brother's girlfriend, Lola, he spelled out her name, just like The Kinks.

In a letter to my mother from Vietnam, written in his scratchy mish-mash of upper and lower case letters, he called her "his little girl" and said "let's not go spoiling this by telling Maddy." Maddy being his fiancée at the time. He asked her, "Can you dig it? You gotta be jivin' me. Hold on, momma, I'm comin' home soon."

He is perverted, but in a way that no one in our family seems to mind. He can pinch his sister-in-law's ass or make a sly comment about the perkiness of her breasts and it doesn't seem to offend anyone. That's the reputation he's established, and the one we've all come to expect.

As a kid, I would hear snippets of my father's language everywhere: Other men on the sidelines of my soccer or football games, burly attendants at the Hess station around the corner from our house, and the slick or heroic guys in mob and war movies on HBO. Though none of these characters spoke exactly like my father, they shared similar phrases: *My old lady's bustin' my stones. Six'a one, half'a dozen of the other. Union's gonna screw the part-timers outta bennies.* I often wished I had a guide book, a Father-to-Son pocket translator, that could define these foreign terms.

For Christmas one year, he made a t-shirt for my cousin, Shannon, who was working as a stewardess at the time. She unfolded the tissue paper and read the front of the shirt while it was still in the box, while my father threw up his hands proclaiming his innocence. Shaking her head, she held it up for all to see: *Stewardesses Always Stay Face Down in the Cockpit.* When I found this scene in one of our old home movies, I watched my ten-year-old self stare at my father, then the shirt, then back to my father, wondering where his ideas came from.

I was twenty when my father had his second stroke. Of course, I didn't know it was his second. The first one had occurred two weeks earlier, on his way to the hardware store with his friend Bobby Haggemeyer. As they idled at a light, he felt the tip of his tongue disappear, a cold stream of drool on his forearm. He couldn't move his lips, form any words, make any sounds. Bobby asked him what was happening. My father rummaged through the glove box for a piece of paper and a pencil. He scribbled a question mark and handed the paper to Bobby.

Halfway to the hospital, his speech returned. He told Bobby to take him home.

The second time, the cold puddle of drool woke him in the middle of the night. He shuffled to the bathroom to examine his face. He looked like he had a fishhook in the left corner of his mouth, as if

God were reeling him in like a bluefish. In the shower, he held his lips to the warm water, but nothing changed. He got out, dried off, and stuck a Winston between his teeth.

On his way to work, he sipped his coffee and it dribbled down his face, onto his lap, and though his hand and leg said the coffee was hot, the left side of his face heard nothing. He was pale when he got to Waldbaum's supermarket. A couple of his co-workers helped him to a bench. He said he just needed some air. They called an ambulance.

Hospitals were his pit stop, a body shop where, every ten thousand miles or so, they pulled him in and threw him up on the lift. Each procedure a quick fix, and as soon as the doctors said he could leave, he tore off his gown, threw on his jeans, knotted his white Waldbaum's apron, laced up his Reeboks, bought a 7-Eleven coffee and a pack of Winstons, and gunned his Chevy pickup into traffic, merging onto the Long Island Expressway until he was indistinguishable from the other commuters. He told us it was no big deal, leaving out or not remembering or just plain never hearing the doctor's diagnoses and recommended treatment.

When he had his varicose veins removed, he couldn't remember why the doctor told him the veins were collapsing or what the name of his new daily medication was. But my father described the veins themselves in detail: how, from his perspective on the operating table, he saw the doctor pulling and pulling a ropey, tangled mess. *Like an eaten cassette tape, boy. God damn.*

His mouth and tongue repaired themselves. His voice returned. Sometimes, though, when he's tired, his speech starts to slur and he moves his mouth like a horse. Soon after the second stroke, I bought a tape recorder and started asking questions.

When I interviewed my father about Vietnam, he twirled his silver dollar in his fingers and told me about a girl in Saigon — *she was kinda like my girlfriend.* The first time he was in her house, in her room, her whole family was sitting in the dining room. After he came out, they served him *pho*, a spicy soup, and my father listened to their strange chatter as he gulped down large spoonfuls.

Before his second visit, he used his GI discount to purchase an iron from the PX. Then he brought her a television. After that, a can of peaches. He'd walk to her home with his duffle bag slung over his shoulder like a Santa Claus in camouflage.

"It wasn't love," he said. "She took the shit I brought and gave it to her family." The silver dollar froze in his fingertips, and for the first time during the interview, he looked me square in the face.

"After a while it was like: Who's screwin' who here?"

In January 2007, I visited my father's mother at her apartment in West Babylon, New York. I had written her a letter several months earlier, explaining that I was working on a book about my father's experiences in the Vietnam War and asking if she'd be willing to answer some of my questions. "Sure," she wrote back. No hesitation, no questions about why I wanted to know these things. All she asked was what I would like to eat.

I walked down the concrete steps to the door of my grandmother's basement apartment. She poked her head of white hair around the corner, cinched her robe at the neck, and shimmied down the hallway. She had that spry, frantic energy old women sometimes have, as if someone is always chasing them. She kissed me, pulled me inside, and locked the door.

Ushering me into the kitchen, she fiddled with her hearing aid, asked if I wanted something to eat, something to drink. She told me to sit, please sit, on a white vinyl chair at the kitchen table. In a skinny wooden box beside me was a clear folder containing a list of phone numbers. *In case of death, call those checked.*

The cuckoo clock ticked above my head. I remembered that clock from her farmhouse in Mattituck, where she cooked me pizza on an English muffin. I'd stand on a chair so I could reach the hands of the clock, wind them around and around until the bird popped out of his house. Or sometimes I'd just stop time and wait for her to notice. She never seemed to mind.

Once she settled at the table, she pulled a narrow piece of stationary out from the soft pocket of her robe. The stationary had a border of bright sunflowers which framed her neat script. Only three or four items on her shopping list of memories:

Would I ever see him again?
Come back safe and sound.
Grandpa didn't say much.

"All I remember," she began. But very soon after telling me what she remembered about Vietnam—what she thought when they took my father to the airport, what she said to him, what my grandfather didn't say—she continued to talk for over an hour about her four bookkeeping jobs. One had been above a beauty parlor and she'd run upstairs, her hair heavy with dye, to balance the books of an asphalt company. I was tempted to stop her, to tell her I came here for a story about my father, a tale no one in our family knew. But then we were talking about her promiscuous old neighbor, the one who had affairs with the mailman, how my grandmother knocked on her door once and told her, "What you do in there is your business, but I want my mail." She told me how she opened bills and flipped through circulars, how she sat by the living room window, wondering when my grandfather would return from his nightshift as an airplane mechanic, and how, sometimes, he didn't come home.

I tried to steer the conversation back to Vietnam. "Did you and Grandpa talk about the war after Dad left?"

"We never talked about anything," she said. "He hardly said anything to me. Like your father."

"Dad talks all the time, Gram," I said. I didn't like the way she lumped my father in the same category as my grandfather, a man who seemed much more imposing than my father. But she didn't seem to hear me. She picked at her palm as if she were digging out a splinter.

"You know, I was trying to think if Grandpa ever told me he loved me."

"He must have," I said.

She shrugged. "If he did, I never heard it."

2

WHEN I TOLD my parents Vanessa and I were going to Vietnam, their eyes widened. As the trip got closer, I talked to them about where we planned to stay, what sites we wanted to see, which restaurants we were going to visit. These conversations usually began like any other about a vacation; my parents were curious and excited for us. But at some point, there was a shift in tone. My mother's lips tightened; her forehead furrowed. My father shook his head.

They never asked me why I was going, which was a relief. I don't know what I would have said. I was between jobs. In a way, I was always between jobs, each temporary position the agency found for me only lasting a couple of weeks or months, if I was lucky. But it was tough to feel lucky while sitting in a cubicle, scrolling through Excel sheets for Liberty Mutual or three-hole-punching documents and organizing them into binders for MetLife's legal department. In six months, I had acquired a stack of ID cards, each one displaying my picture and job title: TEMP.

Vanessa was entering the final semester of her public health program, which meant she had to start developing her thesis. Her work focused on women's sexual health and reproductive rights. She had lived and worked in Namibia, Tanzania, South Africa. Sometimes my father asked her about her experiences. He wanted to know if the "brothas" had running water or what they ate besides grilled monkey paws.

"Dude," I said, shaking my head.

"I say something wrong?" He looked at me, then Vanessa. She smiled and told him that the people ate a few other things.

Vanessa knew I was writing about my father's time in Vietnam, so when her advisor asked her if she would be interested in leading health and anatomy classes for sex workers in Ho Chi Minh City, Vanessa agreed. Her program would cover most of the expenses, and I was able to piece together a few additional temp jobs before we left. Within a couple of weeks, we found someone to sublet our apartment in Boston. After days of photocopying pages of legal jargon, I'd linger in the travel sections of bookstores, thumbing through Vietnamese dictionaries.

The timing was perfect. I had asked my father all my questions and yet I didn't have any answers. I had stories. Bits and pieces of scenes and dialogue, but that wasn't enough. There was some other reason I wanted to go to Vietnam, some purpose I could not name: a desire to stand on the ground I'd seen only in my father's old photographs, listen to his recorded voice talk about Long Binh and Saigon and applesauce, and try to match his audio picture with the actual landscape. My father didn't live in history books or yellowed newspapers at the public library. He didn't keep a journal I could stumble upon in our attic. Scrapbooking didn't exactly fit into his routine.

My mother told me when my father was in Vietnam his personality was "amplified."

"Like Dad now, times a thousand."

I needed to splice the dialogue of the nineteen-year-old kid in his hooch with the fifty-five-year-old man speaking into my recorder. There was too much dead air in our conversation. I wanted to bring it back to life.

My mother suggested that Vanessa and I have lunch with my great aunt and uncle. She said he had served in the Vietnam War and now he goes back every year to teach. I couldn't remember if I'd met them before—my mother's side a forest of "greats" and "seconds"—but they clearly knew who I was. My uncle stood in the doorway and waved us in, then promptly began the tour of his home, which he narrated in quick declarative statements: *This is the guest bedroom. This is the master bedroom. This is the commode.* He told us that when he was fourteen, he used his older brother's birth certificate to join the Marines and fight in the Korean War. Later, he fought in Vietnam. His house was filled with lacquer paintings of Vietnamese women steering basket boats and jade Buddha statues holding unlit incense. In the basement was a red *ao dai*, a traditional Vietnamese dress, he had ordered for his wife in Hoi An. The shiny fabric, stretched over a limbless mannequin, looked brand new.

"We're going out for *real* Vietnamese food," he said and gave us a stern look: *Don't say I didn't warn you.*

Saigon Palace was in a strip mall, sandwiched between a dry cleaner and a dollar store. A teenage Vietnamese girl jogged over to my uncle and bowed several times, then guided him by the hand to a booth at the back of the restaurant. The two of them spoke loudly in Vietnamese and laughed. My aunt smiled and rolled her eyes.

"He's such a show off."

We followed them to the table. The waitress nodded at my uncle, then she giggled, but I couldn't understand them. We sat down and I opened my menu and gazed at the pictures. The grainy images of shrimp and crispy pork were crooked and over-exposed, with an almost salacious quality to them. I thought about my father's Army yearbook, a cheaply-bound collection of photographs, their captions strewn with glaring grammatical and spelling errors. Beneath a picture of a middle-aged Vietnamese woman washing dishes in the mess hall: *Nut Bad.* A young Vietnamese woman typing a report: *Oh yes, ain't it Lookin' Good!* Or two Vietnamese teenagers in the middle of a group of GIs: *Get it on Girls—Do it.*

"Chicken or beef?" my uncle asked us. The words sounded odd in the middle of his conversation with the waitress, the way "Coca-Cola" or an American actor's name stood out in a foreign film, as if these terms were there first and the other language grew around them. He ordered for us and nodded, then rolled his chopsticks between his palms like he was trying to start a fire.

He seemed in control leading us through the parking lot, into the restaurant, guiding us through our first exotic meal, so I didn't have the heart to tell him we had eaten Vietnamese food plenty of times. I looked around the restaurant and saw a man and woman sitting with a young boy by the window. The man tried to talk to him, but the boy pressed his chin to his chest, his face illuminated by his cell phone.

"I go back every year," my uncle said, rubbing his hand over his gray crew cut. "Three, four times. To universities in Hanoi and Ho Chi Minh City." He sat up and patted his hip pockets, then his left shirt pocket and pulled out his business card. *Robert Dalton, Professor of Economics.* "Beautiful country. Just stunning."

"It really is," my aunt said. "At first, I was like, 'Oh, jeez, I don't know about this.' But it really is something."

"Did you notice what kind of jobs the women had?" Vanessa asked.

My aunt looked confused. "Oh, I don't know. I didn't really notice."

"She's going into research mode," I said, rubbing Vanessa's leg.

"I guess waitressing," my aunt said. "Some had little shops and things."

"My colleague, Teddy, he'll show you guys around Da Nang," my uncle said. "Now his wife,"—he let out a long, slow whistle—"is one hell of a cook."

It was quiet for a moment, except for our chewing.

"What was it like when you were over there the first time?" I asked.

"Jeez. Well, I started teaching in '86, so..."

My aunt smiled. "No, honey. I think he means during the war."

"Oh," my uncle said, laughing. "Too many battles. They all blend together."

My uncle didn't seem to be the stereotypical Vietnam Veteran. He wasn't angry. He wasn't indifferent. But he also wasn't my father. I wondered why my uncle was so eager to go to war, why he would forge his birth certificate just to fight, and now the memories were a blur.

When my father found out he was drafted, he considered running to Canada. He decided against it because he didn't want to disrespect his father. *I couldn't shame him like that.* My grandparents drove my father to JFK Airport in 1970. My father sat in the passenger seat, his mother behind him. Their 1951 Chevy Impala hummed down the Long Island Expressway. No music. My grandfather had spent the night crawling around inside the landing gear of 747s, and though he could take the whole plane apart and put it back together again, the only time he had ever sat in one was on his flight to Germany during World War II. He pulled his Impala into the parking lot. My father stepped out and waited on the curb painted white for DEPAR-TURES, adjusting his uniform. My grandmother wrapped her arms around my father, told him she loved him. My grandfather stood up straight. My father leaned in for a hug. His father offered his hand.

"Guess that was about as close as we were gonna get," my father told me.

On our way to the airport, my father bent one wrist over the wheel of his 2001 Ford Explorer, his other hand tapping the SEEK button, searching for a better song. He accelerated, following signs for 495 West, the Long Island Expressway. My mother, the passenger, dragged an emery board across her nails in quick mechanical strokes. From the back seat, I watched her movements. It was as if she was preparing a meal: body hunched over the garbage can, peeling onions or shucking corn. Vanessa sat beside me, her hand resting on my backpack, *Lonely Planet's Guide to Vietnam* jammed into the mesh pocket.

He stopped on 95.9 *The Fox,* home of Long Island's classic rock, though the station broadcasts from Norwalk, Connecticut, across the Long Island Sound. The DJ spoke in a throaty drawl, too tough for a station whose call letters spelled out a furry little animal. Perhaps the DJ was a sly fox, convincing all his fans, if DJs still had fans, that they were slick men on the prowl, one hand snapping out a Steve Miller tune, the other signaling to a sexy *thang* on the corner. This was my father's favorite station.

The Fox played The Chambers Brothers' "Time Has Come Today" and for a second, I thought my father had popped in one of his mix CDs. He picked out the opening guitar riff on the steering wheel, then looked at me in the rearview mirror.

"Tell ya, boy. Never thought this would be happenin'. Not in a million years."

My father had been amazed that it was even possible to go online and buy tickets to Vietnam. *They allow that?* What seemed to puzzle him the most was that we would *want* to go, that this was our choice.

Vanessa stared out the window, the rising sun revealing red streaks in her hair. She sat low in the seat with her legs resting on her giant backpack, which was stuffed with our clothes. Frayed baggage labels hung like tassels from nearly all the zippers. Some labels displayed unfamiliar airlines, in-country flights Vanessa took in Africa or South America. I told myself the nervousness in my stomach was actually excitement.

On Vanessa's lap was a binder the health clinic in Ho Chi Minh City had sent her several weeks ago. The material included the clinic's mission statement, how they hoped to fill the gap in sex education in Vietnam. I had listened to Vanessa speak to her advisor before we left and watched her make small, neat notes in the margins about the women she would be teaching. Some were in their twenties, some closer to sixty. They worked in bars, clubs, massage parlors. Vanessa was concerned about how well she could teach without knowing Vietnamese. Her advisor told her not to worry. They would supply a translator.

Bars, clubs, massage parlors. These words stood out each time I saw them in Vanessa's binder, as if they were written in neon. I thought about my older brother Don and me wandering through Amsterdam's narrow streets the summer I graduated from college. Our faces coated in red light, we stared at the women behind glass, daring each other. Neither one of us had the nerve to actually open the door and speak to the women. The nights were cool, and sometimes when I looked down the crowded streets at people in hooded sweatshirts and jeans, they seemed like Christmas shoppers in New York City, gazing into Macy's window display.

We walked into an old movie theater and sat in the balcony. Men in suits filled the seats around us. Through binoculars, they watched a man dressed as a gorilla pull his penis through a slit in his pants and jump on top of a naked woman. My brother and I leaned over the balcony. The woman closed her eyes and bit her bottom lip. Behind his mask, the man's eyes glowed like an animal caught on the highway. I didn't mention the sex show in the postcards I wrote to Vanessa.

The backpack I used in Amsterdam was the same one on the seat between me and Vanessa. In the side pocket, pressed between the pages of our *Lonely Planet*, were two photographs from my father's going-away party. In the first photograph, everyone sits around a long table full of bread and pasta, extending their wine glasses for a toast. My aunts are slim with dark curly perms; my uncles are slim with slightly more hair. My grandmother looks exactly the same. Beside my father is his fiancée, Maddy, sitting beneath her shiny blonde beehive. My father wears a plain white t-shirt and an expression that says: *All right, Bozo, take the picture.*

The second photograph looked as if it was the same moment shot from a different angle. The back of my father's head, the side of Maddy's hair. In the background, beside the wood-paneled support pole, my grandfather stands, his face half in shadow.

The end of The Chambers Brothers. The tick-tock cowbell returned, the lyrics reduced to *time... time... time.* I watched the back of my father's head as he looked from side to side, then pulled into JFK's short-term lot for DEPARTURES. He shifted the Explorer into park. My mother tried to open the door but it was still locked. Vanessa looked at me and I grinned, pointing to the radio and then my father. The song slowly wound down, and Lester Chambers and my father finished with a guttural grunt.

Vanessa and I stood on the curb. My father held her wrist and gave her a quick peck on the cheek. He handed me my backpack, then pulled me in for a hug: Winstons and gasoline. He stepped back and rubbed my shoulder, grinning.

"Gonna be hot over there, boy. I can tell you that much."

3

SIX A.M. Ho Chi Minh City is a steaming engine. Though I can hear motorbikes toot their horns or a bus grind its gears, the city is dominated by an electrical hum, an audible heat, as if a swarm of cicadas hovers over the restaurants and apartment complexes, the green lakes and street vendors. Conversations break through the din and sound angry, even aggressive, and I wonder what there is to fight about at six a.m.

Last night, I spoke with the owner of our hotel, and as he poured me another shot of rice wine from a plastic water bottle, he said the language only sounds hostile. "Sounds and meanings are very different." He took a sip. I asked him what he hears when we talk—Americans, I meant. Another sip and his smile grew. "I hear R's. All the time R's." He stood up and began to bark, or maybe cheer. "Ra-ra-ra-ra-ra-ra. Very much." He sat back down and shrugged, as if to say it wasn't my fault.

Vanessa and I gather our things and meet our guide in the lobby. He is a thin man in a short-sleeved dress shirt and black jeans, a braided leather belt and white sneakers. He sits in a large, intricately-carved chair, holding a steaming bowl of *pho* inches from his face. The lobby is filled with other travelers, white men and women with enormous backpacks—Australians, Germans, Swedes, my fellow Americans, some French. The hotel staff, in matching mint-green Polo shirts, rush out like a pit crew and surround the new arrivals. They reach up to help the travelers remove their backpacks; the travelers turn and bend down to tip them.

As Vanessa and I walk through the lobby, our footsteps rattle the glass cabinets filled with ceramic Buddhas and lacquer paintings. Our guide stands and bows and reaches for my hand. To him, we are "Antun-nee" and "Ba-nessa." To me, his name sounds like three coins dropping into a glass of water, and I can't imagine what it sounds like to him when I say, "Pleased to meet you, Anh Dung Nguyen." He nods several times, then pulls a map from his back pocket.

"So. You want to see Long Binh, yes?"

"Yes," I say. "And also Bien Hoa."

He nods. "Because you father?"

"Yes."

"He still alive, you father?"

"Yes."

A big smile. "Why he no come?" He opens his arms wide as if offering a hug.

Vanessa and I look at each other and laugh. "I'm not sure," I say. "Too far away, I guess." I realize after I've said this that it's the only reason I can think of. I never asked my father to come and he didn't offer. He hates long flights, can't sit in one place for too long. My father seemed satisfied with his memories: *If I had to live my life over again, I'd go back.*

I packed his voice. His stories live inside the recorder in my pocket, and sometimes during our trip, I'd plug in my headphones and press *Play.*

Anh nods. "Lots of men come back. Lots." He leans forward and slurps down the rest of his breakfast. "First we go here"—taps the map—"then here"—tap—"then we stop here for you to buy"—tap, tap, tap.

"Oh," I say. "That's okay. We don't have to stop."

"Okay, we stop for bathroom only. And maybe you buy," he says, quickly refolding the map.

Ho Chi Minh City's paved veins bleed into one main artery, Highway 1, which runs the length of Vietnam. Motorbikes piled with bamboo or chickens or friends or relatives flow through massive eight-way inter-sections, head-on, and zoom around a rotary, the driver's feet grazing the curb or the muffler of another motorbike. We do not merge as much as we are absorbed into traffic. An opening reveals itself only after our driver pulls out, and suddenly our car is surrounded. Our driver hits the horn—not a honk, but a rapid chirping, like a robotic cricket.

In minutes, the city is gone, and the country opens to infinite green. Farms and rice paddies spread for miles, eventually growing into the mossy mountains painted on the horizon. In the fields are tombs the color of Easter candy. They rise like an exotic crop scattered across the land. A little boy sits shirtless atop a water buffalo, whipping the animal's slick haunches, trying to motivate him around one of the pink and purple stones. "We keep the dead close," Anh says. I try to imagine burying not my hamster but my grandfather, my aunt or uncle behind our pool, beside my mother's flower bed—a colorful stone rising against the seasons, jutting up through leaves and through snow.

Up Highway 1 to Bien Hoa. Behind tinted glass, within air conditioning. Our driver is silent; he doesn't seem to speak English. He hits the funny-sounding horn each time he passes a vehicle, which is often, and as it trails off it sounds as if the car is laughing. The radio quietly plays a Muzak version of the *Titanic* soundtrack. Anh sits in the passenger seat, holding an unlit cigarette in his mouth. When he turns and talks to us, the cigarette jumps like a needle picking up an unstable frequency.

"*Platoon.*" He points to the squat cement buildings capped with corrugated metal, an old movie house, and a dry fountain that form Bien Hoa's center. He holds his hand out straight and sweeps it across the windshield, fingertips grazing the glass. "All *Platoon.*"

Anh knows me. He has never seen me before, but he knows me well. He's driven me up Highway 1 since the late 1980s, when I traveled to Vietnam from New York or Boston or Idaho or Kentucky, when I sat in the back of his car beside a father or a grandfather, a brother, an uncle. He takes us north from Ho Chi Minh City, to small towns whose names we know well, have been to or heard stories of. Anh studies the movies, listens to the music, points to a square of cement where Charlie Sheen once stood or patches of jungle that inspired

CCR's "Fortunate Son." He drives us through the towns, and they all look the same, and perhaps none of us in the car would recognize a thing if Anh didn't mention a movie title or song lyric or speak the name of the town written on the back of the photograph in my pocket, my father standing in front of the old movie house: *Bien Hoa, '71.*

"Many men came here for a woman."

We stand on the cement pier in Bien Hoa, Anh's cigarette now lit, the driver watching us from the road. Anh looks around, paying close attention to the locals walking by, staring. I can tell by the slow pulls he takes on his cigarette, his calm tone, that he is not nervous, just careful. He tells us most tourists don't come here, and many of the locals have not seen a white person since the war.

"Very few women left in Bien Hoa," he says, almost under his breath.

"How come?" I ask.

"Marry soldiers. Soldiers take them home."

I think about the souvenirs we had bought earlier in the trip, the black chopsticks and their ceramic holders, wrapped tightly in tissue paper.

"Did the women want to leave?" Vanessa asks.

Anh purses his lips and stares down the street. "Perhaps some," he says. "Others, maybe not."

We stand on the pier for another minute or so as Anh finishes his cigarette. The stores across the street are different from the shops in Ho Chi Minh City. Instead of pizza and hamburgers, pirated copies of *Dispatches* or *The Things They Carried*, these stores sell scrap metal and lumber and copper piping. One man sits in the only empty space in his shop, as if at the helm of a small ship made of tires and hubcaps. Men laugh on the corner, drinking coffee, playing cards. Men crouch on the pier, pointing into the dark water. Men watch Anh flick his cigarette into the canal, clap his hands together, and their eyes follow us back across the street, into the car, as we disappear behind tinted glass.

The highway is less congested once we leave Bien Hoa and head toward Long Binh. Long Binh is where my father spent his twentieth birthday. This is where he spent most of his nineteen months in Vietnam. This is where he worked as a cook, mixing vats of oatmeal and mashed potatoes, brewing oceans of coffee, baking mountains of donuts. This is where he and the other *spoons* spent one-hundred-degree days preparing soup or baking apple pie. This is where the jokes start: *How long you been in Long Binh? Been too long in Long Binh.* This is where he cleaned and polished his rifle, hung posters of Jimi Hendrix and Playboy centerfolds, drank weak, government-issued Budweiser. One of the sixty-thousand soldiers living within this militarized metropolis, he constructed a hooch out of scrap wood and empty crates. This is where he sunbathed on a lawn chair, somewhere in the dusty divide between two of the U.S. Army's largest structures in South Vietnam: a hospital and a prison. This is where he bought a television and a stereo, tapped off a buddy's extension cord that was tapped off a buddy's extension cord. This is where Vietnamese women went hooch to hooch, waving white rags, speaking the only English necessary.

And this is where a giant supermarket now stands.

"Not many stores like this in Vietnam," Anh says, standing up tall and nodding as he looks around the parking lot. I snap a picture and the driver glances at me. Anh smiles. "Come."

Vanessa and I follow him across the street. He tells us to stay close. A few hundred feet from the store is a long, wide dirt road, which leads to a Vietnamese Army base. Two soldiers in tight uniforms stand in front of the gate. From this distance, they seem fake, like a pair of plastic figures.

"Here," Anh says. "We stop here."

I take a few pictures. Anh looks at his watch. Cars and trucks zip by, their horns laughing. I imagine Anh traveling to the United States, to New York, to Long Island, to Northport, my hometown, where he would pay me to drive him to a place *his* father once lived. I could take him to the loading dock behind Walmart, and point into the long grass beside the dumpsters.

Here, I'd say. *Right here.*

"The government own all this," Anh says. "The soldiers down there, their guns are from United States. After the war, U.S. leave everything." He takes a long pull on his cigarette, exhales. "Leave everything."

The distant figures pace in front of the gate, the barrels of their tiny guns extending above their helmets. I try to picture the exchange of weapons. The Vietnamese soldiers at the gate—did they once open boxes of shiny U.S. guns, or did they pick the dusty weapons off the ground, after the last American troops were in the air? Or was there a day when American soldiers ceased firing, flicked the safety switch, and gave their guns away?

I think of film footage from late in the war. American soldiers on an aircraft carrier, shoving helicopters into the South China Sea. For a moment, they clung to the edge of the deck like cicada shells, then splashed into the water. My father described to me acres and acres of broken tanks and trucks and jeeps. *If it had anything wrong with it, flat tire, anything, we left it.* I found a picture of my father standing in front of a giant lot of tanks. On the back, he wrote: *Mr. Cheapo's Used Car Lot.*

"Okay," Anh says, looking at his watch. "We go."

There was this one, I tell ya, boy. Big friggin' tits. I don't even know if they had silicone back then, but they had to be fake. Had to be fake. She was young, too, maybe seventeen, eighteen. Came in from town to clean the hooches. Every mornin', workin' every hooch. Some days she'd start at this end, other days she'd start on the other side. She knew what she was doin'. Gave every guy a shot. First dude looked out for the rest of us. First dude always stuck his fingers in her, checkin' for razor blades. What you do, GI? *Don't worry what I'm doin', honey. Guys with half the tip of their dicks sliced off. Ain't no purple medal gonna fix that.*

Anh whispers to the driver. The driver nods. We begin our trip back to Ho Chi Minh City.

"That's it?" I ask Vanessa, quietly. "Tour's over?"

She shrugs, mouthing her answer. "I guess so."

Jeep-fulls of Vietnamese soldiers swerve around us. One Jeep pulls alongside and a soldier hanging off the back stares at us. He smiles, perhaps at me, perhaps not. I don't think he can see me through the tinted glass, but he continues to stare. He shifts his rifle from the left side of his body to the right. A slow oscillation of his hand as if he were Miss America. Then the driver hits the Jeep's horn, laughing through traffic.

I feel sick. I've always been prone to motion sickness, particularly in cars. There is a looping video in my head of a young boy chugging two cherry slushies, then puking them up cold on the leather seats of his friend's mother's Jaguar. There are other stories. The heat, the driving, and Anh's perpetual smoke after tiptoeing around a Vietnamese Army base with a stomach full of beef-soup breakfast is my perfect storm. Vanessa hands me a bottle of warm water. I begin to sweat.

"No McDonald's in Vietnam," Anh says, staring out the window.

"Excuse me?" I say.

"McDonald's. No here. KFC, yes. McDonald's, no."

I open the window—the door to a convection oven—and shut it.

"How come?" Vanessa asks.

Anh leans over to the driver, and the driver's response makes Anh laugh. A few moments later, Vanessa asks Anh what he said.

"He say the burgers are too big for our mouths."

We all laugh.

"They're too big for our mouths, too," I say.

Anh takes a long pull on his cigarette. "Perhaps."

We take a different route back to Ho Chi Minh City. Within city limits, we turn left, then right, another left, accelerate into a small parking lot. I don't recognize any of the street names. Vanessa and I flip through our *Lonely Planet*. The car squeals to a halt.

"So," Anh says. "We stop."

"That's okay," I say, repeating the conversation we had in the lobby. "We can wait in the car."

Anh tosses his cigarette out the window. Lights another. "Maybe you need bathroom."

Vanessa and I look at each other.

"No, thank you," she says.

"I need it," Anh says. "Please wait inside for when I come back."

I glance down at our useless guide book. We open our doors and the heat nearly drags us out of the car.

Anh smiles, directing us toward a long, brick building. The driver takes off.

"Where is he going?" I ask.

"He park. No very good for parking here. Go inside. I will meet you there."

Vanessa and I approach the brick building. A small plaque beside the door reads: *Handicapped Handicrafts*. These lacquer-painting-and-chopstick emporiums aren't entirely new to us—we'd been dragged to several of them on other tours, our bus unloading us like prize cattle at warehouses full of small Buddhas, medium Buddhas, large Buddhas. But this one is different. We are the only ones here, and the scent of lacquer is dizzying.

"Welcome! Welcome!" a chubby Vietnamese man says, bowing several times with a wide smile. "Come in. Come in."

We follow him past glistening paintings of leopards stalking eagles on tree limbs or large-breasted Vietnamese women dressed in gauzy *ao dais* or Buddhas smiling so wide their faces may burst.

He hands us two baskets.

"For your convenience," he says mechanically, as if reciting a script.

Then I hooked up with one. Used to see her all the time. Thing was, she didn't want money; she wanted stuff. So I brought her presents.

Whatever they had at the PX that week: toasters, razors, TVs, record players. Chick didn't know Van Morrison from Little Richard, but she wanted that record player, boy. I tell ya. Thing was heavy, too. Lugged it all the way from one side of the base to the other, then took a Jeep out to her shack or whatever. Hut.

Kinda awkward, though. I'm in the next room bangin' her while her whole family's makin' dinner. Whole family, Mom and Dad, brothers, sisters, nephews, friggin' John-boy and little Cindy Lou Who. Everybody's there. So after we finish up and we're layin' there and she goes 'You hungry, GI?' I didn't want to be rude, so I says, 'Sure, I could eat.' Next thing I know I'm at the dinner table with her entire family, fishin' around for some kind of red monkey meat floatin' in my bowl and each time I take a bite her old man starts cacklin'. This guy was really gettin' a kick out of me eatin' this shit, meanwhile I'm thinkin', "Hey, asshole, you cooked it." My girl seemed to be the only one who spoke English so I asked what was so funny and she just said I put too much food in my mouth. So I smile at the old man and he just keeps cacklin', howlin'—old man's got tears in his eyes. When he finally calms down, he looks at his daughter, then he looks at me. He points to my uniform. 'What?' I say. 'What are you pointin' at, old man?' He points at my uniform again, then points at the wrinkles in his shirt.

"Next time," *he says.* "You bring iron."

The chubby man takes us through the store and into the back. He tells us this is a very special program that the government was kind enough to establish. "Help a lot of people," he says. This too sounds rehearsed.

In the back of the store is a large workshop, like a factory. A massive cement room divided into different stations: stools and workbenches, chairs and easels. Empty.

"Unfortunately," he says. "Our workers now eat lunch. They very much like visitors."

Instead of introducing us to the workers, the chubby man guides us through a photo gallery. A legless man polishing chopsticks made of bone. A woman missing both arms sculpting a tea cup with her feet. Children in wheelchairs clenching paint brushes in their teeth.

Vanessa and I are silent. This is not an exhibit, not something to gawk at. The workshop conjures up images of The War Remnants Museum on the other side of the city, the place where Vanessa and I, within a mixed crowd of Asians, Europeans, Australians, and Indians stared at disfigured fetuses floating in formaldehyde jars. On the wall were black and white images of women, men and children, some with half a face or no appendages or an arm growing out of the center of their backs—victims of Agent Orange, white phosphorus, napalm.

Above the exhibit:

We hold these truths to be self-evident, that all men are created equal, that they are endowed by their creator with certain unalienable rights, that among these are LIFE, LIBERTY and the pursuit of HAPPINESS.

Many signs in Vietnam are printed in incorrect English. The original text of the Declaration of Independence capitalizes just the first letter of *life*, *liberty*, and *happiness*. The additional capital letters on the plaque did not feel like an error, but more an inextricable root of Vietnamese—something not lost, but found in translation.

One of the hooch girls gave all the guys the clap. You ever get that? Believe me, you'd know it if you did. Just drippin', all day. Fun while it lasted, though. Not bad waking up to a naked Asian broad. All the dudes, the white dudes, the brothas, friggin' Sittin' Bulls, didn't matter who you were, you were out there, just like everybody else, cryin' over your busted hose. This chick really did a number on us, boy. I tell ya.

Nothing—just get your meds and wait it out. Boy, you shoulda seen some of the remedies these hicks and backwoods hillbillies came up with. Swear to Christ, one toothless asshole came struttin' out the mess hall with his dick dipped in tapioca pudding. Big grin on his face like he just cured cancer. He wasn't smilin' later when I told him he had to mix up a new batch of pudding.

They pulled her body out the dumpster. Throat cut ear to ear. I don't know. No one 'fessed up. Wasn't right. Just one of those things, I guess.

After the chubby man finishes the tour of the workshop, he guides us back into the store. We are still the only ones there. A pretty young woman behind the counter watches us as we browse the chopsticks, tea sets, and Buddhas—the same items we've seen in nearly every store in Vietnam. The only difference is the price. A pair of chopsticks is close to twenty U.S. dollars. A small ceramic Buddha nearly fifty U.S. dollars. Our hotel room, which includes breakfast and dinner, is sixteen U.S. dollars. Holding our empty baskets, we wander the aisles, whispering.

"Will that be all?" the cashier asks.

"Yes, please," Vanessa says. "Thank you very much."

The woman nods and wraps up our thirty dollar bamboo spoon.

Outside, Anh is waiting. He glances at the paper bag in Vanessa's hand.

"Ba-nessa! Very nice for you to buy," he says, exhaling a large plume of smoke.

"Yes," she says. "A lot of nice things in there."

Anh steps closer, nodding. "Yes. Yes. Beautiful things. Very good store."

I'm about to ask where the driver is when his car screeches around the side of the building. He hops out, smiling. He opens the doors for us, pointing to my head, warning me to be careful. I nod, and he gently shuts the door. The car is cool, the air conditioning drowning out the traffic. Behind tinted glass, the brick building looks far away, as if cast in permanent dusk. As we pull into traffic, a bus unloads a large group of men and women and children, each one slowly, carefully making their way to the back of the building. I turn to Vanessa and she is also watching the workers. The chubby man guides the last of them into the workshop. I unwrap the tissue paper and look at our new spoon and wonder which of the workers, if any, have ever touched it.

We are only ten minutes away from our hotel. This provides Anh enough time to smoke four cigarettes. His smoking is an art. He is a master of blowing rings. He displays impressive restraint, allowing the ash to grow nearly two inches before knocking it out the window. Sometimes he performs a French inhale. But Anh is not a showoff. Each one of his smoking tricks I glimpse from the backseat, his face reflected in the side-view mirror.

A group of new arrivals—large white men with backpacks—wait outside the hotel, unsure if they have the correct address. We stand beside the car for a moment, thanking Anh for his assistance. He bows.

I realize we don't have any more cash. Vanessa offers to run into the hotel to use the ATM. I glance at her before she leaves. She smiles, assuring me she won't take long.

Anh lights a cigarette and stares at the men standing outside the hotel.

"They have Heroes in United States?"

I stare at him. He takes a long drag.

"What?"

"Heroes," he says, holding up his wrinkled pack of cigarettes.

"Oh," I say, nearly laughing. "No, I don't think we do."

He nods.

Vanessa returns with the money and hands it to Anh.

"Thank you, again," she says.

He slips the folded bills into his shirt pocket.

"Enjoy the rest of Vietnam."

4

VANESSA SPENDS the next morning at the clinic helping women construct vaginas from colored paper and cotton balls. One woman forms a massive replica out of poster board and cuts a hole in the center through which another woman with spiky black hair pokes her head, as if she is posing in a wooden cut-out of Mickey Mouse. Some of the women are in their early twenties, some late fifties. They are sex workers or partners of injection drug users, or both. None of the women have received an adequate sex or anatomy class. Their knowledge is based on myths and hysteria, perpetuated by stigma and silence.

Stand up after intercourse to prevent pregnancy.

An abortion is when the doctor chops up the fetus with tiny knives and sucks the remains out with a vacuum.

AIDS is transmittable by kissing.

The term "sex worker" sounded odd to me and didn't have the same connotations as prostitute, hooker, or "ho," as my father would say. I pictured naked women in hard hats with tool belts full of dildos, carrying their lunches in red and white Playmate coolers. But after listening to Vanessa describe the women's lives, stories of incest and rape, how many of the women were seen as "damaged goods" and exiled from their families, the hours they spent servicing ten or twenty men a day, their sweaty and dusty commute from village to city, "sex worker" seemed most appropriate. Sex is the job, and they tried not to bring their work home.

I spend my days sitting in cafés or in one of the large wooden chairs in the hotel lobby, flipping through *Let the Good Times Roll*, a collection of oral histories of Asian female prostitutes living near U.S.

29

military bases. I had read the books written by American GIs and Vietnamese soldiers, and the few written by U.S. Army wives and Vietnamese women, but these books gave no voice to Vietnamese sex workers. I could recite Matthew Modine's complete monologues from *Full Metal Jacket*, but I only knew three words spoken by a Vietnamese prostitute in the film: *Me so horny.*

Before our trip, I had searched for recent oral histories of Vietnamese women, but found nothing. Instead, each time I typed "Vietnam" and "prostitution" into a search engine, I was offered opportunities to meet "exotic" and "eager" women. After giving my contact information to hotels in Vietnam, I started getting e-mails with subjects like, *ARE YOU CURIOUS?* or ones that were not so subtle: *FUCK A GOOK TONIGHT!* The body of these e-mails were written in a tone that assumed I had been searching desperately for these women, that I should look no further, that they were waiting and willing. *Here for the taking.*

The women in *Let the Good Times Roll* are from the Philippines, Okinawa, and South Korea. They speak about growing up too poor to attend school. Their elderly parents couldn't maintain the rice fields or coconut trees on their own, so the young girls had to stay home and help bring in the harvest. The girls were often raped by relatives or local villagers. If the man was a relative, the rape was kept a secret, so as not to disgrace the family.

If the girl was raped by a man who was *not* a relative, the woman's family and tradition dictated that the two must marry because no other man would want her. Nan Hee, a thirty-three-year-old Korean woman who worked as a "bar girl" near Camp Casey, a U.S. base in Uijongbu in South Korea, spoke about her husband: "I lived with him half because I loved him and half because he raped me and I had no choice."

I flip back and forth between *Let the Good Times Roll* and Richard Bernstein's *The East, the West, and Sex*, a four-hundred-year history of Western exploitation of the East. In the late 1800s, British soldiers stationed in India—many married, devout Christians—relayed their sexual conquests to comrades in Britain: tales of "nut-brown" women fulfilling every desire, detailing the coveted world of harems in a land where the restrictive moral and religious codes of home seemed not to apply. Reverberations of these tales can be heard in the French's colonization of Indochina in the early 1900s. The French followed Britain's lead and developed their own form of "regulated prostitution," in which sex workers were routinely tested for venereal disease and could not perform sexual labor for any French soldiers until they were "cleared."

Soldiers were not subject to the same testing. If a soldier showed symptoms of a sexually transmitted disease, their supervisors questioned them about recent sexual activity. The woman suspected of spreading the disease to the soldier was apprehended, tested and, if she was indeed infected, forced to undergo treatment at her own expense before returning to work. The soldier was ordered to remain on base, where he received free health care. While prostitution was illegal in France, the laws were not enforced in the colonies.

I take out my tape recorder and listen to my father recount his own stories of an exotic, seemingly lawless place where he balanced boredom with sex. He took R&R in Vung Tau, a fishing village on the southern coast, the town Robert Duvall in *Apocalypse Now* claims has the best surfing in Vietnam. My father lived in a hotel on the beach where women nodded at his words and he at theirs. Accepting his proposals, his promises. His toasters. His televisions.

I replay my father's description of the woman who was murdered in Long Binh: *She was one of the daily hires. Cleaned the hooches, policed up the area, scrubbed the head, shit like that. Then she'd walk by, goin'* "Short-time? Short-time?" *Banged the entire engineer battalion and the next time I saw her, the MPs were draggin' her out the dumpster.* Loud German breaks through my father's voice and I look out the window of the hotel lobby to see two men stumbling out of *Le Pub* across the street. A cyclo driver slowly pedals by, ringing his bell. After bartering in a bastardized sign language, the two German men cram into the cyclo and are peddled away like babies in a big stainless steel carriage.

By the time my father arrived in Saigon, the bars and pool halls—leftovers from the French occupation—were revamped. Owners erected new signs like *Pussycat Café* or *USA Rock Club*. An explosion of

Americana: vanity license plates; red, white and blue beer steins shaped like breasts; posters of Marlon Brando, James Dean, Frank Sinatra, Jim Morrison, Steve McQueen. Much like the inside of my father's hooch or my college dorm room. Vietnam was my father's version of college. It was the first time he lived away from home. He worked a low-wage job for beer money or to buy a gift to impress a girl. There are photographs of my father and Waller in Long Binh, leaning over a table made from plywood and milk crates. They both wear white undershirts and are holding records, trading them like baseball cards. If it weren't for the caption on the back, these photos look like they could have been taken in a record shop near my grandparent's house in New York.

Cyclos carried soldiers to and from the hottest clubs, each driver claiming to know the quickest route. Outside the clubs, Vietnamese teenagers, as if at a concert or sporting event, hawked t-shirts, stickers, patches, pins and coffee mugs with phrases printed in bold, capital letters:

MY LOVE FOR YOU IS RUNNING DOWN YOUR LEG.

ALL RIGHT, I LOVE YOU, NOW SHUT UP AND BUY YOUR OWN DRINK!

YOU WON'T GO DOWN IN HISTORY, SO MIGHT AS WELL GO DOWN ON ME.

Other items the teenagers sold were a bit tamer: *Shit Happens* inscribed on Zippo lighters; simple plastic American flags; or pins the bar girls wore that shouted: MONEY TALKS!

Inside the clubs, Janis Joplin offered another piece of her heart. My father leaned close to the sounds coming from a woman's lips, until she was quiet. She pressed her ear to the notes and vibrations in his mouth, his throat. He bought her several "lady drinks," expensive beverages on which she received a small commission. After she met her quota, the papasan allowed my father to pay her "bar fine," the bulk of which covered the room she rented above the club. Her room had to be furnished: a bed, a dresser, a fan, a sound system and a television. To pay for these required items, she took a loan from the owner at five, sometimes ten percent interest. The woman and my father ascended the stairs to her eight-by-eight room. Maybe he hummed along to Janis or maybe she, having heard the song over and over, mimicked the lyrics: *Didn't I make you feel like you were the only man?*

I meet Vanessa after she gets off work at the clinic. I place the recorder on the table, stick the right earpiece into my ear and give her the left one.

She leans over the table and presses her finger into her open ear. I hit *Play.*

"What's that clinking sound?" she asks.

"He kept flipping his silver dollar. He was kinda fidgety."

I had listened to the recording so many times I could recite it from memory. The din of the café seeped in through my left ear: the chatter of porcelain tea cups and saucers, motorbikes idling at the curb, the horrible Muzak that followed us everywhere, each song the synthesized sister of a familiar tune.

Eight weeks into Basic in South Carolina. Run run run. All day. Hit a few of the bars. All the locals knew you were military and the girls kinda stayed away from you. They could tell by your haircut or whatever and it was just like anything else. You hittin' on 'em, and they know. If you live in a base or around a base, it's the same crap. Guys come and go and they be hittin' on the girls and they ain't lookin' for romance or to go out and buy furniture. They just wanna pop ya.

There was a few places that the sergeant warned us about before we went into town the first time. Any hotels of, uh, ill-repute. Bordellos. If you gotta go—and I'll never forget him sayin' this—if you gotta go, go to the Hotel de Soto. Best one in town. And the cleanest.

The hiss of dead air. Vanessa looks down at the table and slowly spins the salt shaker. My voice breaks the silence: "So did you guys go there?" My father speaks through a yawn:

Nah, we were still stateside. Wasn't necessary yet.

Vanessa looks up. "What does that mean? 'Necessary?'"

I open my mouth, but my voice on the tape speaks for me: "Right, it's not like you were on the other side of the world yet."

5

WHILE VANESSA is at work, I wander around Ho Chi Minh City. I can only walk for so long before the heat becomes unbearable and the straps of my backpack cut into my shoulders. Then the rain comes and cools the city and I watch, from beneath an awning, as motorbikes beep and slide, but never slow down. When the rain is gone and the sun returns, the streets steam like a giant manhole cover.

Sometimes while I wait for the rain to let up, I duck into a café and look at my father's old photographs. The city he caught on film was then called Saigon. Aside from the year, make, and model of the cars and motorbikes, Ho Chi Minh City looks very similar to Saigon, and many locals still call it that. There are differences, of course, but the old butts up against the new, and in some places it's almost possible to draw a line between the past and present: a crumbling pastel apartment building beside a nightclub whose entryway is guarded by a massive neon bull's head, or a rusted bicycle parked outside a gleaming Kentucky Fried Chicken. Many parts of the city look like Paris; French presence lingers in the architecture, the cafés, the language. The older generations speak French and some pass it down to their children.

My father sometimes uses words like *beaucoup*. *Boy, I put beaucoup mus'tid on ya sandwich.* Or in the summers he'd tell me I had *beaucoup time on my hands.* For years, I thought this was a goofy term my father invented, but then I heard it in movies and in French class and now it rings out on street corners or is shouted in restaurants in the middle of high-speed Vietnamese conversations. The first couple of times I hear it, I half-think my father is standing behind me, holding up cue cards from which the city is reading.

One afternoon, I sit in a park and read *Lonely Planet*. Across the street is an old hotel. The metal balconies bleed rust down the side of the building. Two Vietnamese women in tight, short skirts stand in the doorway, passing out flyers. A neon light in the window flashes the word MASSAGE. Some men stop and start talking to the women, take a flyer and leave. Couples or women do not stop and are not offered flyers. I can't hear what the women are saying, but the smiles they wear when talking to the men fade as they turn to face each other.

I cross the street. The women are older than I thought and their clothes seem like last-minute Halloween costumes, something pulled from the clearance rack. I walk by once and don't stop. Then I turn back and walk by them again. They call me *sir* and *mister* and say my shoulders *seem have beaucoup stress*. I smile, but don't say anything. They hand me a hot-pink flyer that is written in English but is nearly unreadable, a mish-mash of italicized terms and bolded phrases wrapped around headshots of Vietnamese women that seem oddly familiar, like the photographs that come with picture frames. *Relax for you after long hard business!!! Take load off and feel comfort!!! What's the hold up?*

I almost laugh, partly because of the translation, but also because I can't help but read the last sentence in my father's voice as he waits in line at the auto parts store. I look up at the women, who are nodding and nodding and nodding and I think about how the Career Center in college told me to always nod when negotiating, that nodding is contagious and if I nod enough, I can convince my client to do what I want, to give me what I need. I shake my head at the women and their smiles fade, their eyes searching for someone else on the sidewalk.

"You weren't tempted? Not at all?" Vanessa asks as we search for a place to eat dinner.

I tuck the flyer back into my pocket and shrug. "No way. There was nothing tempting about it. Plus the place was gross."

"So if it was clean it'd be okay?"

I felt I was approaching a slippery slope where my words could no longer express my intentions. "No, it's not that. You know what I'm trying to say."

"Where is this restaurant?" she asks, looking up and down the street.

"I know as much as you do, babe. The place is owned by a deaf and mute family. Book says it's got the best *bun cha* in town."

She doesn't answer. I glance down at the map, then back at the street signs, then back at the map.

"Let's just ask someone," she says.

"Nah, we got this. Come on."

We walk down a long alleyway that leads to another one and another. The alleyway brings us to a street filled with restaurants, but none of them are the one we're looking for.

"Almost there," I say.

I look at the map again. Street signs. Map. Street signs. Map. The map is colorful and detailed, but when I hold it up against the dark city, it doesn't help. Vanessa shifts her bag from one shoulder to the other.

"I'm asking this guy," she says.

"Wait a second."

"Hi. Excuse me? Excuse me? Do you speak English? We're looking for this place." I pass Vanessa the guide book and she points to the name of the restaurant. The man squints at the words and nods. He opens his palm and draws an invisible map. He stops a few times to point at the map in the book, then points out into the street, then back at the map in his palm, then back at the map in the book. He smiles and nods. "Not far."

We head in the last direction he pointed and eventually come to a busy intersection. "According to the book," I say, "there are two restaurants. One is the real place and the other is a scam, run by people who aren't really deaf or mute."

"As long as they serve food," Vanessa says.

Somehow, we find the right street. It is packed with tourists. Two Vietnamese families, on opposite sides of the street, stand with their hands clasped in front of them. Two mothers, two fathers, two daughters, two sons. As we walk by, the families reach out their hands and speak in strained, warped voices. Their bodies appear strained, too; sinewy necks and stretched fingers, forcing each limb to speak. A small child tugs on my backpack and points to his family.

The real restaurant is also known for their homemade bottle openers, a long piece of wood with a bolt driven through one end so that you could fit it snugly around a beer cap, slap the opposite end, and send the cap flying off into the air. Each family member waves a wooden bottle opener. They hold them up as indisputable proof. We stand in the street, making our choice.

I lean forward and whisper. "Do you think this is it?"

Vanessa shrugs.

We feel mute everywhere in Vietnam, so I wonder what difference it makes if the family here really is deaf and mute. In a way, a weight is lifted, and we don't have to worry about talking. The children seem much more daring than other children we've seen. Instead of shying away, tucking their faces behind their mother's legs, the kids on this street hold menus and bottle openers high above their heads and run after us.

"So. Do we stay or do we go?"

"I don't know," Vanessa says. "I guess we're already here."

Our whispering excites the families, as if Vanessa and I have become a deliberating jury. By this point in our trip, we are used to shouts and stares, but this is new. Another child runs toward me, tugging on my shorts. Then the other kid who yanked on my backpack returns and pulls me in the opposite direction. Neither child says a word.

A man who looks like a Vietnamese Harvey Keitel steps out of his restaurant. He draws a piece of wood from his back pocket, digs a shiny silver bolt from his apron, punches the bolt through the wood, twirls a beer bottle in the air, catches it, fits the opener on the cap with one hand, slaps the wood and pops off the cap. He takes a long, audible gulp.

We follow his family inside.

Each time Harvey Keitel's little girl approaches our table, she points to the menu and nods. Vanessa and I smile and order another round of *bun cha* and two more beers.

"So if it wasn't tempting, then why did you stop?" Vanessa asks.

"Huh?"

"The massage place. Why did you stop?"

"I don't know," I say, chewing. "I just wanted to hear what they had to say."

That sounds like a lie and I know it, but I don't know what else to say. I don't know what I'm supposed to be doing in Vietnam and often, on very hot days when I am hungry and working up the courage to eat alone in empty restaurants, the voice in my head tells me I'm just tagging along with Vanessa, that she has a real purpose here and it just happened to work out that I am unemployed, again.

Some days I concoct fantasies where an old prostitute would see me sitting on a bench, shuffle across the street and take my hand. She tells me a story about my father, the expressions he wore as a teenager, the words he used, the plans he had. Some hidden tale that would replace the shrugs and flippant responses he gave when I asked him what he wanted to do with his life: *Damned if I know.* She tells me things my father had told her that he never told anyone else, and when she takes me back to her apartment, she tells me to sit on the bed. She pulls out a dusty old book filled with my father's secrets, printed in the same chicken-scratch I used to see on the notepad in our kitchen: *Pick up milk, boy.*

I look across the table at Vanessa, wondering where to begin.

"A woman from the clinic works at a massage parlor," she says.

"I doubt it's the same place."

Vanessa shakes her head. "Guys are so weird."

I laugh. "What does that mean?"

The waitress comes over and nods. We nod back.

"Nothing," Vanessa says.

We eat the rest of our meal in silence, though inside I am defending not just my father, but all males, all across the world. But my defense seems shallow and clichéd, founded on random phrases I've said myself, or that I've heard my father or my brother or my guy friends use when confronted with a direct question about sex or gender: *It's a guy thing. Chicks don't understand. All dudes do it.* Or, like my father said about his "extracurricular activities" during the war: *Still stateside. Wasn't necessary yet.*

Through the front doors of the restaurant, I see the other family across the street trying to convince customers that they really are deaf and mute. I look back at Harvey Keitel and his family standing by the bar, backs straight, hands clasped, lips pressed tight. I imagine the fake family practicing their routine at home. "We must not talk. Listen, but do not let on that you can hear."

When we leave the restaurant, the rain is pounding hard. Beneath each awning, huddled in every store entrance, are packs of tourists, some laughing and cheering, gazing up at the rain as if it were a fireworks display. Others are Saran-wrapped, like leftovers, in thin, brightly-colored ponchos, their faces scrunched. Even the motorbikes acknowledge the rain and idle at the curbs and street corners. Some cars pull over; others plow through the flood, tires almost completely submerged, their hazard lights flashing.

Vanessa and I are still in front of the restaurant when Harvey Keitel's little girl comes rushing out. I think she may have found my passport or wallet beneath the table, but instead she offers to sell us a poncho. We shake our heads and smile. She pulls out an umbrella.

"No, thank you," Vanessa and I say in unison and move beneath the awning of the neighboring restaurant.

The water is sloshing over the curb, spreading onto the sidewalk, lapping at the entrances to stores, restaurants, bookshops, travel agencies. Many of the entrances have no doors, only open airways connected to the street by concrete ramps. The water moves up the ramp like an incoming tide, and I can feel a shallow yet powerful undertow around my ankles. I think about how I used to beg my mother to let me swim in our pool during rainstorms. I loved sinking under the water and staring up at the boiling surface. As long as there was no lightning, my mother said it was okay.

There is no lightning now, the sky expending its energy solely on the rain. We watch Vietnamese boys and girls splash in the water or fill up plastic squirt guns and spray each other. Soon, tourists inch out from beneath awnings and entrances and step gingerly into the water. Some laugh and hold on to each other. Others grit their teeth as if sinking into a hot bath. I put my arm around Vanessa.

"After you, m'lady."

She smiles. "Yeah?"

We look up and down the street, men and women and children carrying their belongings over their heads, taking high, exaggerated steps. The water on the sidewalk is as deep as the middle of the street.

"I don't think we have a choice."

She holds my hand tightly as we step down the ramp. I feel the warm water move up my thigh. At its deepest, the water hugs Vanessa's waist and ripples outward like a vast black skirt. Her eyes are wide. She gives me an uncertain smile, but I don't think my expression is doing her any good.

But we warm up to it. We take big steps like the rest of the people in the street, sometimes stumbling, but for the most part, our footing is sure. I slip and fall forward and nearly go under, but another tourist grabs my arm. We laugh and I thank him in English and he says, "No worries, mate." I imagine this is what it's like in Spain, during the running of the bulls or the big tomato fight. Or like Mardi Gras or Carnival, the right place, the right time where something that seems irrational in everyday life suddenly becomes a care-free experience where everyone lets loose. For the first time since I've been in Vietnam, I feel a part of something.

"What is that?" Vanessa asks, pointing to a white piece of material bobbing in front of us. We move closer. It's a dirty diaper.

"Oh, gross," I say. "Head that way."

To my right are clumps of dead cockroaches. To my left is another dirty diaper. We move quicker and the water feels deeper. Sweet'N Low packets and coffee filters and egg shells. A bloody tampon wrapped in tissue. Chicken bones and more roaches. Cigarette butts and an unopened box of Trojans and water-logged books. We step faster, harder, but our movements are slow and awkward, the way one runs in a dream. I look to the sidewalk and see how high the tide has risen, flooding all the stores and restaurants, and each time the water laps at the concrete ramps, the undertow pulls the insides out.

6

FOR SEVERAL WEEKS, Vanessa helps the clinic prepare for a sexual health and reproductive rights conference in Hanoi. She takes off from work a week early, and we buy tickets for a three-day bus ride north. The bus drives through the night. We stretch out as far as we can on the five-foot-long sleeper beds, the driver blasting loud Muzak nearly the entire ride.

I put my earphones in and listen to my father. He talks about one of his last days in Basic Training where the sergeant takes all the guys to a mock Vietnamese village behind the obstacle course. *That there gave ya a lil' slap in the face, reality-wise.* The sergeant led them through several thatch-roofed huts. I imagined the scene as if it were in a museum, my father peeking over a velvet rope at a wax family gathered around the hearth. He reaches out to press a red button beside a plaque on the wall and from somewhere a voice tells the family's story.

All the soldiers stood in front of the village, the sergeant droning on and on about always being alert, keeping all your senses tuned to the war. My father stretched his neck and licked the sweat from his lips. He put the butt of his rifle on the ground and leaned on the barrel like a cane. Then from beneath piles of dry grass, two Vietnamese men in conical hats sprang up and unloaded their AK-47s. My father and the rest of the men dropped to the ground and covered their heads. When the rifles were silent, my father heard laughter and looked up to see two Army sergeants remove their conical hats. The bullets were blanks.

Then they took us to the dream room. And the dream room was where you picked the country you wanted to go and the occupation

42

you wanted to do. They had all places where the U.S. was stationed, all over the world. So I put down Korea, cuz I figured dat was close to Vietnam and I said I'd be a medic or a cook. So, they said I gotta pick one, so I says, all right, cook. The orders get cut and he calls your name and what you gonna do. Johnson, 11-bravo. Hernandez, 11-bravo. Those are all infantry. Calls me, says 94B20. Never forget that number. This lil' hodee drill sergeant, he looks at me and says, "You a spoon, boy. You ain't nuttin' but a greasy spoon."

Around two in the morning, I hear the *Titanic* soundtrack. I roll over to see Vanessa rolling over to look at me. Outside, yellow and red lights flash like lightning bugs, but it is too dark to see where they are coming from. I look out the windshield. The bus's headlights seem to bounce off the night as we follow the highway's sharp turns; the driver toots the horn to alert oncoming traffic. Motorbikes' headlamps burn like spotlights. I can hear the driver gently singing along with Celine Dion as he accelerates into a blind turn.

"How are you?" I whisper to Vanessa.

She smiles and stretches her shoulders up to her neck. "Good. You?"

"Good. This music is god awful."

She laughs. "And it's everywhere."

Sometimes Vietnam was a peaceful backdrop, a pleasant hum in my ear: a street vendor's sizzling wok or the Mekong patting the side of a basket boat. Other times the country was invasive and re-lentless: engines and horns and yelling and rain pounding on metal roofs. Speakers attached to telephone poles blasted tinny music and daily announcements from the government at six in the morning. The owner of one hotel told us the announcements say things like *Keep our country clean; do not spit on the sidewalk.* At first, Vanessa and I did not know where these announcements were coming from, but after we discovered the speakers, even when they were silent, the gray, bullhorn-shaped plastic cones appeared poised to shout.

"Are you nervous about the conference?" I ask.

"No, not really," Vanessa says. "One of the women was scared because she thought I was going to show everyone her paper vagina."

I laugh and want to ask her more questions: What else are the women scared of? What do they do when they're not at work? What kind of music or movies do they like? But several people on the bus are talking on their cell phones and the Muzak seems to get louder and the bus engine roars and the tires slam down into potholes as if pounding out a brain-jarring Morse code. We look at each other, silently agreeing to close our eyes and fake sleep.

We arrive in Da Nang at four in the morning. One of my great uncle's colleagues, Teddy, picks us up in his 1984 Chevy Cavalier. Never has a stranger been so excited to see us. He nearly claps his hands as he scurries out of the car, grabs our bags, and tosses them in the trunk.

"Welcome! Welcome to Da Nang!"

"Thank you," I say. "It's great to meet you."

He bows. Then he opens the back door for Vanessa, the front door for me.

We drive through the center of Da Nang. Strands of white lights stretch over the street, which Teddy explains are from last week's festival. When I ask what kind of festival, he says there are too many to remember.

"China Beach," he says, pointing to the dark shoreline.

I smile and think of the television show of the same name, a team of female Army nurses stationed along the coast. It is too dark to see what the real China Beach looks like. But even if it were mid-day, I wouldn't see the beach Teddy saw. For him, it is the place where he met the first American Marines who landed in Da Nang in the mid '60s. Teddy was in his late teens, and he hung around the base looking for work. His outgoing, funny personality caught the soldiers' attention. They never called him Phan Ngoc Thiet, but instead nicknamed him Teddy.

"'Teddy Bear,' they say to me. 'Come here, Teddy Bear.'" He smiles.

Perhaps Teddy's China Beach is not the real China Beach, either. Perhaps the real China Beach is the one described by Eliseo Perez-Montalvo, an air force sergeant whose oral history depicts China Beach as two beaches: American and Vietnamese, separated by razor wire. Marines bought sheets from the PX and gave them to the Vietnamese women on the other side. The women draped half of the sheet over the razor wire, propped up the other half with a stick, and dug a two-person wide trench. At night, the moon rippled across the ocean, and Eliseo watched green pants bunched around black boots twitch within the trenches.

The television series *China Beach* didn't show Teddy's beach or Eliseo's beach or the beach known by small Vietnamese boys, the ones who collected used condoms off the shore, washed them in seawater, stuffed them into little containers and resold them to fresh Marines, along with Zippos and t-shirts and pins.

Teddy's tour is epic, his voice loud and animated. Vanessa and I feel sleep deprived. We drink coffee at breakfast and lunch. I feel bad because I want to see everything, but after a long bus ride, a nap is much more tempting. We make it through, though, and Teddy doesn't seem to mind when our eyes glaze over.

We pick up his wife that night, and she rides in the back with Vanessa. I turn around and make brief eye contact with Vanessa, but she seems far away. Teddy circles a large parking lot in front of Da Nang's many seaside restaurants. As he eases his Chevy into a parking spot, the *Titanic* soundtrack bubbles to the surface. Teddy hums a few notes and shuts off the engine.

I can't take it anymore. I ask him why that music is always on the radio.

"I haven't heard it on U.S. stations in years," I say.

"I'm not sure," he says. "American things sometimes come late."

After dinner, Teddy takes us to his home. The first thing I see is his impressive collection of shot glasses on top of his grand piano.

"Coke and Jack?" He points at me, then at Vanessa.

We nod and his wife leaves and returns with mini bottles of Jack Daniels, the kind served on airplanes, and two cans of Coca-Cola. She mixes our drinks, hands us our glasses, and walks out of the room. We don't see her again.

"My favorite drink," he grins, proposing a toast. We smile and thank him.

He finishes two Coke and Jacks and leaves to grab another bottle. When he returns, he sits at the piano and uncovers the keys and begins to play *The Star-Spangled Banner*. The song booms off the marble floor, and he turns and grins as if he were giving the crowd their money's worth. Tilting his head to the ceiling, he sings louder. He stares back at us and motions for us to stand. We glance at each other, then stand, holding our sweaty glasses, and sing. I feel like an elementary school kid reciting the pledge of allegiance. Teddy adds a long interlude, like at a Billy Joel concert; his fingers dance a cartoonish ditty after he sings the final words. Silence. Vanessa and I set down our drinks and clap.

"Now!" he says, out of breath. "The best part!"

Best part of what?

He leads us upstairs to a door at the end of a long hallway. The door handle is stainless steel, unlike the ornate glass knobs on the other doors. He reaches into his pocket for his keys.

Tiny red and green lights blink in the center of the room. A fan whirs. Teddy tells us to wait in the doorway. He flicks a switch and a massive model airport comes to life, taking up nearly the entire room. Sounds of air-traffic controllers and planes landing and taking off blast from little speakers. A metal sign on the wall reads: *Phan Ngoc Thiet International Airport.* Teddy stands with his arms spread like a magician.

"This is amazing, Teddy," I say.

"It is!" he says.

Teddy guides us into the room with his hands on our backs, then turns and shuts the door.

"TOM CRUISE!" Teddy shouts, eyes wide, as if he too is surprised to see the framed *Top Gun* poster hanging behind the door.

For several minutes, Vanessa and I walk around the room, looking at the airport's intricate detail. Lego men stand on the tarmac holding red batons or sit behind the wheel on handmade wooden baggage carts. I kneel down and inspect hundreds of holes that Teddy has drilled into the plywood, and see that he has inserted a small blinking light into each one. Behind me, on the wall, are at least a hundred small planes, each one on its own shelf, arranged alphabetically by airline.

The speakers in the corners of the room announce a connecting flight to Kennedy. Teddy nods when I smile at him.

"I record all this," he points to the speaker. "Every time I fly, I record new announcements."

He opens a small closet and shows me his tape recorder and the stacks and stacks of little tapes, the date and airport written on each label. Teddy holds up his pointer finger and reaches into a box with his other hand. The photo album is full of pictures of him posing in dozens and dozens of airports around the world. A newspaper clipping falls out. Vanessa picks it up and unfolds it. Another picture of Teddy, this time standing in front of his own airport, the caption beneath announcing his induction into *The Guinness Book of World Records*.

Vanessa smiles. "You're famous!"

"Yes," Teddy says. "Celebrity."

There is a long pause. Teddy glances at his watch and yawns, which spreads to me, then to Vanessa.

"So," he says, a smile rising on his face. "Time for karaoke?"

7

IN LAOS, it costs one U.S. dollar to shoot an M-16 at a paper target. For ten U.S. dollars, you can throw a grenade into a haystack. For fifty U.S. dollars, you can fire a bazooka at a live cow. An Englishman on holiday showed me the brochure. There are rumors that, for a certain price, you can shoot at a human being.

The Demilitarized Zone (DMZ)—the border that once separated North and South Vietnam—is now a popular tourist attraction. Here, for thirty U.S. dollars, one can visit The Rockpile, an infamous Marine landing zone. On the same tour, one can also glimpse Khe Sanh, the small village made famous in 1968 during the Tet Offensive, when nearly forty thousand North Vietnamese soldiers surrounded six thousand Marines. In nine weeks, the U.S. dropped one-hundred thousand tons of bombs, in addition to hundreds of gallons of napalm and Agent Orange. Air strikes occurred every five minutes, resulting in the most intense bombing period of the war. Only recently has grass begun to grow.

Vanessa and I take a tour of the Vinh Moc tunnels, just north of the DMZ. A jeep carries us down a long dirt road, past vendors selling Coca-Cola and bottled water. *Very thirsty in tunnels! Buy now, save later!* Some of the vendors sell frozen Snickers or extra-large t-shirts exclaiming: *I survived the Vinh Moc tunnels!*

At the end of the road is a small museum filled with U.S. artillery and pistols the Viet Cong made from bamboo that are capable of firing American bullets. Live ammunition once sprinkled the dirt roads and jungle floors, scattered like loose change. Some bullets are buried deep in the earth; others emerge like stones dug up by a farmer's shovel. Before we reach the tunnels, the tour guide pulls over, leads us a few feet off the main road, parts vines and tall grass and reveals an abandoned U.S. tank, undamaged save for patches of rust.

I think of a photograph of my father standing beside a tank in Bien Hoa. He looks like me when I was little, posing next to a purple stegosaurus. The tank is clean. The bright-white Army star below the gun barrel reflects the sun. My father smiles as if the tank is an animal at the zoo, a big beast that, for a moment, has allowed my father to touch it.

Images like these remind me that there was a war going on around my father. So many of his stories from Vietnam are about sex and boredom, as if he spent nineteen months inside a brothel, ticking off days on a calendar. He did keep a "short-timer's calendar," a color-by-number picture of a naked Asian woman. On the last day, my father filled in the space between her legs with a red pencil. I imagine my father sharpening each colored pencil, killing time before his shift in the kitchen. In the distance, bullets echo through the jungle.

The topographic maps of the tunnels on the wall look like giant ant-farms. A pair of German girls in short-shorts and tank tops bend over the rope barrier, gazing into the barrel of an AK-47. I want to pretend I'm not as curious as they are, but I am. Like everyone else, I have paid to be here.

A petite Vietnamese woman enters the museum and gives a brief history of the tunnels. She is dressed in a black long-sleeved shirt, heavy pants, and boots. Vanessa and I are dripping with sweat, and so are the other people we've met on the tour: the heavy-set couple from Missouri in denim shorts and t-shirts, the young guys from Norway with thick eyeglasses and strappy leather sandals, the middle-aged widow from Vermont in weathered hiking boots.

Though expanded to accommodate Westerners, the tunnels are still very tight. My shoulders brush against the walls, and sometimes we turn sideways to squeeze through a particularly narrow section. The walls drip. Our guide leads us into a five-foot-wide room that was once the tunnels' hospital and birthing center. Clay dummies with broken ears sit in the corner—one pregnant, the other wearing a white surgical mask. An Indian man with a video camera holds his lens less than a foot from their faces.

I am suddenly reminded of my family's vacation to Howe Caverns in upstate New York. I was eight years old. My parents had recently purchased their first video camera, and my brother and I shot hours and hours of shaky footage that gave my parents motion sickness when they watched it. My mother often narrated the scene, talking to me or my brother, or describing the beautiful weather. Later, she'd complain about the sound of her voice. "If it bothers you so much," my brother said, "don't talk."

We took the camera inside the caverns, which were lit by yellow and red and purple flood lights, casting long shadows on the slick stone walls. Most of the footage looked like it was shot with the lens cap on. In the darkness, the tour guide's voice echoed. I asked my brother if it was my turn to hold the camera. My family wandered in the cave for almost an hour, whispering.

Here, our Vietnamese guide explains that many children spent their whole lives in the tunnels, surviving only to age three or four due to food and water restrictions. Some never saw daylight. The Indian man disappears around a turn, following his camera's red glow. I imagine him watching the footage when he returns home. His family will sit around a high-definition, flat-screen television, sipping tea, captivated by crystal-clear darkness.

At one point in the tunnels, I have to hold my breath to squeeze through a passageway. When we resurface on the shores of the South China Sea, the tour group is relieved.

"So sorry if you came here for guns," the guide says.

I stare at her, wiping my forehead.

"In Cu Chi Tunnel, south from here, you shoot gun after tour. But no here. Very sorry."

She smiles, turns away from the sea and leads us up the hill, as the Indian man's video camera captures our return to higher ground.

After buying bottled water from one of the vendors along the dirt road, I pull out *Lonely Planet* and look up Cu Chi. For a dollar a bullet, you can fire an AK-47, the official weapon of the North Vietnamese Army. Afterwards, you can eat boiled-root soup, drink bitter tea, and pretend you are the enemy.

8

IN HANOI, Vanessa works with a translator, Ngon, who is around our age. When she introduces herself to me, she tells me her name means "soft and nice communication," and asks me about mine. I hear Bruce Willis in *Pulp Fiction* answer for me: "I'm an American; our names don't mean shit."

"I looked it up once," I say. "Think it means 'priceless.'"

She nods, then turns to Vanessa. "Vanessa, I never asked what your name meant. What does it mean?"

Vanessa blushes. "Butterfly."

"Why are you embarrassed? That is very beautiful."

"My father used to call me that." I turn and look at Vanessa, but she's still looking at Ngon.

Ngon thinks for a moment and then her eyes light up as if she's made a great discovery. "Do you guys like pizza?"

That night, as Vanessa and I get ready for dinner, I skim *Lonely Planet's* restaurant index. *Apocalypse Now. DMZ Bar. The Raging Bull.* I imagine Ngon flipping through a guide to Vietnamese restaurants in the U.S. and reading: *Saigon Palace, Lucky Grasshopper, Pho Getta 'Bout It.* Ngon's parents often spoke to her in French. Perhaps Ngon remembers enough to walk through Boston, gaze at *Au Bon Pain* and imagine opening a restaurant in Hanoi called *To the Good Bread.*

"Think Ngon would be up for a "roadhouse?" I yell to Vanessa while she's in the shower.

She laughs. "They serve pizza?"

"Of course," I say. "Just like a good Vietnamese roadhouse should."

"It's your call."

We tell Ngon we want the restaurant to be a surprise.

I hear The Cowboy Saloon before I see it. Michael Jackson had died the week before, so they are blasting a re-mix of "Smooth Criminal." As we approach the brightly-lit saloon—a two-tiered building with wooden railings, wrap-around porch, and spring-loaded doors—I see a banner advertising a Michael Jackson tribute show, an arm-wrestling competition, dollar drafts, and personal pan pizzas.

"Wow," I say.

"Nice work," Vanessa says.

Ngon giggles. "You picked here? This place is very loud."

I look up the block at the long row of dark store fronts.

"Give it a shot?" I ask.

They stare at me as if my question answers itself. We walk up the steps, pay the ten-dollar cover charge to the Vietnamese bouncer dressed in a pink cowboy shirt and Wranglers, and push our way through the saloon doors.

The inside is dark save for flashing neon lights. A massive disco ball spins above the bar. Vietnamese women in cowboy shirts knotted above their navels deliver glass boots full of beer to the dimly-lit tables. We appear to be under-dressed. The customers are mostly white men in suits, ties loosened around their necks, top buttons undone. On the wooden stage, beside haystacks and wagon wheels, several Vietnamese women move back and forth, swaying to the music.

We sit away from the bar, in line with the stage. The three of us lean close and yell in each other's ears. The laminated drink menu offers margaritas, sangria, Long Island Iced Teas, Sex on the Beach, Fuzzy Navels, and something called "Hot Screw against Wall." I pass the menu to Ngon and look around the bar.

"See anything you like?" Vanessa asks.

"Hey, I didn't know it was gonna be like this."

"I was talking about the menu." She grins.

"This place is different now!" Ngon yells. "One time, it was a family place! Now different!"

I can't imagine families sitting here, even if the lights were bright and the cowgirls only served juice. Our waitress, an older Vietnamese woman, moseys over and tips her white straw hat. We pass around the menu and point at each drink. Ngon speaks into the waitress's ear. They giggle.

"What did you say?" I ask.

"I say no tequila in Hot Screw."

We eat our pizza and have several drinks. A man dressed in black, wearing a heavy, rubber, Michael Jackson mask, moonwalks onto the stage. He grabs the microphone with one hand, his crotch with the other. The crowd goes wild.

As he brings the microphone to his lips, I notice the rubber jaw has been cut out, allowing him to sing without removing his mask. He sounds exactly like Michael Jackson. Even the yips and squeals seem as if they are coming from the jukebox, and not the speakers at his feet. His backup dancers are young Vietnamese women who move like this is the first time they've heard the song.

Perhaps it's the opening chords to "Beat It" or the several empty glass boots on our table that encourage me out of my seat and up to the bar to request another round. The place is jammed and many of the waitresses are no longer circulating among the tables. Instead, they are perched on stools, yelling into the mens' ears beside them. I peel a wet menu off the bar and point out my order to the bartender. She wears a black cowboy hat with an LED screen on the front that flashes H. O. T.

Beside me, a red-headed man who looks to be about my father's age balances a young Vietnamese woman on his knee. He shouts at her over the music. She also wears a black cowboy hat, as did each of the young girls talking to the men in suits. I look back at Vanessa and Ngon clapping and singing. The black lights at the foot of the stage flash on, illuminating the white cowboy hats on the older Vietnamese waitresses, as they wipe dirty tables and stick their fingers into empty glasses.

After the arm-wrestling match between a short Vietnamese man dressed as Rocky and a stocky Irishman pretending to be Ivan Drago, Ngon asks for the check. Vanessa and I pay the bill.

I feel embarrassed, but can't say why. I don't own the saloon. I didn't choose the entertainment. I don't know for sure that the waitresses doubled as prostitutes. But I feel connected with the jumbled, distorted assortment of American pop culture that pulsed between the faux-wood tables and plastic cacti. I grew up on it. I know all the lyrics and movie quotes by heart and, though I hate to admit it, a part of me was comforted by the sights and sounds of it all. It felt similar to seeing McDonald's golden arches rising high over New England back roads, how on a long scenic drive that bright "M" elicits a mixture of guilt and ease.

We walk Ngon back to her apartment and she thanks us repeatedly.

"I hope it wasn't too much," I say.

"No," she says. "The pizza was very tasty."

She and Vanessa speak for a few minutes. They hold hands. I watch them talk, amazed by Vanessa's ability to connect with people so quickly. She has only known Ngon for a couple of days. Perhaps the hand-holding is a custom I am unfamiliar with. But then I remember a photograph from Vanessa's trip to the Philippines: Vanessa sitting on an old woman's couch, their hands clasped tightly between them.

"I feel bad," I say to Vanessa on our walk back to the hotel. "I hope I didn't offend her."

"No, not at all," Vanessa says. "She's fine. It was an experience."

"I wonder what my Dad would think of that place. This whole place. It's like walking into one giant Hard Rock Café. All the stuff that once meant something else is on display or for sale."

"It *is* weird," Vanessa says. "But what did you expect?"

"I don't know. Not this." It was quiet for a moment. "It's amazing that you and Ngon are so close already."

"She's a really smart woman," Vanessa says. "And she's been through a lot. She lost her father during the war. That's how she put it. 'I lost my father and I look for him all the time.'"

I reach over and hold her hand. She looks up at me, then gently presses her cheek to my shoulder. It makes sense now why Vanessa is so open with Ngon. The word "father" sounds different to me when Vanessa says it, as if when the word moves between her lips, it does not have the same meaning. If Vanessa happens to mention "father" in an e-mail, the word seems to glow, cast in permanent highlighter. Sometimes I feel a little uncomfortable even saying the word "father" around her. From what she's told me, her father was a loud, dominating presence: His incessant yelling from the sidelines of her soccer or basketball games, his fits when the orange juice cap wasn't twisted tight enough, or his tirades over Vanessa's hair in the shower drain. Once, knowing he'd use the shower after her, she spelled out her name with long wet hairs on the tile wall. He didn't talk to her for three days.

The night Vanessa moved away to college, he wouldn't open the door to his apartment because she was five minutes late. He yelled out through the window, but refused to see her. She left. Soon after, his body rejected a second liver transplant, and he died.

Perhaps if I met the man I'd feel differently, but each time I visit Vanessa's family, her mother and sister sitting close on the couch chatting like girlfriends, it's hard for me to imagine him in the family. I know his death is a wound, but the three women seemed to have healed, in the way a scar pulls taut the healthy skin that remains.

I think about Ngon's father and Vanessa's father and the ways we choose to describe the dead: passed on, or in a better place, or lost. If I know exactly where my father is, then what am I searching for?

By the time we find the hotel, the sun is rising over Hoan Kiem Lake. We stop at a small convenience store for water. We wait in line behind a Vietnamese man who is also buying two bottles of water. The cashier rings him up and the man pays with a few small coins. When we approach the counter, the cashier smiles, rings up our water, and asks for triple the amount. Vanessa and I look at each other. The cashier nods. We look at the man with the water. He nods. We pay.

Lonely Planet encourages me to barter, but I feel ridiculous, squabbling over a few thousand dong, the equivalent of pennies. My life in the United States is devoid of bargaining. I was raised to accept face value. Besides, the Vietnamese salespeople were slick: pushy men on the corners hawking U.S. dog tags or children selling Zippo lighters. A man working at the War Remnants Museum in Ho Chi Minh City offered me the same fake souvenirs. His upturned palms gestured to the dog tags in the display case as if he were a model on *The Price is Right*. I imagined a massive sheet metal factory tucked into the city, stamping out the social security numbers and blood types of soldiers that never lived.

Before Vanessa and I leave the convenience store, I see a tray of Army pins and patches. As I dig through, I discover another tray, this one filled with coins. U.S. coins. I wish I could say that the Eisenhower silver dollar—the same year as my father's coin—glows like the Golden Ticket or casts a halo around the store or burns in my hand like coal. But it doesn't. It's dirty and dull, buried beneath wheat pennies, buffalo nickels and a gilded Sacajawea glancing over her shoulder.

9

"I DON'T THINK I'm helping at all," Vanessa says. "They're either sleeping or talking on their cell phones."

We stand on the corner of a large rotary and watch the whirlpool of traffic. Earlier that day, one of her students received a call in the middle of Vanessa's lesson on STDs. She stood up from the conference table and walked to the corner of the room. Vanessa hesitated for a moment, then continued her lesson.

"Just when I was about to start talking again, she starts smiling and clapping and jumping up and down."

I lean close to hear Vanessa's voice. Motorbikes sputter past, some hopping up on the sidewalk to bypass traffic. Cyclo drivers ring bells or yell *Hey!* until we gaze in their direction. We shake our heads.

"So she jumps up and down and announces that her T-cell count is high enough for her to get pregnant."

A teenager tries to sell me a wallet with POW/MIA stamped into the leather, then he offers a Zippo that reads *Wine 'em, Dine 'em, 69 'em.* By now, I've learned the Vietnamese word for "No."

"That's good news for her, right?" I ask.

Vanessa wipes sweat from her forehead. "Yeah. But she basically told the whole class she's HIV positive and now she wants to have a baby. This is a woman who was taught it was wrong to look at herself naked."

We play a frightening game of Frogger as we try to cross the street, then follow our map through side streets of crumbling French villas and people of all colors eating croissants and drinking wine at open-air cafés. The movie house is tucked down a narrow alleyway lined with bicycles. At the end is a Vietnamese woman shaded by the Oscar Mayer umbrella on her hotdog cart. Before we attempt to ask her where we can buy our tickets, she points to a window.

"What are we seeing again?" Vanessa asks.

"*Casualties of War.*" She looks at me as if I still haven't answered. "Michael J. Fox? Sean Penn?"

"Oh."

"It's good. You'll like it." I smirk, thinking about when I went away for a week and Vanessa hijacked our Netflix account. I'd check my e-mail and see that *The Good, the Bad, and the Ugly* had been replaced with *Orgasmic Birth*, *The Big Lebowski* with *The Business of Being Born*. She'll humor me and watch my movies, but she's never as captivated as I am. Once, in the middle of Steve McQueen's famous car chase in *Bullitt*, she started flipping through a magazine. I wanted to shut it off. It's like when you're dying to play your favorite song for someone during a road trip and the person doesn't like the song and now you don't even want to listen to it anymore. Somehow their response affects yours. Sometimes I wonder if the films I like are just "guy movies," as my mother would say. Or perhaps the movie I'm seeing is not the movie Vanessa sees. We don't have the same connotations. Perhaps the movie I see is the movie of me watching the movie.

Carrying frosty mugs of Tiger beer, we enter the small dark theater and sit near the back. The crowd is mostly older white couples. Several people walk in as the house lights fade and I wonder where they're from.

Michael J. Fox is on a trolley in San Francisco. An Asian woman boards, takes a seat further down the car. A wood flute that could either be the original score, or one lifted from *The Karate Kid* soundtrack, fades in, and we prepare ourselves for a flashback.

I remember watching this with my father years ago. He sat on the couch, cracking open peanuts and popping them in his mouth, prefacing the action scenes with: "Good part coming up, boy." The film follows a platoon of U.S. soldiers after they kidnap a Vietnamese girl. Sean Penn plays the psychotic, trigger-happy sergeant; Michael J. Fox is a scared young man fresh out of boot camp. The soldiers take turns raping the girl. Michael J. Fox is the only one who refuses. That, to the other soldiers, is evidence of his homosexuality. Two things the platoon can't trust: a snitch and a faggot.

I look over at Vanessa during one of the rape scenes, which is as disturbing as it is loud. She raises her eyebrows and mouths the words: *Nice choice.*

In the middle of the movie, I want to reach into my pocket for my headphones, drown out the actors' lines with my father's words. I must have missed something in the recording. I remember scenes in mystery movies where detectives turn up the volume on a crackling 911 call and reveal a hidden voice, a faint sound, an unidentified person in the background, breathing. I often lose track of time listening to my father's voice, my neck stiff from leaning forward, as if pressing my ear to a door: *Who's there?*

The flashback that opened the film subsides to present day, where Michael J. Fox runs after the girl on the train and turns her to face him, but—*sigh*—it isn't the same girl. Music swells, the screen fades, and we know everything will be all right. Someday.

"That's really weird," I say as we leave. "I remembered it being a lot better."

Vanessa walks a step or two in front of me, her hands in her pockets.

"Wait up."

"It's hot," she says. "I just want to get back to the hotel and shower." She tries to hail a cyclo driver. "An hour ago, we couldn't walk ten feet without one of these guys yelling at us." She walks closer to the corner and waves her hand.

"What are you doing?" I ask. "They'll screw us. We're better off walking."

She looks at me. We had wandered around Hanoi enough times. I can find our way back.

I start walking up the street, but Vanessa stays on the corner, waving. I stop and look back. A cyclo driver pulls up and rings his bell. "Very cheap," he says. "Very cheap." He repeats the words over and over until they lose their meaning. I hold my arms out by my sides. Vanessa looks at me, then the driver and shakes her head. As we walk away, the driver peddles slowly beside us for a few blocks before he gives up and coasts across the street.

We are lost. Again. My sense of direction is never any good, but in Vietnam, it's pitiful. We have been here for three months and just when I think I know where we're going, the city clicks like a Rubik's Cube and nothing is where it should be. Vanessa lets out a long exhale and I decide to keep walking straight. I open *Lonely Planet*, but it's too dark to read. I stare at the tangle of streets in front of us.

Several street vendors are still open, selling ginger, exotic mushrooms and baskets of raw meat. Couples browse the selection and the vendors smile when the customers point to what they want. I give in and walk over to one of the vendors and point to the name of our hotel in the book. She nods and smiles, draws an invisible map in her palm, but this one is clearer than the man's in Ho Chi Minh City. She traces the lines on her palm. I read them like street signs.

We are almost there. A man holding two baskets overflowing with leafy vegetables steps into our path. Vanessa lifts her head off my shoulder and smiles. He pushes me with both hands and I stumble back. I hear Vanessa shout "No!" and I echo her, but the man reaches out for her and I push Vanessa behind me. The man's swollen cheeks and dry, cracked nose look like a tree grown around a wiry smile. He pauses when I say "no" in Vietnamese, but then holds up his basket of vegetables and points to my pockets. We quickly cross the street and at first the man follows, then he turns away. At the end of the block, I look back and he's gone.

In our room, we lie in bed with the door locked. I keep picturing the man's angry face, the way he held up the vegetables as if they were the only thing I would ever need and he was outraged that I didn't understand that. His body screamed, "What are you waiting for, you idiot? BUY THESE!" Vanessa and I had been cornered by beggars or belligerent drunks in Boston plenty of times, but this man was different. His aggression seemed specific, focused, as if he had been waiting for us.

Vietnam, the past and present, the truths and replicas, the images I see and the stories I've heard—none of it... This isn't working out the way I planned. Perhaps it's my Hollywood education that makes me assume the man with the vegetables was anything more than a random event—the wrong place, the wrong time. My father often said he didn't trust any of the Vietnamese: *They help you during the day and shoot at you at night.* But the Vietnamese were not trying to kill me or Vanessa, and Ngon and Teddy and plenty of others have been kind and generous to us, so why then do I still have this persistent suspicion or, even, fear? Is it because I've never traveled this far from home? Or that Vietnamese is the most difficult language I've ever attempted to decipher? Or is it that for years, Vietnam was not a country to me, but only a war?

Vietnam was the first televised war. One of the first reality shows, before actors were paid to act like real people. In living rooms nationwide, Americans watched bombs green as watermelons tumbling above patchwork farms. Villagers in conical hats and *ao dais* running silently from Pac Man pellets. Thatch-roofed structures, ignited by Zippos, crackling like Duraflames. For most of my generation, Vietnam remains a televised war.

I thought I came here because I was sick of war films and still-shots of my father in his hooch. Yet I retreated to a movie theater, as if the Vietnam outside offered no insight. In my father's Vietnam, women walked from hooch to hooch, *buffin' their snatches* with white rags. Old fathers sold their daughters for household appliances. Children made weapons out of Coke cans. They didn't seem related to the people outside the movie house: the families waiting in line for a puppet show; an old man guiding Vanessa and me across a busy intersection; a group of hip teenagers in a Mercedes idling at a red light.

Even the women in The Cowboy Saloon, pressing themselves against men in suits, seemed to have little in common with the women my father dealt with thirty years ago. The younger Vietnamese we chatted with in hotels or on tours didn't care about the war, and the older generations were calloused or indifferent or dead. As in most of the world, the Vietnamese we met were busy people who worked to support their families. It is disturbing yet ingenious that many Vietnamese businesses now capitalize on the war. In a single day, Vanessa and I could take a bus tour through Khe Sanh, shoot Vietnamese and American guns at paper targets, drink cocktails called Napalm or Agent Orange, eat dinner at the DMZ Bar, and catch a late-night showing of *Hamburger Hill*.

I sit up in our bed and reach for my recorder.

"Babe, you gotta hear this. My Dad once told me about this Vietnamese dude who—"

"I'm really not in the mood right now."

"It's not that long."

She sits up. "I don't want to hear anymore. I don't care about the girls he was with or what he spent his money on. I don't get why you're so obsessed with it."

"I'm not obsessed with it. It's not like I'm getting off on these stories."

Vanessa reaches for her water bottle. Then she stands up and tries to turn up the air conditioner, but it's already on high.

"Have you even been listening to *yourself* on that tape? You snicker each time your Dad says "beaver" or "jugs.""

I fight the urge to snicker now. "Oh, come on. Those words are hilarious. I don't condone his behavior."

"Whatever. You stare into every massage parlor we walk past. You take us to that saloon. Then, after I spend all day talking to these women with horrible stories of rape and whatever else, you take me to a movie that's basically a 90-minute rape scene. And you keep playing me these stories about your Dad doing whatever he did here."

"Yeah, but there's a big difference, babe. He didn't rape or kill anyone." My voice echoes off the low ceiling.

"I'm not saying he did, but those women he was with—"

"He was only nineteen! Show me another nineteen-year-old guy who would have done any different."

She shakes her head. "You really think we're only talking about your father right now?"

My face burned. "What?"

"You can't think of any other sketchy situation where a guy doesn't question his behavior?"

I shake my head. "Sure I can. And I can also think of a situation where a woman keeps bringing up the same shit even though the guy and the woman have talked about it a thousand times."

Vanessa nods her head, but not in agreement. She walks to the bathroom and slams the door. The room hums like a phonograph, the needle hissing between tracks. I want to pound on the bathroom door and unload every curse in the book, or knock gently and apologize and tell Vanessa I love her. My mind and body struggle like two negative magnets—a pair of objects that could fit together or push each other away.

I feel fire move inside my head, burn down my throat, smolder in my stomach. I take a long sip of warm water. I want to close my ears. I want to mute my brain. I want to reclaim my spot beside my father on the couch, crack open another peanut, and let Hollywood return me to a Vietnam I remember.

Before we left, I couldn't articulate my purpose for traveling to Vietnam. Now that the trip is almost over, I still can't. Maybe I should have brought him with me. Maybe if he was here now, I could point to the places he stood and ask, "What happened here?" But no matter how romantic I am in my imagination, I can't pretend that my father would suddenly have the answer, that he would turn and look me in the eye and say, "Son, here's what happened. And here's why."

II

STATESIDE

*You listenin' to me, boy? He's dead. Believe me, he's dead. Tell ya,
though, when I found him, coulda sworn he was sleepin'. Sometimes
these tractor trailers they chew 'em up, and then they're no good. Air
horn gets 'em all herky-jerky and they don't know which way to go.
Bumper musta just clocked this guy cuz he's in pretty good shape.*

Pass me my knife.

*Cars zippin' by, hot cup of coffee in my hand, tryin' to scrape him
up without breakin' his neck. I had to touch him a little bit; so what,
I'm touchin' him now.*

*No, I didn't put him in the backseat—what was I, takin' Grandma
to church? I put him in the cooler in the trunk.*

*Right here, okay? See how the fur parts between his ears. Along the
spine. Down to his tail. Now this might not be textbook or whatever,
but I like to hang him upside down. Easier to skin that way, instead of,
you know, holdin' em up with one hand and tryin' to cut with the other.
He ain't gonna bite ya. He's dead. Anyways, I sewed his mouth shut.*

*Watch. No blood. No guts. Just strippin' the hide, like takin' off a
coat. Little slimy under there, but that ain't nothin'. And I just keep
slicin', over his ribs, his belly, down each leg, slicin' the membrane.
Nice and easy.*

*Gimme those shears, will ya? Oh, what do we got, a little Ted Nu-
gent? Turn this up, boy! Those look like shears to you? Those are them.
Hold'm steady. And when I clip'm, keep that pan under his throat.*

*The body's not so tough but the head's a bitch. Gotta be really
careful and just use the tip of the knife around the mouth. The nose.
Especially the ears.*

There we go.

Toss the body. Cuz we don't need it anymore. 'Less you want to eat him? Tie up that bag, too, or Mom'll freak. Then we dunk the hide in this pickling solution. Wring'm out good and keep'm in the fridge 'til we get the mannequin set.

Some guys use plastic eyes, but I've always liked glass. The way they reflect. Both are tricky, though. If you don't get 'em centered, he'll be all cockeyed, one lookin' for a garbage can, the other caught in headlights. Won't look legit. Put a dab of clay in the socket, then push 'em in.

Now we just wrap the hide around the mannequin. Pull it up around the legs like a pair of Levis. Stretch it over the back. Gently, real gently, pull the skin on the face, get all the features right. Pretty soon you could put him in the backyard and never know the difference. Hand me that needle and thread. Linen thread, not cotton. Cotton'll rot.

We can make him hold somethin', if you want. Drill a lil' hole in his paws and squeeze in a pine cone or some shit. Paws got wire in 'em; we can shape 'em anyway we want. Go outside and see what you can scrounge up. I gotta take a breather anyway.

10

MY FATHER ROSE at 5 a.m., shuffled his calloused feet to the bathroom and slid open the pocket door. After a brief coughing fit, he hocked into the sink. The exhaust fan rattled. A fart kick-started his long piss. Then he blew several quick, hard blasts into his handkerchief. Pocket door slid open, down the stairs, wood creaking and popping, sandpaper hands rubbed along the banister. Muted Weather Channel's blue glow. Silverware drawer, running water, coffee pot. Back up the stairs, bathroom, mug placed on the permanent coffee ring on the sink. Sparked a Winston, let it burn like incense on the wicker shelf. Shower. Scraped his jaw line with a razor, slapped Old Spice onto his cheeks. Down the stairs, checked the weather, coffee cup thunked in the sink. Into his Chevy, first gear, second, third, and I didn't see him again until four in the afternoon, when he coasted the Chevy back into the driveway, tossed his bloody white apron over his shoulder, and carried the scent of nearly forty years of tobacco and coffee and cold cuts inside.

Seven a.m. My mother officially rose, though she'd been awake for hours, tossing, turning, mumbling. Shuffled out of bed in her pink nightgown. Into the bathroom for a bout with IBS, expelling yesterday's swallowed air. A sigh. Tossed my father's burnt Winston filter into the trash, down the same stairs, same Weather Channel, same coffee pot. Sparked a Marlboro Light. If she were cleaning houses, she took her rags from the dryer in the basement, packed them into a canvas tote, then collected the rest of her supplies: Windex, Lysol, an all-purpose spray called Simple Green, which she swore by.

Perhaps these were her yacht club years, and instead of Windex and rags, she loaded a rectangular plastic bin full of restaurant checks, an enormous printing calculator balanced on top. Or she was a secretary for the dermatologist, so she'd been up since six, showering, blow-drying, ironing, heels clicking on wood, then tile, wood, then tile. Perhaps arts and crafts, wedding albums with thick cotton covers and lace trim, or something called *poofs*: little, flower-shaped puffs of satin with a metal clip glue-gunned to the back that one could attach to shoes or blouses or use to cinch a pony tail. Or the beauty parlor in the basement, fully-equipped hair-washing station and spaceman dome, which she assured me was for drying the hair of the strange women who entered our home and not for transforming them into a *Jetsons* character and blasting them into another galaxy.

Maybe this day she worked two or three jobs, loaded all of her equipment into the car, took a final sip of coffee and burst off the porch like Superman from his phone booth, returning hours later for a quick costume change before shooting back out into the world once again. A different role. A different identity.

When I was in elementary school, my father would sometimes let me go to work with him. I sat on the edge of the tub at 5 a.m., stealing sips of bitter coffee in his mug while he shaved. The residual shower steam swirled with his cigarette smoke like the off-shore storms we glimpsed on the Weather Channel. As my father splashed water on his face, I watched the exhaust fan suck the tiny hurricane through its golden grate and wondered what happened to the storms off the coast of Florida or Cuba that never touched land.

"Chilly willy, today, boy," he said, tossing me one of his wool hats, which smelled like everything else he owned—Winstons, coffee, gasoline, a hint of Old Spice, a whiff of bologna. I pictured him on a billboard, straddling a dusty horse, cowboy hat tipped over his face, leather reins clenched in his left fist and in his right a small bottle of amber cologne. *Work* by My Father.

As he finished his routine, I watched the thick exhaust pouring out of his Chevy in the driveway. He dug his old sneakers out from beneath the couch. He held his shoelaces between his callused fingertips, and as he tied, I could almost feel his rough skin guiding a heavy hammer or a baseball bat in my hands. The deli took a piece of almost all his fingers, the flesh slivers ending up "in somebody's ham sandwich, I guess."

He sparked a Winston in the driveway, told me to tie my shoes and hop in the truck. *The Fox* kicked on: Bob Seger's "Still the Same." My father jiggled the shifter into reverse, and we were off.

We stopped at 7-Eleven, where my father bought a coffee for himself, and a hot chocolate for me. He always peeled off the lid on the walk back to the truck and took several quick sips, as if there were some secret ingredient, something more than caffeine that satisfied him. My hot chocolate was sweet and made me feel like a little kid, which I was. As we pulled out of the parking lot and headed toward the Expressway, I timed my sips with my father's.

A few miles before our exit, my father jerked the wheel right and skidded to a halt on the side of the Expressway. My hot chocolate splashed out of my cup and onto my jeans.

"Sorry," he said, staring out through the windshield.

The white line cut through the middle of its body. The head and paws stretched onto the highway. Its legs and tail lay in the breakdown lane. Cars rushed by, shaking the truck and whipping the gray and black fur. My father looked in his rearview mirror and stubbed out his cigarette.

"Hang here for a sec."

He stepped out; I locked my door. The sun was rising, but the highway was still dim and damp. I looked over at the rusty guardrail splattered with tar, never having been this close before. My father stood between the headlights. His long shadow cut across the breakdown lane and stretched into the pine trees.

The animal lifted its head. Slowly moved it side to side. One paw stretched further into the highway, then pulled back, back, back. My father knelt beside it. The animal lifted its head again and looked as if it were chewing, working something from behind its back teeth. Then it stopped.

My father walked past my window and reached into the bed of the truck. He came back with a short metal shovel. The metal scraped the pavement, and a large black part of the animal fell out and slapped the ground. Heat rising like smoke in the cold air.

When he brought it closer, I saw it was a raccoon. I continued staring at the animal until my father dropped it into a black garbage bag. As we pulled back onto the Expressway, I watched the black bag slide from one side of the truck bed to the other.

"What's in the bag, Don?" said a man stocking shelves as we entered Waldbaum's supermarket.

"Special delivery, Tommy. Mind your business." My father smiled.

He carried the black garbage bag down the empty aisles of gleaming linoleum, past orange signs proclaiming deals on Doritos, Entenmann's cookies, Cheerios. Kicked open the scuffed saloon doors marked EMPLOYEES ONLY, passed through a series of heavy plastic strips hanging in the doorway. *Just like the car wash*, I thought.

My father set the raccoon on a stainless steel table, then tied his apron around his waist. He grabbed another apron from a milk crate beneath the table and tossed it in my face. I slipped the neck loop over my head and tried to tie the strings around my waist but ended up knotting them around the middle of my thighs. Then he put on a paper hat; I put on a paper hat. He put on his name tag; I put on a name tag. My new name was *Jesus*—"a shit-bag part-timer who banged in sick Super Bowl weekend." I looked down at the name on my chest, thinking about all the times I pretended to be sick, tricking my mother into letting me stay home from school. Technically, I had "banged in" sick to school today, but I believed that because I went to work with my father, I wasn't doing anything wrong. We'd tell her later.

"Okay," he said. "Let's get this guy squared away."

He carried the garbage bag over to the walk-in freezer. The large metal handle was coated with frost. My father yanked it open; cold fog billowed out, carrying the sulfuric scent of freezer burn. Frosty steel shelves held piles of carcasses and animal parts: cow ribs, chicken breasts, lamb shanks, pig's feet. We walked past all the other animals, to the back of the freezer. My father picked up a canvas tarp and placed his raccoon beside a frozen deer head wrapped in cellophane—eyes caught in permanent headlights, specks of black tar clinging to its fur.

I spent the rest of the day watching my father slice bologna or make roast beef sandwiches. He gave me a look when an elderly customer requested 1/16th of a pound of low-sodium turkey breast, or when a man asked if my father could slice his ham thin. No, thinner. A little thinner, buddy.

"Perfect," the man said, accepting his order with a toothless grin.

He gave the male customers funny nicknames: *Rocko, Charlie, Butch, Guy, Chief, Boss.* The female customers he called *Toots, Hun,* and sometimes, *Miss.* But as the day went on, the nicknames dwindled, until it was three o'clock, a half-hour before quittin' time, and my father called everyone the same way: "Next!"

Earlier that week in school, an overzealous guest speaker had come to our class to teach us about fingerprints. I believed the man to be a private investigator or secret agent, but most likely he was a criminal justice major from one of the community colleges. He distributed ink pads and pieces of paper which had a box for each one of our prints. Fighting the urge to smear each other's faces or leave a permanent high-five on a friend's back, we listened to the man identify the loops and whorls and arches, explaining that each one of us has a unique print unlike any other person in the entire world. He told us about desperate criminals slicing off their fingertips in hopes of eluding the law.

"But," he said, holding up an inky finger, "they always grow back."

"How long does it take?" one kid asked. We all nodded, anticipating an expert's response.

The man paused. "Not as long as you'd think."

I wanted to ask more questions, but, as usual, I kept quiet, my face burning for answers. How many times can you slice your fingers before you alter your prints? What if this guy was wrong? What if my father's whorls have become loops, arches into whorls, or if now there's nothing at all, no unique markings, the skin as smooth and common as sausage casing?

We punched out. My father slung the black garbage bag over his shoulder, and I followed him out to the parking lot. On the ride home, I dozed off, my head knocking against the passenger window. We pulled into the driveway. My father grabbed the raccoon and walked into the house, through the kitchen, into the basement, through the laundry room, beyond his rack of Army jackets with our last name sewn above the pockets. I followed him around his workbench strewn with scalpels, hypodermic needles, and glass eyeballs. As he opened a long, casket-like freezer, I watched him drop the raccoon beside a frozen zoo of squirrels, big-mouthed bass, rabbits, and a hawk.

Mornings sounded painful. Stretching, groaning, shuffling, showering, shot of caffeine, sigh after sigh after sigh—all in preparation for leaving the place you loved, the place you felt comfortable, and venturing out into a dreadful world. I watched television shows where the mothers and fathers sat around a marble island of pancakes and eggs and bacon and fresh-squeezed orange juice, chatting about their plans for the day. None of them swore beneath their breath or paced the house searching for a missing shoe. While I knew these shows were fake, there were parts that felt very real: a science teacher who acted just like mine or a kid who said the same things I did. I second-guessed myself: Perhaps I'm wrong. Perhaps all of it could be true.

A lot was required to break my parents' routine. When it was temporarily broken for a long weekend or a trip to visit relatives, the first day was spent leaving the routine, the last day was devoted to reentering the routine, and much of the time in between was spent in limbo, neither one sure what to do or how to act. So my mother scrubbed Simple Green on her sister's stove while everyone slept and my father took long walks to 7-Eleven, returning with a 12 oz. coffee cup clutched in his hand.

Our home was an integral component of my parents' routine. They seemed unable to operate at full capacity without first loading themselves inside our home, as if the floors of our house were circuit boards, their morning rituals a computer's processes. While they seemed to need their routines in order to function, I never noticed them deriving any pleasure from these essential habits. Perhaps in my mind I lump together their preparation for work with the work itself, envisioning my mother pacing and sighing through the dermatologist's office or my father breathing Winston after Winston as his fingers work a ham across the slicer. But it's hard not to. I cannot remember my parents ever saying anything positive about their jobs. Work sucks. Work is life.

I once asked my father what he wanted to be when he was younger. He looked at me.

"What do you mean?" he asked.

"I mean, was there anything you wanted to do?"

He paused. Chewed the inside of his cheek a few times, then raised his eyebrows.

"Not that I can think of."

I believed his animals were alive. The way he handled a freshly-killed raccoon or squirrel was different from how he moved a hunk of ham or roast beef across the deli slicer at Waldbaum's. When he'd work the slicer, the meat was sterile, no hint of life. My father would move his right arm back and forth in a quick, isolated motion, while his left hand supported his body weight against the slicer.

In his workshop in the basement, his technique for handling dead meat was different. He'd flick on his magnifying lamp and hunch over the animal. With a scalpel pressed between his fingertips, he'd gently slice through the fur, then the membrane, careful not to puncture the animal's veins or organs because if he did, the hidden interior fluids, the blood and the bile, would spill out and ruin the exterior.

When I asked my father how he became a taxidermist, he paused for a moment. He squinted, like he does when he's stumped by a piece of music or movie trivia. "Well, I was hoping to take the boiler repair class, but it was all filled up." My father's days off were sacred, so for him to spend his free time doing something and not get paid, there had to be a good reason, but I didn't know what that was.

A rabbit perched on our mantel; a pair of mallards hung from the wood paneling in the living room, a squirrel held an acorn on the shelf above my bed. The squirrel often rode shotgun as I raced my plastic go-cart down the driveway. What could be better than a wild animal sitting patiently beside me, gazing up as if to ask: "Where to next, brotha?" There's a picture of me in sunglasses on our back deck, sitting in my go-cart, wheels angled, raising the squirrel above my head like a trophy.

"It was pretty creepy," my older brother, Don, said. "I'd catch you in the backyard trying to feed Dad's squirrel a piece of your peanut butter and jelly sandwich."

I didn't think it was creepy. Why would it be? My room was already filled with fuzzy dinosaurs and turtles dressed as ninjas. Is a squirrel holding an acorn any creepier than me inserting a cassette tape into the back of a bear wearing suspenders and singing Teddy Ruxpin songs? And if I wanted Teddy's friend—a worm—to sing along, I simply plugged an AV cable into Teddy's spine and the worm wiggled to life.

11

I LAY in the grass, my sneakers against the red barn door, onion weeds and dandelions tickling my neck. Above, the black branches of the dead oak stretched like thin fingers, cracking the flawless blue sky. The cars on Route 25 *whooshed* by the house and followed the s-curve past the animals and the silo. My mother and my father were somewhere, laughing. A silhouette of a man stood over me, blocking out the sun, the oak, even the sounds.

"What are you doing?" the silhouette asked.

"Nothing."

"Well, time to do something."

Grandpa picked me up and carried me to the animals. Not rough, but not gentle, he held me like a sack of chicken feed. I bounced in his arms as he climbed the slight hill, his bad breath whistling through his teeth. He set me down and opened the gate to the chicken coop. I liked the goats and the pigs, the cows and the sheep, the slow harmless animals. The chickens frightened me. There were so many of them and they'd get excited when he came in and they'd squawk and run and try to fly. He scooped out chicken feed using an old Clorox bottle sliced in half. The loyal, hungry chickens followed him, pecking the pellets out of the mud and crying for more.

"Ant, come here!"

I walked out into the mud. He gave me the scoop. I held it upside down and he grabbed my hand with both of his and corrected me. The Grandpa I now see in my mind has no face. All I see is tan, swollen biceps, veins bulging like blue hoses, and callused hands. I used to watch his hands: the black tractor grease buried beneath his remaining fingernails and in the creases of his knuckles and palms; stubby fingers wrapped around a ratchet or a hammer; stumpy thumb holding a tape measure in place. My father had the same hands.

When we drove out to Grandpa's farm, my father bent his wrist over the wheel of his Chevy, the rough tips of his fingers dancing to the oldies station like wooden wind chimes. His thumb was busted and split, never healed. It got tired of repairing itself and chose to stay ripped and raw, awaiting the next blow from a hammer. Their hands were like history books, scars of Braille. Some people hope to inherit money or land; I wanted hands like my father's.

I dug the scoop into the bucket and before I could throw it, the feed dribbled into a pile around my feet. The chickens swarmed me, running around my legs, lifting off the ground and flapping beside my ears, pecking, squawking, screaming. Grandpa walked over slowly and scolded the chickens. The chickens reluctantly broke up like a pack of bullies, and I swore they were giving me dirty looks. The chickens liked my grandfather. They followed him everywhere, even when he didn't have any food. He treated them well and, in return, they offered him their eggs. I didn't understand why they didn't like me.

My brother told me about the time my grandfather took him out to the chicken coop. He sat Don on the fence, told him to stay there. Grandpa chased all the chickens into a small wire pen. There were so many chickens and the pen was so small that they climbed all over each other, flapping their wings and pecking up through the holes in the wire. He let one out, choked it silent. He pressed its body against the fence where my brother sat and bent its neck around the wooden post. He slid the axe out of his back pocket, held the chicken's body with his boot.

"Hold his head. Like this."

Don held the chicken's head, pulling the neck tight around the wooden post. The axe cut through the chicken and thumped into the wood. The chicken's body took off into the mud, running in circles, then zigzagging before it slumped on its side. Don held the head in his finger tips, blood dripping on the dirt. The beak was shut and its right eye blinked once, drowsily, and then remained open. Grandpa took the head and tossed it over the fence, into the tall weeds.

Don told me what chicken eggs really were. They weren't gifts to Grandpa, thanking him for his food and care. Grandpa was stealing their babies and eating them. I had watched my grandfather pick the shells off hardboiled eggs, peel the whites from the yellow yoke ("the baby," Don said), and put the pieces in his mouth. There used to be a little dog that hung around the farm, but somebody drove by one day and stole him. I wondered if really Grandpa had stolen the dog and eaten him. I wondered if I had any other brothers and sisters that Grandpa had stolen before I could remember them. Had he cooked them in a pot and then eaten them on the back porch, too? Maybe afterwards, he had smoked his pipe and rocked slowly in his chair beside a bucket of tiny bones.

"Everybody was afraid of him," my mother told me, "but not you. You could always get to him."

Soon after our trip to the farm, my cousin Matthew died in a car crash. He was nineteen. It didn't make any sense. How could a soldier die here? There was no war, no tanks rolling down our street or helicopters hovering over our pool. And soldiers only die from bullets, not on dark highways leading back to their bases.

On the morning of Matthew's funeral, my father bleached his white Reeboks. That was a habit of his. First he removed the laces and let them soak in a bowl of hot water. Then he moved them into a bowl of bleach. After that, he placed the sneakers in the sink, their tongues pulled back. He placed his hand inside the sneaker, wearing it like a glove. Then he dipped the orange scrub brush first into the water, then into the bleach and began rubbing it along the sides of the sneaker in quick scratchy strokes. He stood barefoot at the sink in jeans and a white tank top, a Winston hanging limply between his lips. From my seat on the counter, I saw the black soapy water run off his sneakers and swirl in the drain. The bleach and smoke stung my nose as he exhaled and dipped the brush in the water again. When he was finished scrubbing, he wiped them with a rag and placed them on a paper towel next to the sink. The laces soaking, he stared out at the backyard.

He only bought white sneakers. When they became too worn for daily use, he bought a new pair and put the old ones under the couch, wearing them only on weekends for yard work or painting. He'd come home from work on Saturday, switch sneakers and head out into the backyard to rake leaves. Eventually, the new sneakers became the old ones, and the old ones got thrown out.

"You don't have to come if you don't want to," he said, resting his Winston on the edge of the sink.

I nodded, relieved. I didn't want to see Matt's body. I thought about the movie *Stand by Me* and wondered why all those stupid kids would risk so much just to stare at a dead person. I had been sitting on the back deck when my father came home from work and told me. The expression on his face, the tone of his voice, made me feel like I had done something wrong. I had started to cry. "That's not how it was when Dad told me," Don said, years later. "I grew up with Matt. I was a lot closer to him than you were. Dad just walked up to me when I came home from school and said, 'Hey, listen, Matt died.' Like he was telling me dinner would be late."

I wonder if this is really how my father told him. Maybe my father thought that Don was old enough to handle a blunt sentence better than I could. Maybe by then Matt's death was starting to affect my father more than it had before and he wasn't paying much attention to his tone and just wanted to spit out the news. Maybe after he told my brother, he saw something change in Don's eyes, like a tiny fluorescent light flickering, and my father couldn't think of anything else to say.

My mother walked into the kitchen wearing a black dress and black shoes, neither of which I'd ever seen her wear before. It was odd to see her standing there in the kitchen, rummaging through her small black handbag. A few hours before, I had been in the garden with her, watching her stab the earth with her silver shovel. I sat on the bag of fertilizer, racing my Matchbox cars up and down the deck. Before she had cut open the bag, she told me to go play somewhere else.

"This stuff is poison," she said.

From the other side of the lawn, I stood watching her poison her flowers. She wore a white facemask that protected her nose and mouth, and bright gardening gloves to protect her hands. I walked around the side of the pool, closer to her flower bed. The fertilizer fell like snow in the warm air, the petals catching some of the white granules, the rest falling to the ground.

"Hey," she said, wiping her forehead, "I told you to stay away."

"Why are you putting poison on your flowers, Mom?"

She looked down at the bag and then at her flowers, as if the answer lay somewhere between.

"It helps them grow," she said. "Sometimes things need a little poison to grow."

On the way to the funeral, they dropped me off at school. The three of them sat in the Chevy, looking straight out through the windshield. Each of them gave me a half smile. I turned and walked into the low brick building.

I was quiet for most of the day, but that wasn't much different from any other day. Mrs. Flood kept looking over at me throughout her lesson on long division, squinting, as if I was too far away to see. When we took our afternoon snack break, the rest of the kids unzipping baggies of apple slices or cheese and crackers, she touched my shoulder and guided me toward the hallway.

"Is everything okay today, Anthony?" I found her densely-freckled face soothing in a way and didn't mind how she always leaned over and spoke very close to me.

I nodded and smiled, then shrugged a little.

"Because you seem a little distant. A little glassy-eyed."

I thought about the boxes of glass eyes my father kept in the basement. They were mostly brown or black. I couldn't remember the color of Matt's eyes.

"I'm fine," I said. "Everything's fine."

The rest of the day my head felt huge and weightless, like a balloon attached to my neck by a thin string. Mrs. Flood's voice echoed in my head: *A little glassy-eyed.* I imagined a chisel pointed at my face: a swift smack of a hammer and my eyeball would burst into shards, scattering across my desk.

12

AND WE'RE BACK! Comin' at ya live from Beneath the Sink, I—.
Wait, I messed up. *Okay. Comin' at ya live from Beneath the Sink, I'm
your host, Anthony, here once again to bring you all your favorite mov-
ies on the radio! Um* (rustling of cereal boxes and potato chip bags).
Today... uh, for your listening enjoyment, we have the great movie
Goonies. *Now I have to say this is one of my favorites. A classic, really.
I love it. You love it. We all love it. If you don't know it, you will love it.
So for all you fans out there and also the people who haven't seen it
and you're driving home from work now in beaucoup traffic, this one
goes out to all of you. Okay* (rustling). Shoot. Why won't this stupid
thing—okay. *Here we go! See you all next time! Enjoooy the movie!*

A television flickered. Canned laughter from the living room or my
room or my brother Don's room or my parents' room. I pulled 'fridge
duty,' so I got out the salad dressings, ketchup, applesauce. My mother
opened the oven and heat rushed out, filling the kitchen with invisible
fire. The television laughed. She set the bowl down and stabbed a
wooden spoon into the fleshy macaroni, and I thought of a behind-
the-scenes show I had seen about the soundmen in movies—how it was
actually some lucky guy's job to sit in a soundproof recording booth
and make audiences believe that a knife stabbing through watermelon
was Anthony Perkins slicing up Janet Leigh or crunching eggshells was
Harrison Ford stepping down a path crawling with insects. I remembered the soundman in the show as a wild-haired, hyper little man who
seemed to love that it was his job to use whatever materials necessary to

convince people that these common sounds meant something more.

I loaded my plate with macaroni, topped it with a pork chop, grabbed my juice and began my slow balancing act down the hallway, up the stairs, toward my flickering blue light. My father did the same— dinner a chance for him to refuel, then return to Clint Eastwood or Sylvester Stallone in the living room—as did my brother, retreating to his room across the hall from mine to gaze at Ozzy Osbourne or the Beastie Boys on MTV.

I placed my plate on a folding dinner tray. With my Fisher-Price tape player—a brown plastic device with chunky white buttons—I recorded an audio version of *Goonies*. The tape player had all the fundamental features of a grown-up's recorder: *Play, Rewind, Fast Forward, Pause,* and *Record*. I discovered that if I pressed *Pause* on my recorder gently, the audio slowed to a warped, wobbly dialogue. Over and over, I forced the audio to a place between *Play* and *Pause*, changing all the characters' voices: Mouth's squeaky voice deepened and the evil Fertelli's gunshots boomed like cannons. Chunk did the "truffle shuffle" in slow motion. With a flick of my finger, the tape could go as fast or as slow as I wanted.

I sat inches from the television, holding my recorder to the speaker. My old Zenith television was huge, encased in an ornate wooden shell. It looked as if only the screen had been unpacked and the rest was still in its crate. Beneath the screen, brass rings offered access to false drawers. Sometimes I played with the brass rings, my bare feet tugging the cold metal as if the drawer might open.

During my intermissions, I paused the tape recorder and the VCR at the same time and ran downstairs to refill my juice. My mother was finishing her meal at the table. Sometimes I didn't take a break and came down hours after dinner and saw her in her worn recliner smoking a Marlboro Light, flipping through *Better Homes and Gardens*, my father nodding off to *Easy Rider* with his hand in his pants.

Above the *Play* and *Record* buttons on my tape recorder was a red bracket indicating that the two buttons must be pressed simultaneously. How can you play and record at the same time? It didn't make sense. With the pointer and middle finger of one hand hovering over the tape recorder, the pointer of my other hand poised before the VCR's *Play* button, I pressed all three at once. I was proud of my seamless transition. Though later, when I crawled beneath the sink and broadcast my tapes all over the country, I detected the changeover's soft click and hoped my audience didn't notice.

There were no movie restrictions in my house. My parents did not censor me, so in elementary and middle school, I taped *Full Metal Jacket* and *Goodfellas* and *Taxi Driver* and *The Doors* and *Platoon*. My best friend Marlon, who my father called Brando, wasn't allowed to watch R-rated movies. His father didn't believe I had seen *Full Metal Jacket*, so he quizzed me.

"All right, so what do the soldiers chant in the barracks?"

I smiled, chewing over the snap-crackle of my Rice Krispies.

"You mean before the sergeant gets his head blown off?"

"Yeah."

"But not before they leave Parris Island?"

"Uh huh."

I looked at Marlon, then back at his father. I finished chewing and stood up; my spoon in one hand, my crotch in the other.

"This is my rifle, this is my gun! One is for fighting, one is for fun!"

We laughed: his father at my response and me at Marlon's face as I recited the lines, knowing that he knew all the words, too, but couldn't let on that he'd seen *Full Metal Jacket* at my house.

I had my basic movie groups: Mob, War, Rockumentary. A film pyramid. A steady diet of explosions and curses and stage dives and full frontal nudity, with a sprinkling of comedies at the apex that I viewed sparingly. This was my foundation. Where I set my life.

I did not read. Books were set decorations, mere objects on a shelf, no more or less important than my mother's ceramic Christmas village on the mantel or my father's collection of antique beer cans in the basement. I did not spend afternoons tucked away in the public library nor did I read Chekhov in between bites of meatloaf at the dinner table. I did not keep journals or take notes or write stories. Reading and writing did not interest me because these activities seemed to require a great deal of thought and silence. I had more than enough of that. I preferred a retreat into the ready-made world of image and sound.

When I came home from school, I didn't have to think. The television screen brightened, the MGM lion roared or Paramount donned its crown of stars, opening music faded in, and I hit *Record*. Soon I was in another world, an atmosphere dominated by Sylvester Stallone's accumulating sweat and Robert De Niro's cool laugh and Joe Pesci's boiling temper. They all used words like my father. Though I was particularly tuned to their curses, their racial and sexual slurs, I replayed words like "ain't" and "brotha" and almost any I-N-G word where the actor dropped the final G: "kickin', walkin', talkin'". I collected these words like another kid might collect coins or stamps, then repeated them in my own voice, into my tape recorder.

Testing. Testing. One, two, three. Is this thing on?

I taped *The Karate Kid*. I taped *Top Gun*. I taped *Stand by Me*. I taped *Raiders of the Lost Ark, Back to the Future, Field of Dreams*. Lesser known titles: *Over the Top*, an early Stallone masterpiece in which his character, Lincoln Hawk, must compete in arm-wrestling matches in order to regain custody of his son. *Armed and Dangerous*, a comedy about two wanna-be cops who can't cut it, so they end up as armored car drivers in a plot full of cocaine and corruption and a tractor trailer full of rocket fuel (not to mention Steppenwolf's "Born to be Wild" as John Candy wobbles through traffic on a motorcycle). *Willow*, starring Val Kilmer as a renegade swordsmen hired by dwarfs to battle an evil sorceress who threatens to kill a baby, and that baby is destined to lead the eventual coup that will topple the sorceress and her wicked empire. A rare fantasy in my filmography. I preferred true stories, or at least ones that seemed real.

Recently, I found a tape. The label reads: *Creative Project, Mr. Martin, Period 2*. Mr. Martin was my fourth grade teacher. For our final project, we had the choice of an oral presentation or a "creative experience." I dreaded creative projects because they often involved poster boards and glue sticks and doilies. I was a horrible painter. I couldn't seem to transpose the images in my mind onto paper.

"I'd like to see some of you choose the creative experience," Mr. Martin said from his desk, glancing over his glasses. A broad-shouldered man in a tight flannel shirt, with bushy white hair and a beard. When he leaned forward and rested his chin on his hand, he looked like the cover of my mother's Kenny Rogers holiday CD, *The Gambler Does Christmas!*

"Perhaps you'd like to make a movie or produce a radio program? Think about it."

So I brought my tape recorder over to Marlon's house. He lived in a stone house set deep in the woods off a busy main road. Ivy reached up from the foundation, stretched along the stone, and gripped the green gutters. I coasted down his long dirt driveway on my bike, listening to the traffic fade behind me. When I reached his patio, I couldn't hear a single car, only giant oak leaves brushing above me.

The interior had a thick smell ("incense," Marlon explained) and there were all kinds of weird paintings and sculptures hanging on the walls, none of which looked like the Norman Rockwell collector plates that decorated my house. Marlon's mother came rushing out of her "studio" and greeted us with hugs and loud kisses. When she heard about my creative project, she gasped.

"Oh, I love it! Love it! How phenomenal this experience will be for you. And what will your radio show be about?"

She often used words like "phenomenal" and "extraordinary," words my mother never said. When they stood opposite each other in the school parking lot or in each other's driveway, it was as if they appeared on a split-screen: the same actress portraying two very different characters.

"Mom, shut up, all right? He doesn't know yet."

She slapped Marlon's shoulder. Hard. They laughed.

"Well, if you boys need help, I once did some theater in—"

"Thanks, Mom!" Marlon said, pulling me down the stairs into the basement and slamming the door behind us.

A massive cement cave. Pipes dripped above our heads, bags and bags of cans and bottles, brand-new power tools on the workbench beside rusty hand drills and wooden clamps. The over-stuffed clothes dryer looked as if it had puked jeans and dress shirts all over the cement floor. We'd pee in a bucket, set fire to small objects and, as we got older, puke in the slop sink. We didn't talk much in Marlon's basement. Instead we blasted classic rock, sometimes sitting in his father's old MG Midget, pretending we were outrunning the law.

When I told my mother about my creative project, she bought me a new recorder. She came home from work one day and placed it on my bed. It was a black rectangle with a plastic handle and buttons like piano keys. The kind *Magnum, P.I.* might use to interrogate hardened suspects: *Start talking, Bozo.*

I still marvel at our ability to create something from nothing. That was my project, and I had no clue what it was about when I asked Marlon to help. We never questioned each other. Tape something? Come on over.

"I got it," Marlon said. "I got it! I'll be this psycho Vietnam Vet who flips out during an interview." I thought about the time Marlon had asked my father if he had ever played any sports in school, and my father had told him, "No dice, Brando. My blood pressure was too high. And then I got drafted." Marlon's eyes widened. "You mean you went straight to the pros?"

I laughed at Marlon's suggestion for my project. "That's perfect! We just read something about war last week."

We didn't have a script. I just hit *Record* and started asking Marlon—Bud Montgomery—questions about what it was like rotating back to "The World." He told me Charlie was out to get him and explained how he got some shrapnel in his ass when he sat on a land mine. I asked him if he had any thoughts about how the war was portrayed in the media.

"Let me tell you something, Geraldo, the government screwed me! They screwed me!" Marlon waved a staple gun as he spoke. He clenched one of his father's burnt cigarette filters in his teeth. I held the recorder up to his mouth.

"Yes, Bud. Yes, I know. I know this must be painful for you. But take us back to that time, that time in your life when you were so innocent. One might say you had the whole world in the palm of your hand."

"Sounds great, boys!"

"Jesus Christ, Mom! We're fucking recording here!"

"Watch it, Marlon. Just watch your language, okay? Anthony, do you need anything?"

"No, thank you, Mrs. Ziello." It seemed okay for Marlon to curse and demand things from his mother, but I always felt weird. I couldn't imagine speaking to my mother that way. Marlon and his mother often yelled and swore, then soon after they were laughing and kissing, all while I sat on the couch wondering if I should call for help.

Mrs. Ziello exhaled sharply. "Call me Joanne, please, huh?"

When I heard the door close, I rewound the tape and repeated my question to Bud.

Our interview continued for another ten minutes, full of slang and jargon and coded messages we picked up from movies and classic rock. We had no idea who this Charlie dude was, just that he was out to get Bud and was usually up in a tree or down in a hole. Bud got progressively angrier until he reached into one of the black garbage bags, smashed a Perrier bottle against the floor, and held the broken neck up to Geraldo's cheek.

Technical difficulties. Please stand by.

Geraldo got back on the air and apologized to the audience.

"Bud is calm now, ladies and gentlemen. Isn't that right, Bud?"

"Yes. Yes. I'm calm. My apologies everyone. Friggin' Charlie. Shrapnel."

The interview ended peacefully, Bud and Geraldo making plans to grab a cold one after the show. Joanne came downstairs with grilled cheese sandwiches.

"What's all this glass? What broke?"

"Relax, Mom. Okay? Just props."

13

CHRISTMAS MORNING, 1991. I was nine years old. My father, my brother and I were on the couch watching *Goodfellas*. The smell of my mother's pancakes drifted from the kitchen, down the hallway, over piles of crumpled wrapping paper, and into the living room. I wore my stiff new baseball mitt, pounding oil into the palm, as Ray Liotta repeatedly bashed his gun into a young man's face. My father laughed.

"Broad daylight, too. Jesus," he said, sucking on a candy cane, the cellophane wrapper crinkling in his hand.

"Great scene," Don said. He leaned forward and added another new CD to the stacks in front of him: Rolling Stones, Led Zeppelin, The Doors.

Ray Liotta walked back to his wife's house, where she'd been standing in the doorway, watching him pistol whip her disrespectful neighbor. He placed the bloody gun in her hands and asked her if she was okay, but she didn't answer and he didn't wait for a reply; his eyes were still locked on the man across the street.

I mouthed her interior monologue while tightening a leather knot on my glove.

"You guys want bacon?" my mother yelled over the gunshots.

We looked at each other as if silently electing a spokesman for the group.

"I don't care," my father said to me.

"I do," Don said, not loud enough for my mother to hear.

"Well?" she yelled.

"We all do, Mom!" I said.

I heard the bacon pop and sizzle in the frying pan. My father turned up the volume. Often when we watched movies, before a particularly funny or violent scene, my father would say, "Hey, Ant, watch this." I'd turn toward the TV and not look away until Stallone knocked out Mr. T or Clint Eastwood loomed tall on the screen and asked if I felt lucky. I wanted a name like Sylvester or Clint. Most guys named Anthony were chunky minor characters, guys that pushed papers while Bruce Willis fought terrorists, or else they were the snitches that got whacked by Joe Pesci.

Sometimes my father received mail that was intended for my brother. They had the same name, even middle names, and sometimes when my mother called their name from across the house, a single "Huh?" rang out in stereo. Sometimes my father opened packages and said, "Hey, I didn't order any of this Red Hot Chili Pepper crap." He'd toss the box in a basket beside the couch, full of credit card offers and sweepstakes notices all addressed to my brother.

Sometimes I asked my mother about my name. She said she had wanted to name me Jake. On the brown paper bag covers of my text books, I would write Jake D'Aries in tiny letters, look at it for a while, and then cross it out. Even now, I sometimes say the name in my head. If I had been a girl, she once told me, my father would have named me Tina Marie.

"Can you imagine?" she said, shaking her head. "He wondered what you'd look like if you were a girl, but I think that's as far as it went."

My father always liked the name Anthony but I wonder if my mother, or anyone else, ever knew that. My father's interests and desires often remained a mystery to all of us, until one day he'd say, "I always liked that," and we'd discover his new-found fondness for Native American jewelry or Melissa Etheridge.

"Why'd you have to give me the same name?" Don once asked my mother.

"Dad always wanted that," my mother answered.

"Fucking annoying. Anytime I try to sign up for anything or do whatever, they think I'm Dad."

I thought it would be cool to have the same name as my father, to be a junior. I could look at him to see who I'd become and he could look at me to remember who he once was. In the summer, my brother stretched out on a lawn chair, his hair dyed ice-pop blue; my father slid out from beneath his Chevy, hands caked with grease. They glanced at each other. I don't think they believed what they saw.

"I think *Goodfellas* is De Niro's best," my father said.

"No way," Don said, "*Taxi Driver.*"

"You think?"

"Definitely."

"*Raging Bull,*" I said.

"Pancakes are done!"

"You think so, bud?" my father asked me.

"Without a doubt."

"Yeah, he's a mean bastard in that one," my father said.

"And he wasn't in *Taxi Driver*?" Don said. "Come on."

Big Italian men in white tank tops, suspenders and no shirts, stood around in tight groups. Loud body language punctuated hushed words. A secret code, a football team in a huddle. My father often called me over to his spot on the couch and whispered cryptic messages for me to whisper into my brother's ear. But by the time I would get over to my brother, his whisper had disappeared and I would just laugh in Don's ear.

"It's getting cold, guys!"

One scene that always cracked us up was at Ray Liotta's wedding. All of the wise guys were dressed in fine suits, hair slicked back. The camera panned the reception hall, showing dozens of conversations around the table: *I took care of that thing. You talk to that guy? Forget about tonight, forget about it.* In the middle of these conversations, Joe Pesci's mother stared out at the dance floor, speaking to no one: *Why don't you get a nice girl like your friend. He's married, he's settling down now, and you're still bouncing around from girl to girl.*

My father always laughed.

"Who's she talking to?" he said. This white-haired woman reminded me of my father's mother, who spent much of Christmas Eve fiddling with her hearing aid, gazing at her four loud sons laughing in the kitchen.

"That's Scorsese's mother in real life," my father said.

"Really?" I asked.

"Yeah, he gives her small parts in his movies sometimes."

Finally, my mother came into the living room, glanced first at the tower of CDs in front of my brother, then at the television. "Come on, guys, it's ready." She waited in front of the large bay window, the sill lined with her ceramic Santa Claus collection. The tinsel she put on the tree sparkled like long drops of frozen rain; the red and green bubbler lights boiled in their plastic tubes. Snow muffled the tires of passing cars. The wind swirled in tiny cold tornadoes on the front lawn and in the driveway. Some of the neighborhood kids were already outside, pulling shiny new sleds up the block, their mothers standing on porches and sipping steaming cups of hot chocolate.

Joe Pesci's head popped like a party favor, misting the air with blood. The three of us let out a half groan, half cheer.

"Jesus," my mother said, "why are they playing this on Christmas?"

I picked up mixed signals from my mother: one minute she paced the house, muttering to herself about us watching the same movies, the next she would tell us what time *Casino* was on HBO. In the kitchen, she often complained about my father's TV-marathons, but that Christmas she bought him a wide-screen television. "It's what he likes to do."

My father pointed at the VCR. "It's a tape."

She sighed. "Pancakes are ready."

My father looked at me and grinned. "So bring it over."

"What?"

"*Bring it ova' here.*"

"*Don't ova' cook it,*" I said, leaning back in my chair like De Niro. "*You ova' cook it, it's no good. Defeats its own purpose.*"

"I never know what the hell you guys are talking about."

My brother joined in. "*It's like a piece of charcoal, bring it ova' here!*"

We laughed as my father paused the movie and headed into the kitchen.

"*Raging Bull*, Mom," I said, picking a piece of crispy bacon from her plate.

If it wasn't the TV, it was the radio. My father quizzed us on song lyrics, turning up the music in the middle of my mother's sentences—*wait, wait, hang on, Kathy*—looking at me and my brother. An impromptu *Name That Tune*. He turned up the song with a grin on his face, as if he were the one who picked each song the DJ played. Most of the songs had been written twenty, thirty years before I was born—Beatles, Rolling Stones, Otis Redding. My brother, seven years older than I was, hijacked my father's record collection when he was twelve; he had a slight advantage. But even at eight or nine years old, I nailed "Love Me Do" after a few blasts of the harmonica, or listened to the melancholy trumpet give away "Try a Little Tenderness." My father gently sang, *oh, she may be weary*...as my mother's unfinished thought hung in the air like a struck piano key.

My father often quizzed me in the driveway while we washed his Chevy. Soap suds clung to my forearm as I dug my hand into the bucket, then squeezed the big yellow sponge over the truck, the water running down the hood in sheets. My mother knelt in her garden, silver shovel glinting in the sun. I watched the clean water form black rivers on the driveway and flow out into the street.

"You paying attention, boy?" my father asked as I popped the soap bubbles in my hand. I looked up and nodded.

He walked into the garage and eased up the volume on the long silver radio. What sounded like a church choir poured out from the speakers.

"You got it?" he asked.

"I've never heard this song before in my life," I said, wishing my brother was there to give me a hint. The choir sang on; my mind was blank.

"Anthony, could you bring me that bag of topsoil?" my mother asked.

"Yes, you have," my father said. "One second, Kath." My father stood in the doorway of the garage, an unlit Winston clenched in his teeth.

My mother stood up and brushed the dirt from her knees, exhaling in a faint whistle like her tea kettle. Her sighs were her songs, the solos she sang softly in the kitchen, wrenching out the pots and pans jammed in the drawer beneath the stove, searching for that second sock in the wicker laundry basket, writing checks and stuffing them into envelopes on the kitchen table, carefully wrapping each Christmas present and signing each tag, "Love, Santa."

The song played on and I still had no clue. My father walked over to my mother's garden and picked up a stone. He bent his knees, rolled the stone down the driveway, then looked at me with a big grin.

I laughed. "What?"

He did it again. "Come on, boy!"

My mother stretched her back and walked into the garage. She took off her flowered gardening gloves, gripped the twenty-pound bag of top soil, and started to drag it across the driveway. I heard her whisper, "Rolling Stones," and give the bag a sharp tug.

"Rolling Stones?" I asked.

"Yeah! Told ya you knew it."

By the time Mick Jagger went into the chorus of "You Can't Always Get What You Want," my mother had dragged the bag of topsoil across the driveway and into her garden, a tiny stream of dirt betraying her path.

"Oh, Kath, I would have gotten that for you," my father said.

"No, no," she said, stretching, "it's fine."

Later on, in middle school, I would become obsessed with our home movies. Holidays, vacations, my old soccer or football games. I was fascinated with the past, the shaky footage my mother had filmed. I sometimes tried to get my brother to watch them with me, but he wasn't interested. Alone, I stayed up late and sat inches from the screen with the volume on low. Rewinding and playing, rewinding and playing. What was I looking for?

I was especially curious about the events occurring just outside the scope of the camera's lens, the elusive footage I could only hear. A conversation between two of my uncles. A neighbor's lawn mower. Someone laughing. I wanted to see beyond the frame.

If there had been footage of the Christmas morning we watched *Goodfellas*, I would want the camera to pan across our conversation in the living room, down the hallway, and into the kitchen, zoom in on my mother's hands caked with pancake batter, cooking spray smoldering in the hot frying pan. As one batch of pancakes cooks, she mixes more batter, cracking an egg and carefully picking out slivers of brown shell that have dropped into the bowl. Gunshot after gunshot blasts from the living room. The camera's microphone picks up her quiet sigh, and then her loud, unanswered questions about bacon. As if bored, the camera slowly pans back down the hallway, into the living room, past the bright tree and piles of presents, and across the mantel. Each of the stockings that my mother knit hangs full, bursting with candy and little toys, my father's overflowing with shaving cream and razor blades and Old Spice. My mother's stocking is empty.

From there, the camera lifts up through the roof of our house as if connected to a crane or a helicopter, lifting higher, higher. An aerial shot showing the other houses in our small Long Island suburb—each roof, each above-ground pool almost identical. Our street connects to a main road, which connects to another, past the high school, over the train tracks. Parkway bleeds into Long Island Expressway. As the camera pulls back, the docks and charter boats along the north and south shore, the trees and smokestacks, cars and Mack trucks are reduced to Legos. Higher, and the Manhattan skyscrapers crop up like acres of glass and steel, until the asphalt grid blurs to pulsing blue and a child's finger could almost trace on a screen the borders of New York and Connecticut and Massachusetts. Higher. Higher. Stare long enough and the continents move, their jigsaw edges drifting together. Deserts and mountains appear on the surface like scars. The Earth hums within a force field of blues and greens. Fade to a blue and white marble floating in the dark, stars flickering as if a universe of light burns behind an old black cloth. The colors and light are suddenly condensed into a single glowing line across the screen, fading, fading, fading. Beyond the boundaries of the frame, beyond what the camera can capture, the microphone picks up the sound of bubbling bacon and a woman's unanswered song.

14

WHEN I WAS in elementary school, Don was in high school. When I was waking up, he was going to sleep. We used to share one room, with bunk beds, and I sometimes thought he might fall on me in the middle of the night. Eventually, we split the bunks into two twin beds. Then my parents moved from their room across the hall to the first floor. Don took apart his bed and carried it over, piece by piece, and set it up in their old room. He screwed a hook and eye lock into the door.

That didn't keep me out. I snooped around his room every chance I could, which was often because he was rarely home. I found a videotape in his closet. The black cassette was painted with swirls and circles and stars in bright psychedelic colors. I peeked out through the dusty blinds, then pushed the tape into the VCR. Our living room flickered on screen—the couch on the ceiling, the fan blades spinning on the floor. Someone whispered, a girl laughed, and the camera flipped right side up.

Something like fear surged up my neck when I saw the pale girl with black hair sitting in the corner; a more animated, more clothed version of the girl that appeared in the photos Don hid in his bookcase. A few guys huddled around our kitchen table, which was littered with little plastic baggies. I didn't know their names but I had seen them before—they were part of the caravan that gathered in front of our house most weekends. Strange, droning music played in the background. Our house looked odd on tape; everything was slightly off. It reminded me of those books where you're shown two similar photographs and have to circle the differences. On the tape, I would have circled the fluid haze beneath the kitchen lights, the block letters of our WELCOME sign on the mantel rearranged to say COME WEL, and each one of those plastic baggies.

Don was filming, so I couldn't see his face until he turned the camera on himself, asked if anyone had a lighter, and then shut it off. A brief burst of static, then our living room flicked on again. Now the room was empty. The radio was off. I heard people whispering. Two guys carried another guy into the living room, his head slumped forward, arms spread across their shoulders. They walked him around in circles, whispering to him while he slowly shook his head. No one was filming; the camera rested on the table. I wondered what Don was doing. Before I could find out, the camera shut off.

I watched that tape many times, trying to figure it out. There was something to learn there but I didn't know what. Or perhaps I just liked the control I had over my brother and his friends. Speed up. Okay, now slow down. Do it again. Stop.

I rewound the tape to the part when my brother leaned over the front of the camera, briefly dipping his head into the frame. It took me a few times to find the right place, to get him into focus. I scooted forward on the rug. When I paused the tape, two white lines of static vibrated at the top and bottom of the screen, and Don's face, each feature, was perfectly clear in the center. Leaning close to the screen, I moved my pointer finger toward him, like the little boy reaching out for E.T., and as my hand neared his face, static electricity snapped at my finger.

The sky was bright blue, clouds like cotton ripped from the stomach of my stuffed tiger. My brother watched the man pull the vinyl straps across my waist as my whole body shook "no." "Lock 'em down," the man yelled, walking along the row of crazy people, some laughing, some crying. Men and women, all ages. Kids, too, even younger than I was. What were they doing here? They seemed so innocent. I worried about them only for a second, then the other man at the end of the row nodded to the man who strapped me in, and the heavy metal bars locked in front of us.

I heard screams in the distance. To my left, a firing squad pumped holes through their targets, one man leaning over the shoulder of a young boy, teaching him how to hold the rifle. To my right, parachute after parachute fell from the sky, the jumpers' sleeves flapping like wings. Something jolted behind me, and I was moving. I closed my eyes. I heard my brother yell my name but I wouldn't look at him. He had brought me here. I held him fully responsible for whatever this place would do to me.

I was brought to the top of a steel mountain, machinery ticking beneath me. At the summit, a row of colored flags slapped in the wind. As if to tease us, the machinery moved us closer, closer to the edge, then hung us there for a moment. "It won't be so bad," was the last thing I heard my brother say.

I dropped into a black cave, falling, falling, falling, everyone around me screaming, begging for their lives. I hoped it was true that the fright of a fall kills you before impact, but I fell deeper and deeper and was still alive. Right before we crashed into the asphalt, we shot back up again into the sky, flipped around once, twice, then dove straight down, but veered away at the last second. I imagined my brother holding a joystick, controlling my fate. *Murderer*, I thought. *My brother is a murderer.*

We screeched to a halt. A man vomited. A child gasped for air. The man freed me, unstrapped me, and raised the bar over my head. I stepped woozily onto the platform. My brother slapped me on the back. "I knew you'd like it."

One day in my brother's room, I slipped my bare feet into his black Doc Martens. The worn leather rode high on my leg, consuming the cuffs of my jeans. Sunlight cut across the rug like a golden guillotine. It was noon. The house was empty. I was supposed to be sick.

I walked like Frankenstein. I was alone, but I was being watched: The blood-shot, glow-in-the-dark eye Don had painted on the closet door; the melting face of Pink Floyd's *The Wall* locked into a silent scream; black and white World War II photographs of hollow-eyed bodies bulldozed into mass graves. Dust sparkled at the window—a final warning. I put on Don's favorite shirt.

It was a long-sleeved, brown-and-white-striped shirt with thumb holes cut into the cuffs. It was these minor alterations I envied most: the flannel patches stitched onto the knees of his jeans; paint speckles on his second-hand tweed blazer; stickers of bands I'd never heard of covering his wallet. Once I stole a sticker from the top drawer of his dresser, but when I stuck it on my wallet, it was crooked, and the glossy image buckled.

I watched myself, too, turning side to side, studying my reflection. Before I stepped in front of the mirror, I half-expected not to see any image at all. The mirror knew me, knew these clothes did not fit me, did not belong on my skin. *You're back again? Why?* The mirror was bored, sick of my feeble attempts to transform myself, so it accentuated my chubby features, squished and stretched me, cast shadows on my face. The mirror wouldn't let me pretend.

Patchouli, jasmine, stale pot, acrylic paint. If I couldn't look like him, I could at least breathe like him. I stomped my way to his dresser, taking him into my lungs, and opened the top drawer. Though the mish-mash of ticket stubs, rolling papers, lighters, incense, matches, coins, pencils, receipts, and paintbrushes gave me no new insight into his life, his drawer would contain answers. I was sure of it.

I stood over the drawer, waiting for the objects to move: ticket stubs could tremble, twitch like moths, spread into a loud concert; Zippos might spark, illuminate a trap door in the room, shed light on a secret; rolling papers would twist into night, with teenagers in an open field gazing at a sky of falling stars. But nothing moved. I had to reach into the junk, pull something out and hold it up to the light like an archaeologist.

In the back of the drawer, I found his gun. I took my thumb out of the sleeve of his shirt and grabbed the long silver barrel. The metal was cold against my hip. I walked like John Wayne back to the mirror.

My image was powerless. The real weapon was in my waistband; the mirror held only a reflection, a copy. I slipped my thumbs back into the sleeves. We paced in front of each other, my hand hovering over my right hip, the image over his left. I squinted my eyes. The image narrowed his gaze. I licked my lips. He licked his. We held our breath. The music swelled.

I reached and the gun fell down my pant leg, into my brother's boot, clacked against my ankle bone. We dropped to the rug, cursing, still struggling for the first shot. I took off the boot and the butt of the gun stuck up like a prosthetic ankle. Breathing heavily, I stared at the weapon. The image in the mirror. The weapon. Our bullets collided, the mirror shattered. One image became a million, shards of eyes and fingers, denim and leather, long-sleeved striped shirts and bulldozed bodies, glow-in-the-dark eyes, Pink Floyd's *The Wall*, and the air dense with falling stars.

Take a bow. Remove your costume. Return your prop.

Exit.

It was the most realistic gun I had ever seen. Heavy and cold, the way movies tell you it's supposed to be. My BB gun—the long black barrel dented and chipped from many leaps off the deck, the tinny click when I pulled the trigger—was no match for Don's pistol. I needed two fingers to pull the trigger.

In a shoebox beneath his bed, I found a series of black and white photographs. In one, Don stood naked behind a bed sheet, holding the gun. In another, he aimed at the camera. To the left. To the right. At the ceiling. At the floor. There were several copies of the last image: head down, gun up, barrel pressed against his forehead.

My brother was armed. We handled him like dynamite, tried our best not to set him off. My father had brief conversations with him in the dark kitchen; the beginning of my father's day was the end of Don's night. My mother tip-toed to his bedroom door each morning before school and knocked lightly. She answered his muffled reply through the locked door. *Are you getting ready for school?*

Sometimes, when she got tired of standing in the quiet hallway, she'd come into my room and ask me if, when I was done getting ready, I could wake my brother. I sat on the edge of my bed, slowly tying my shoes, and listened to my mother's footsteps echo down the stairs.

There was a mirror in the hallway where I tried to project the image of a boy who had the guts to wake up his brother. I started across the hall, but returned to the mirror, making sure the boy was still there. *Why did she always make me do this?* I wondered. I heard him breathing. His lips stuck together; each breath forcing them apart in a faint *pfft.* I pressed my ear to the door. Maybe my sheer presence would wake him. Maybe I wouldn't even have to touch the handle. Maybe he would just suddenly appear in the hallway, dressed and ready. I waited, but nothing happened. I whispered his name once and backed away from the door.

When I was ten, my brother took me to see *Edward Scissorhands.* He was sixteen. These hang outs were sporadic. One day he'd threaten to beat my ass for wearing his clothes, the next he'd ask me if I wanted to go see a movie. His friends scared the crap out of me. But that made it fun, in a way. They were all huge and hairy and loud, even the girls. They sat me on their parked cars like a hood ornament, and I listened to their plans for the night. Wherever they decided to go, I was coming along for the ride.

I was a whiney little red-cheeked bitchy pain in the ass who watched my brother from a distance. Watched and listened. Watched him pile his friends ("clowns," my father called them) into his 1978 Volare. Watched the car spit sand onto the front lawn. Watched it zoom down our street and take a right just before the dead end. Listened to the front door creak as I was falling asleep. Listened to the Volare back-fire in the street. Listened to my brother in the CDs I snuck from his room: Pink Floyd, The Doors, Nirvana. He appeared and spoke like a character in a foreign film, a singer vocalizing in a smoky bar.

Don and I stood outside his Volare, waiting for the rest of his friends to show up. Several cars pulled into 7-Eleven. A dread-locked blonde hopped out of her El Camino.

"Aww. Are you little Donny?" she said to me. I nodded. She wore a flannel shirt and ripped jeans. She leaned over and gave me a hug. She smelled like my father's ashtray.

Don elbowed my ribs and grinned. When the rest of his crew arrived, Don pushed me into the Volare. He gripped the plastic penis he'd slid over the shifter, jerked it into drive, and we were off.

The theater on Main Street only charged a dollar, and that attracted a lot of high school kids on the weekends. Up until then, I had only glimpsed the theater from the backseat of Mom's car, as we drove around town looking for my brother. I wondered if she knew my brother's secret hiding places, back roads I'd never heard of or parking lots for stores like Odd Lot that had gone out of business. Though she drove fast, her hands tight on the wheel, our path felt haphazard. When we gave up, we weren't at a dead end or approaching the last exit on the parkway; we were often in the middle of a road she drove on every day. She eased her foot off the gas and we turned around and headed home. On those nights, she would sleep on the couch, and when my brother arrived, she'd roll over and glance at the clock on the stove. After she heard him close his bedroom door, she would gather her pillow and blanket and join my sleeping father in their bedroom.

Don dug a dollar from his ripped jeans and pressed it in my hands. I whispered to him, asking him if he could just buy the ticket for me.

"No," he said. "I think you can handle it."

I folded and unfolded the bill in my hand as I approached the ticket counter. The guy behind the counter wore a paper hat and had terrible acne, as if he'd dipped his face in Jujubes. I whispered.

"What?"

"....please."

"Speak up, little man."

"*Edward Scissorhands*, please."

He nodded. I passed my brother's dollar through the ticket window. The machine punched out a ticket and, when I held it, I was careful not to bend the perforated edge.

I passed through the heavy red curtains and into a party hosted by my brother. The house lights lit up groups of kids sitting on seatbacks, standing in the aisle, throwing popcorn, sipping something from brown paper bags. I thought of the scene in *Gremlins* where all the critters had taken over the movie theater.

I hesitated in the doorway.

"Come on," Don said, grabbing my wrist, pulling me into the crowd.

I met Jason and Adam and RJ and Rob and Ben and Larry. Allison and Christine and Meghan and Beth and Jessica. Jessica. I remembered her. The pale girl in the leather jacket who starred in the movie I had found in my brother's room. Fingerless wool gloves. Ripped jeans over white thermals. Doc Martens. Dark circles beneath her eyes like a Tim Burton character. It was strange to see her in person, and I couldn't think of anything to ask her that didn't sound rehearsed. She held out her hand and I stared at it. She smiled.

"Shake it," she said.

I reached out, and she moved my hand up and down. Up. Down.

The lights dimmed.

"Move it, dude," my brother said. The kid beside him got up, and I took my place next to Don.

I was afraid of Edward Scissorhands. Seeing the coming attractions at home or walking past the movie poster at the mall gave me the chills, even though I had no idea what the movie was about. A pale man with wild, greasy hair dressed in a tight leather jumpsuit, brass rings and buckles dangling from his shoulders, his chest, his arms, leading down to his gleaming metal fingers.

The first few minutes fulfilled my expectations: the dark castle, the dismembered mannequins, Vincent Price. But later I found comfort in scenes of falling snow, the soft music-box tune playing in the background, the panning shots of the suburban streets. I remember watching the Avon lady pull her tiny car into the castle's thorn-canopied driveway, and thought of the years my mother had worked for Mary Kay. The woman got out, walked to the door, and lifted the black iron knocker. It was a moment when I wished the characters would listen to me—run when I tell them to run, duck when I tell them to duck. I watched her, wondering how such a small woman had the strength to open a castle door.

"You stupid bitch!" one of my brother's friends yelled and smacked the screen with a piece of candy. An older couple gave us a look, a look I'd usually shy away from, but I was in the middle of the row, protected by this pack of flannel shirts and Converse All-Stars.

Later in the movie, Edward is trying to protect a little boy. He crouches over him, his sharp metal fingers clicking frantically. Other people see this and think Edward is attacking him. A man knocks Edward off the boy, and Edward is moving so fast that he cuts the boy, almost as badly as he cuts himself.

"Get the fuck out."

"I am!"

My father stood at the beginning of the driveway. Don walked backwards, almost in the street.

"I don't care where you go, just get the fuck out."

My father said the words over and over with a calm, trained authority. I was in Don's room, watching from the window like it was a giant tennis match and I was the judge, sitting high in my chair. Don walked down the street but turned around every few steps and yelled. I looked to Don, then to my father, then to Don. Don yelled some more. My father watched, blowing streams of smoke from his nostrils. Don slammed the door of the Volare and turned the ignition. The car revved and revved but wouldn't start. My father nodded, taking another long drag. Don got out, told my father to go fuck himself, walked down the street, parted the fence beside the DEAD END sign, and disappeared. My father took one last pull of his Winston, inhaling through clenched teeth, and flicked it into the grass.

Where did Don go? I'm not sure how long he was gone but I know he didn't come back that night. It was one of the few nights my father didn't fall asleep in front of the TV. He took a shower and went to bed.

The fight had something to do with a video my brother had shot at the pizza parlor on Main Street. He and a group of his friends, ten or more, had ordered one or two slices, shared one or two Cokes, and hung out for hours. The owner peered at them. He pounded his floured fists into the dough as my brother and his friends balanced salt shakers on the table, then watched them fall to the floor. The red light on the camera glowed. The owner had told them to leave; they didn't. He had told them to shut off the camera; they didn't. He had asked them again; they laughed.

Cut to our phone ringing: My father picked up. He nodded as the owner told him the story.

Flash forward to Don's side of the story: *That guy's a fucking asshole. We weren't doing anything.*

I don't know for sure what happened at the pizza parlor. Maybe it wasn't even the reason why my brother got thrown out that time. It could have been because my brother failed gym, which completely baffled my father. Or it could have been because of the time my brother's friend called, mistook my father's voice for Don's, and asked him if he "dropped it yet."

"Don drops anything other than his drawers, and I'll break your legs," my father said and hung up.

There were days when I didn't say a word to anyone. On my walk home from school, I'd practice talking, regurgitating a day's worth of swallowed words. The cars rushed beside me, their hot, loud exhaust drowning my voice, but I could still feel the vibrations in my throat. It felt strange, oddly painful, like walking out into the sun after a long movie. I didn't want my voice to sound awkward during a driveway talk with my father or as I gave my mother the summary of my day, as she stood over the foamy rush of water in the kitchen sink.

My room was my decompression chamber, equalizing the me the world saw and the me I really was. On very bad days, when my anger swelled like a kinked hose, I'd bite the brown headboard of my bed and shut my eyes. My jaw trembled. My teeth broke through the brown varnish, leaving a chemical taste in my mouth and deep white impressions in the wood. It only took a few seconds to satisfy me. Then I'd open my mouth wider, pulling my teeth out of the wood. I remember the sun shining through my windows, illuminating the dust in the air, while I scratched the varnish off my teeth. I felt guilty and relieved. I worried more about the times when I didn't bite the wood, and the anger swirled in me like carbon monoxide filling up a small room.

I did weird, secret things. When I was about nine, I went with my parents to visit their friends, Bobby and his wife, Linda, who lived a few towns over. Linda collected Coca-Cola memorabilia. While they played cards on the patio, I wandered around their house, reading that classic red and white script on t-shirts, buttons, coolers, lamps, plates, jackets, books, picture frames, and stuffed animals. The old wooden floor creaked beneath me as I moved from item to item. I found an expensive-looking watch on the table, lots of dials and silver buttons, a watch I imagined a deep-sea diver would wear. On the face, two smiling polar bears gripped long, full Coke bottles. I wrapped the leather strap around my wrist but it was too big, even on the first hole. I swung my arm and felt it dangle and spin. When I turned the watch upside down, the Coke seemed to drain from the bottles into the bears' mouths. Backing out of the room, I shut off the light, closed the two glass doors, and slipped the heavy watch into my pocket.

At dinner, I ate with one hand. The other felt the watch, spun the dials, pressed the buttons. The grown-ups were all laughing loudly and smoking cigarettes. I watched Bobby cut his steak and Linda sip her wine while a dizzying dose of adrenaline pumped through me. For a little while, I thought I'd put the watch back, but when we got in the car at the end of the night and started to back out of the driveway, I slid one end of the watch out of my pocket and moved my gaze from the watch to Linda waving from her stoop.

I put the watch in one of my socks and stuffed it in the back of my top dresser drawer. Each week I'd pile new clothes on top of it, pushing it further and further into the back of the drawer, burying it.

One day, I was watching TV in my room. My father called me downstairs. He was on the couch, the phone pressed between his cheek and shoulder. I was halfway down the stairs when he looked at me.

"You didn't see Linda's watch, did you?"

"No. No, I don't think so."

"He says he hasn't seen it." He spoke into the phone while his eyes peered up at me. The tips of his fingers slid up his neck in slow, scratchy strokes.

I went into the kitchen, poured a glass of orange juice, and asked Mom what she was making for dinner. She said pot roast and I asked how she made it. What spices? How long did it take to cook? Was the meat frozen or fresh? I couldn't think of any more questions so I walked back into the living room and headed upstairs. Before I reached the top, I knelt down and stuck my head through the wooden bars.

"I think I actually did see it. Next to the snow globe on the little table."

"Little table?" my father asked.

"Yeah."

I sipped some orange juice, stood up, and went back to my room.

The next day, I sat at the end of our block, drawing lines in the sand on the side of the road. I took the watch out of my pocket, placed it in the sand. I found a smooth, fist-sized stone and bashed the face of the watch. The silver dial broke off. I turned the watch on its side, supported it with two small piles of sand, and bashed it again. It cracked, and the two polar bears fell out, the sun gleaming off their silver bodies. Then I gathered the parts in my hand and tossed them into the bushes.

My father's Chevy rumbled around the corner. He drove a few feet up our block before the brake lights glowed like two red eyes. The truck idled on the side of the road. A cloud of smoke billowed out the window; a Winston pinched in his fingertips. I ran over to him.

"What are you up to, boy?" he asked.

"Not much, just waiting for Marlon to show up."

"Uh huh." His eyes were hidden behind his dark sunglasses. He bit the filter of his Winston and spoke through clenched teeth. "You be careful, ya hear?"

I watched from the end of the block as he drove up to our house and made a sweeping turn into the driveway.

A few days later, I searched the bushes and couldn't find any pieces of the watch. I don't think he took them but I knew exactly where I threw them and they weren't there. We never talked about the watch again.

15

BILLY LIVED down the street from me, near the dead end. I was ten and he was eight, but he had a way about him that made him seem older. He lived with his mother and two sisters—Mary, eleven, the oldest, and Josephina, five. His father showed up every other week or so. We could hear the music blasting from his white Camaro when he pulled around the corner. He parked in the street, wheels angled toward the road. I remember him walking across the front lawn—a tall thin man with short, dark, curly hair, white sweater, black jeans, and tennis shoes. He stopped to pick up a bright yellow Tonka truck off the lawn and carried it to the front of the house.

"Hiya, Bill," he said, dropping the truck in the patch of dirt beneath the front windows. There was no garden, no bushes in front of his house like mine, no tall flowers or pine trees—only a strip of dirt and a chipped gray foundation.

Billy and I sat on the front steps, crushing small rocks with larger rocks. His Dad slid his iridescent sunglasses into his hair and squeezed the back of Billy's neck. He called me "Tony," the only one who used that nickname, and it always made me feel like he knew some secret about me. I smiled politely as he walked past us and into the house.

The inside of Billy's house was like a wound, something delicate ripped wide open. Josephina's juice boxes and melted ice pops left hard, red blotches on the beige carpet. Crushed saltine crackers dusted the stairs. The big red couch was stained with Coca-Cola, and one of the cushions was torn so badly it looked like it was sliced with a steak knife. When we watched TV, Billy pulled chunks of cotton from the couch and threw them on the floor.

Billy's father didn't seem to notice. He walked down the hall and into the bedroom. I heard him say something to Billy's mother and shut the door behind him. Billy nudged me with his elbow, thin black hairs curling over his top lip as he grinned. He muted the television and crept toward the hallway. Mary sat with perfect posture at the kitchen table behind a fort of math and science textbooks. Josephina was alone with her bucket of chalk in the driveway. Billy beckoned me toward the hallway.

We got down on our hands and knees and crawled toward the bedroom door. I was right behind Billy, the dirty bottoms of his bare feet almost touching my fingers. He turned around and slid backwards on his butt until his back was against the wall. I crawled forward and sat next to him. Billy put his finger to his lips.

His mother moaned—a soft whimpering, the whispers of a foreign language. Steady and breathy, as if there wasn't enough air in her bedroom. Billy giggled quietly, thrusting his hips into the air. I'd heard these sounds in the movies Billy and I watched on cable late at night, men and women rolling in bed with sweaty, painful expressions, but I had never heard them in real life. She moaned louder; I pressed my ear to the door.

"Billy!" Mary whispered, peeking over her history textbook. "Get away from there."

Billy looked at her, gave her the finger. She shook her head and looked at me. I shook my head, too, with half a smile as if I didn't want to believe what was happening. Part of me didn't. Part of me was frightened of what went on inside their house. The other part was curious.

Her moans quickened and for the first time I heard the bass of his father's voice, then silence. Normal sounds slowly broke through the blood-rush in my ears—the scratching of Mary's pencil, Josephina's singing in the driveway, the cool outside air blowing through the curtains. The bed creaked, and we ran back to the living room.

A few minutes later, his father came out of the bedroom and walked into the kitchen. He stretched in front of the refrigerator, then reached in and grabbed a can of Diet Coke. He popped the top and took a long swallow—each gulp audible in his throat. I pretended to watch TV, but I kept glancing at him. He absently flipped through Josephina's drawings, which were stuck to the freezer with magnets shaped like fruits and vegetables. He held up a family portrait: the mother in a long bathrobe with wild hair; Mary standing up straight, neat clothes, arms full of books; Billy holding a toy gun, spraying bullets in the air like a cowboy. The father in the drawing smiled in his white Camaro, three lines shooting out from the back of the car to show how fast he was going.

He put the portrait back on the freezer and finished his soda. The delicate echo of the empty can hitting the counter was followed by the papery slap of an envelope filled with money. He kissed Mary on the cheek and walked into the living room. He said goodbye to me and Billy. Then he took a quick look around the house, put his sunglasses on, and closed the door. I heard him whistle as he walked across the front lawn. Through the window, I watched him get in his car, the convertible top blossoming as he drove up the street.

Billy's mother shuffled out of the bedroom, her bathrobe never completely closed, always revealing too much. A blotchy breast, a pale veiny thigh. She seemed to sleepwalk everywhere she went—the kitchen, the backyard, the elementary school to pick up Josephina. In the evenings, Billy forced her to walk to McDonald's and get us food. Screaming and cursing, he told her to get a pen and write down our order. He said it was okay, that I could go ahead and tell her what I wanted. She knelt beside me with a pen in her hand, looking up at me with exhaustion, as if my answer could save her. I told her what I wanted.

As chaotic as Billy's house was, I didn't feel threatened. His life was so completely different from mine, so exotic and incomprehensible, in equal parts, that it seemed too far away to do any harm. I was a voyeur, an extra. I hardly said a word in his house. Even when his mother asked me if I wanted barbecue or sweet and sour sauce for my McNuggets, I would wait for Billy to answer and order the same. I couldn't imagine my brother and me sitting on the couch, telling my mother to "walk her ass down to Mickey D's" and buy us food. At my house, the food my mother cooked was ready by the time my father came home from work.

I rode my bike home from Billy's house, and as I crossed the railroad tracks, I pulled hard on my handlebars, hoping to lift my tires off the ground. I skidded to a stop in our driveway and parked my bike on the side of our house. On my way inside, I stared at my mother's garden. The finely-trimmed lawn. The blue sky shimmering in the pool—a reflected world washed clean of consequence. At the dinner table, I ate with visions of Billy's house safely tucked away inside me.

Josephina was five, but still couldn't talk. She communicated in one-syllable sounds and hand gestures. She'd point to a cheeseburger on the table and open her mouth wide, waiting for someone to feed her. She'd squeal and scream, reaching for a can of soda on the counter until someone boosted her up. When she wanted to go outside, she scratched at the door like a small dog.

With her bucket of multi-colored chalk, she drew bright worlds on the hot black driveway. Smiling yellow suns coaxed laughing purple flowers from tall magenta grass. Herds of unicorns and giraffes and dinosaurs ran together through open fields. She sang songs to herself in her own language, baby-talk much too young for her, as if there were an infant ventriloquist hiding behind her, controlling every word she said and lyric she sang.

Billy rode his bike up and down the driveway, screeching to a stop over her drawings until her worlds were blurry and his bike tires were coated with chalk. His mother and sister yelled and chased him down the driveway as he peddled just enough to stay ahead of them, laughing. I sat in the grass, the urge to stop him surging up in me, to kick Billy from his bicycle with the tip of my sneaker like a knight suddenly spearing the dragon with his sword. But I didn't. I watched Josephina stand above her world and cry, a stub of chalk in her hand.

Since Billy was younger, we never saw each other in school. I was closer in age to his sister, Mary, and sometimes I'd see her at the bus stop or in the corner of the library. If the hallway was empty, sometimes we'd wave to each other, our hands never any higher than our hips. Most of the time, we looked the other way.

My mother and I often saw Billy's mom walking in her bathrobe. Limping up a quiet side street, her face caged in black hair. Or shuffling along the white line, cars whipping by at forty miles an hour, her bathrobe undulating in heavy waves like a waterlogged cape.

"That poor woman," my mother said, her tongue clicking on the back of her teeth.

We never stopped to give her a ride. We thought about her only when we saw her and drove on.

I didn't want to associate with Billy or his family outside of his house. Inside his house, I was not myself. I was Billy's protégé, his understudy, learning how to be bad. Outside, I was the polite, chubby, red-cheeked child with the permanent smile. Always polite, always got along with others. I was known for my ability to share. But inside, I longed to learn Billy's language, to understand the way he communicated with the world. Because after his mother got us our Happy Meals or fetched us another round of Cokes, I quickly forgot about the look on her face. Billy's way of communicating worked like a charm, and though he often called his mother "Bitchy" or "Fat Ass," the name that he used regularly, the one that seemed to insult her the most, was her real name: Jeanie.

Billy was the opposite of me. Outside his house, he felt vulnerable and weak. Once, I invited him on a trip to visit my grandparents. He agreed. I guess I felt comfortable with the situation because we'd be far away from home and no one would know us. My parents asked me if I wouldn't rather take another friend, someone I knew better. They didn't know as well as I did what went on in Billy's house, but they sensed something, as if a sinister soundtrack became audible as soon as Billy appeared. As my father loaded Billy's backpack into the car, he looked at me as if I might still change my mind.

"Sure you wanna bring that peckerhead with us?"

I thought about Woody Woodpecker and heard the theme song in my head.

"Yeah, Dad."

Billy didn't talk the entire trip. Not one word. Nor did I see him eat anything. When my grandmother asked him if he'd like some lasagna or a slice of meatloaf, he just shook his head and sat at the table with his head down. Though he was obviously uncomfortable, I marveled at the power he had over the table, none of us sure how to behave in his presence.

One day, Billy and I were in Mary's room. Mary was downstairs. Jeanie was asleep. Josephina sat on the edge of Mary's bed as we flipped through a dirty magazine and dialed the numbers in the back. We used Mary's telephone, the trendy kind made of clear plastic so all of the inner workings were visible. The transparent receiver blinked in Billy's hand.

"What's that?" he said. "You want to speak to Anthony? Okay. Here he is."

Billy tried handing me the phone but I ran to the other side of the room, tripping over Josephina's Twister mat. He laughed and gave the phone to Josephina instead. I picked up the cordless phone on the table and listened. A woman on the other end moaned softly, asking Josephina what she wanted. She said she wanted to please Josephina and make all her fantasies come true. "You'd like that, wouldn't you, baby?" Josephina seemed soothed by the voice, as if listening to a nursery rhyme. Billy hung up the phone and Josephina screamed, holding the phone to her ear, slapping all the buttons, trying to make the voice come back.

That was when I would leave. Josephina would scream and Billy's mom would wake up and run to her—"What? What is it? What's the matter?"—but Josephina couldn't tell her, couldn't speak her language. She'd just scream and reach out in the air for some invisible savior. I'd slip out the back door and run home.

Once, while Jeanie was out buying us McDonald's, Billy and I snooped around her bedroom. My parents' room was spotless—the alarm clocks dusted and angled toward their pillows; the bed, wrapped tightly in blankets, rested high off the ground in its wooden frame. Jeanie's room was littered with shoes and underwear, and the bare mattress lay on the floor. Someone had thumb-tacked two bed sheets over each window.

I stood in the doorway while Billy opened drawers and rummaged through Jeanie's stuff. Then he started tossing around the clothes and makeup on the floor. One part of the room was piled so high with clothes that it reminded me of the ball pit at Sesame Place.

"Come on," Billy said. "Help me look." He threw more clothes over his shoulder, then bent down and pried the mattress up off the floor.

I didn't know why Billy thought I'd be any help searching his mother's room. He seemed to know his way around. But I was glad that he invited me in. He gave me permission.

I went straight for the closet because that was where Don hid all the good stuff in his room. He had a canister of Fart Spray that didn't really smell anything like real farts—more like garbage in the sun. Jeanie didn't have any Fart Spray, just shoeboxes filled with papers and some clothes half-hung on hangers. One piece of clothing hung in a plastic zippered bag. I opened the bag and touched the soft white material.

"Got it!" Billy yelled.

I ran out of the closet and stood next to Billy. He was holding a long white box, the kind that were often filled with roses and delivered to women in offices on TV. Billy walked over to the bed. I heard something knocking against the inside of the box. I thought maybe there was a gerbil or guinea pig inside, but there were no holes in the box. Billy hummed the Star Wars theme as he held the box high above his head, flying it over the mattress. He looked over at me and grinned.

"Ejector Seat!" Something flew out of the box and hit my arm, then dropped in the blankets.

"Ow, man. What the heck was that?"

Billy reached into the blankets, taking his time, making a show of it, then held up what looked like a pink rubber sword with two ends. "Bitchy's boyfriend."

I laughed and watched Billy wrap one end of the sword in a pillow case. He held it up as if he were leading a marching band. Each time he moved his arm, the sword flopped from side to side, like some animal whose neck was too weak to support its head. Billy stood in the doorway, gave the sword a jiggle, then walked out into the hall. I heard Mary scream.

"Billy! That's disgusting. Put that back."

I ran to the kitchen and saw Billy, humming and marching around the table, holding the sword high above his head. Mary chased him and Josephina chased Mary. Josephina was giggling and holding her piece of chalk up in the air like Billy. Mary grabbed hold of Billy's shirt and shook him, hard. His collar ripped.

"Fuck off," Billy said, then continued humming. He opened the screen door and marched onto the deck, his sisters close behind. I stood alone in the kitchen for a moment. I could do whatever I wanted, I thought. I could run back into the bedroom and look for more stuff. I could sit on the couch and watch anything I pleased. I could walk out the door right now and no one would notice.

I followed them onto the deck and saw Mary and Josephina chasing Billy around the pool. Mary quickly gave up and went back inside. Out of breath, Billy sat in a folding chair while Josephina watched him, waiting. I dragged a small plastic chair out of the sandbox and sat beside them.

"She ripped my shirt," Billy said, picking at his collar. I stared at the sword.

"What are you going to do with that?" I asked.

"This?" He launched the sword out into the grass and it hit the ground with a solid thud. Josephina jumped up and ran after it.

"Josie, leave it," Billy said. But she didn't listen. She held the sword with both arms and brought it back to Billy. "I said, leave it." Billy said, tossing it back out into the grass, but again, Josephina chased it.

"God damn it," Billy said. He stood up and walked over to Josephina and took the sword from her. "I said, no!" He flung the sword high in the air. I watched it tumble, end over end, then slap the pool's surface. Josephina ran to the side of the pool, but the railing was too high for her to see the water. She started to cry.

"Let's go," Billy said.

When we walked back into the kitchen, Jeanie was unpacking our cheeseburgers and French fries. Her forehead was sweating and she kept rolling up her sleeves, but the elastic was stretched out, so the material kept slipping down her arm. She crumpled the paper bag into a ball. When the kitchen was quiet, she heard Josephina crying.

"Where is she, Billy? What happened?"

"I don't know," Billy said, chewing. "She's outside."

Jeanie ran out to Josephina, who was still standing beside the pool. She was reaching her arms up above her head. We watched Jeanie kneel down and talk to Josephina. Jeanie picked her up and climbed the steps to the pool. She leaned over the water, then looked back at us in the kitchen. Billy asked me if I wanted ketchup, as I stared at Jeanie, extending the skimmer's long metal handle, stretching out over the water.

If I kept going there, kept watching, I felt I would somehow be responsible. Billy's life would rub off on me and people would know where I'd been, like a miner covered in soot emerging after a long shift.

But I continued to go over there. All I had to do was stay away for a little while, sometimes a day, sometimes even as little as a few hours, before I felt invincible enough to go back. The feeling was similar to when my brother took me on the roller coaster. After I had gathered up enough courage to ride it once, the next time and the time after that and the time after that were easier. I might have to sit on a bench and wait for the world to stop spinning or drink a soda to calm my stomach, but eventually I'd walk back up to the roaring, twisted metal and get in line.

16

A PHOTOGRAPH: Don and my mother at JFK Airport. He is twenty. He has his arm around her, pulling her close, as if, a second before the picture was taken, my father shouted, "Get your arm around your mother, boy!" She is squished, and so is her smile, tight-lipped. Dressed in the magenta track suit that became popular with her and her sisters around that time. Comfortable. Easy to move in. My mother is afraid to fly.

Don looks ready to hop a freight train or hitchhike. Green duffle slung over his shoulder, frayed denim shorts, long-sleeved white thermal shirt. Chain wallet. Black boots. A cocky grin, perpetual squint—*can't see where I'm headed, but I'm going.* He is not a destination man; it's not about that. Just move. Just go. Fill out the college application as long as the address at the top contains a California zip code, a place as far from Long Island as possible. The sky is purple. Is it dusk or dawn? I can't tell.

There is no picture of me and my brother at the airport, but I imagine he pulled me in for a side-hug, my shoulders scrunched up beside my ears. I was about thirteen when Don left, so I was probably wearing my Raider's hat and Raider's jersey. My father loved the Raiders, so I did, too, if only for the colors and the logo. All of my sportswear beside Don's grunge gear made us look like mascots for opposing teams. He probably unhooked his arm from my shoulders and turned toward the gate. As he walked away, he glanced back at us like a driver changing lanes. No signal.

"He's out in California. Drawing stick figures or some shit."

My father knelt on the garage floor, the rotary phone's red receiver cradled in his shoulder, telling Bobby Haggemeyer about Don attending art school. He worked a rusty lug nut free from his Chevy, applied a white chemical, and scrubbed it with an old toothbrush.

"I haven't the slightest clue, Hag." Bobby was the only person my father spoke to on the phone for longer than five minutes. His voice changed. Bobby brought out the redneck jive that lay dormant most of the day. At the supermarket, between the hours of five a.m. and three p.m., my father spoke in quick choppy statements: *Got it. All set. Ma'am, can I help you? Number sixty-two. Now serving number sixty-two.* After work, in the hazy garage, Winston dangling from his lips, the levee broke. He opened up.

"You gots to be foolin' me, Hag. I know you ain't bin messin' wit my tunes. Yup. Dats right. Dats right. I want 'Tenth Avenue Freeze-Out,' then 'Night Moves,' THEN 'Beast of Burden.'"

He laughed.

"Uh huh. Nun'a dat Eagles shit, friggin' Neil Young's cryin', or any'a dat new shit you bin listenin' to. Chimp Biscuit. Friggin' Marion Manson."

I heard Bobby laughing. My father spat on the lug nut and worked it into the chrome.

Bobby was more computer savvy than my father, if only because Bobby called it a computer instead of "the machine." *I ain't messin' wit dat machine, boy. Punch this in for me.* At the time of this conversation, Bobby and my father were deep into a Napster binge—Bobby having discovered the program after his nephew e-mailed him a link and explained what Napster could do. My father and Bobby had been downloading songs for months.

"Yeah, boy. Good call, Hag. Great call. 'Against the Wind.' Dat one slipped my mind."

I sat on the vinyl stool, feet dangling, listening to their conversation. His wide workbench spread out in front of me. In the corner was a long silver radio, always tuned to *The Fox*. The radio was plugged into an outlet that was powered by the light switch, so when the garage lit up, the radio immediately kicked on. *The Fox* offered the same dozen or so artists every afternoon, a predictable rotation of Led Zeppelin, Rolling Stones, Doobie Brothers, Steve Miller Band, Jimi Hendrix, Janis Joplin, Eric Clapton. Once in a while they'd surprise us and throw in some Otis Redding or Wilson Pickett, and my father would strut over to the radio and ease up the volume, as if he didn't want to scare "the brothas" off.

"Yeah, boy. 'Mustang Sally.'" He slid back beside the tire. "Ol' Sally can ride wit me anytime."

I laughed and shook my head, knowing all the lyrics, but shying away from singing with my father. Instead, I spun on the stool and tapped my foot and took inventory of the tools on the wall, the items on the shelf.

Fishing poles lined the walls like an armory, his green and black Army knife stabbed into the wall. Posthole diggers stood with their mouths shut. Birthday card on a nail, giant breasts holding a lit candle, Bobby's handwriting asking: *How'd you like to suck on these, you old bastard?* Pictures cut from magazines: centerfolds of muscle cars. El Caminos. GTOs. 442's. The car my father loved the most, his "mudda fucka:" a 1941 Willys. A rare, stubby little hot rod. When a Willys entered a car show—gleaming hunk of obsidian absorbing the sky—people turned their heads. The car was expensive. My father played the lottery.

Secret items. Stuff I couldn't see then, but knew was there because I snooped around the garage while my father was still at work. An old crumpled pack of Kent cigarettes. His father's brand—the same brand the Army issued to my father with his rations in Vietnam. I also found a dusty brown eyeglass case containing my father's green sunglasses. He wore the same pair in most of his pictures from Vietnam. The lenses were loose in the case, but I popped them back into the frame and tried the glasses on. The world was emerald, the sun shining like a precious stone. The water in our pool became green. The brown grass, burnt by the sun, appeared fresh.

"Listen to this drum solo, boy. John Bonham is nasty." He laughed. "God damn."

The Fox had entered its "Stairway to Seven" routine, which meant my father and I would be enjoying a solid rock block of Led Zeppelin, but also it was just about time for my mother to come home from work. My father lit another Winston, bent his knees, and went to work on another rusty lug nut.

Wednesday was junk day. It was also my father's day off. He let me ride around our block and look for cool things in our neighbors' trash: radios, televisions, food processors, anything. Most people threw out furniture or records or boxes. I had no use for that stuff. I needed electronics, wires and motors, appliances that, with the turn of a few screws, revealed their inner workings.

One hand on a coffee maker or blender, the other steadying the handle bars, I coasted down my street in sweeping S's, drunk with anticipation. If my find was too large to carry, I tied it to my bike with rope and dragged it home. Once, I pulled a small electric lawn mower three blocks. Items too big to drag—a microwave or mini-fridge—I stashed in the woods, where they waited until my father drove me back to pick them up.

I parked my bike and carried my VCR, my electric typewriter, my walkie-talkie into the garage. If my mother was working in her garden, I hid behind my neighbor's bushes until she stood up, stretched her back, and went inside for a glass of water. She wasn't angry when I brought home junk; she just wasn't as encouraging as my father. We often kept secrets from her—the cost of a new power tool, pork sausage instead of turkey. *Just between you and me, boy.*

Stale-sweet scent of gasoline, coffee, cherry cigars. I believed the garage and my father were created from the same material, at the same moment, separated at birth like a freakish set of Siamese twins. The garage was alive in the summer, when I had all day to scour the neighborhood for items to dismantle.

One Wednesday, I spent the morning at Billy's house. On my ride home, I searched the streets for something to take apart, but couldn't find anything good. I came home and went upstairs to the attic and dug through Christmas decorations and old photo albums, some boxes filled with my baby clothes. One box contained canisters of 16mm film from my parents' wedding. I held the negatives to the light and saw a tiny couple on the dance floor. I slipped the reel onto my finger like a giant ring and pulled out more and more film, but the tiny couple seemed frozen in the same position. Carefully, I rewound the spool and shut the metal canister. Behind the box was my old Fisher-Price tape recorder.

I flicked the switch in the garage, spotlighting the Chevy. My father had started restoring his truck. He had smeared Bondo, a goopy paste, over the rust holes on the front and rear fenders. When it dried, he sanded them smooth, wrapping sandpaper around a wooden block so as not to leave fingerprints in the metal. The garage maintained its scent of oil and tobacco, but the Bondo had added a chemical scent, like the pickling solution he used on his animals in the basement.

His long silver radio on the workbench glowed an emerald green. Springsteen barked about the skeletal frames of burned-out Chevrolets. I searched for a Phillips-head screwdriver. First, I removed the brown plastic shell without much trouble. The recorder could either run on batteries, or I could open a small door in the back and unravel a power cord. The cord was a nuisance now, so I cut it with a large pair of tin snips. With the turn of a few screws, the recorder lost its form, began to look like something completely different than what it was. I switched out the Phillips with a short flat head and poked around the recorder's insides. Tiny blue wires, soldered at each end, connected all the different parts. I cut each one. All that was left was a tiny motor. I jabbed at the pieces of plastic that kept the motor in place, until it finally broke free. A two-inch cylinder. No more screws. No more wires.

I held it to the light, but I couldn't see through it. I tossed the cylinder on the workbench and stared out the window. Now what? I grabbed my father's permanent marker and quickly wrote a list of curse words. Right in the center of his workbench. I didn't even have to think:

Cocksucker

Motherfucker

Asshole

Shithead

Twat-kisser

Dick-face

When I was done, I was out of breath. I felt empty. Not hollow, but satisfied, relieved. The way my father must have felt after cursing out a driver who cut him off or a telemarketer who called during dinner. The curves and angles of each letter were shiny, but soon the slick ink faded to a dull black. I hid the marker behind the workbench. I sat on the vinyl stool for a moment. My breathing returned to normal and I could almost pretend the words were not on the workbench. I stood up and grabbed my father's Army knife and sliced up the stool, cutting it into strips like a Fruit Roll-up, then pulled out the dry-rotted yellow foam. I carefully returned the knife to its spot in the wall.

I rode my bike back to Billy's house. As soon as I stepped onto his front lawn, I felt safe. Jeanie had already picked up pizza for everybody, so when I walked in, she pulled the ottoman over to the dinner table and gave me a paper plate.

Soon, the phone rang.

"Get that, Bitchy!"

"Billy! Don't talk to me like that." She reached for the phone. "Hello? Yes. Oh, yes. He's right here." Jeanie offered me the phone, but I shook my head and stood up.

"Tell him I'm on my way."

My father was waiting for me in the driveway. His eyes were hidden behind black sunglasses. As long as he kept them on, I could pretend he didn't see me. I pulled my bike into the driveway, and he pushed the sunglasses up onto his bald head.

We didn't talk. I followed him to the garage and we stood above the words for what felt like hours. Then he pointed to the stool, the stuffing scattered on the floor, just as I had left them. I felt like the whole garage should be wrapped in CAUTION tape, like a crime scene. My father lit a Winston.

"I don't get you, boy. Just don't get it." He exhaled. "Did you think I wouldn't see this?"

I stared at the words and the pieces of yellow foam on the floor.

"And this," he said, pointing at the stool, "this here's the kicker. What did you use for that?"

"My Swiss Army knife."

"I gave you that to use for other stuff. Not to destroy shit."

I nodded and waited. A part of me thought if I waited long enough, the director would yell "Cut!" and this whole scene would be over. He took another long pull on his Winston and exhaled as he stubbed it out.

"Get some soap and water, boy. Start scrubbin'."

As he walked away, I realized the radio was playing faintly, but I couldn't tell what song it was. In the doorway, my father stopped and turned around.

"Got an A+ for spelling, though. God damn."

17

IN THE SUMMER, my father was indestructible. He stretched himself out on a lawn chair and baked in the sun for hours. My mother turned red walking from the house to the car but my father, without a drop of sun block, could work outside all afternoon and never burn. Occasionally, his shoulders would peel, but all he had to do was rub his hand over the dead skin and it flaked off and disappeared.

I watched him drive a posthole digger into the ground. His vein-laced biceps trembled as he wrenched the handles apart. Bending at the knees, bracing himself, tendons in his neck pulling the tan skin taut across his throat, he extracted the digger, its mouth shut, metal lips clamped on brown soil and severed roots. The digger left a large hole in the earth, and the root's frayed white ends were bright against the dirt. He emptied the digger into a pile, measured the distance between posts with footsteps, then slammed the digger into the ground once more.

"Gonna look good, boy," he said, twisting the digger deeper. "Not like that plastic piece of shit Mitch put up."

Our neighbor's fence suddenly appeared ridiculous to me, so clean and fake. White plastic passing itself off as wood. It even had phony grain and knots, as if somewhere in the world, white synthetic trees were harvested for this purpose, to give Mitch and a few others on our block the impression of wood, the illusion that plastic could protect them. My father and I used real wood.

Hurricane Gloria had recently torn through Northport, burying the streets in broken tree limbs. Hard rain had pasted oak leaves on the sidewalks like green hands. The Long Island Sound swelled above the docks downtown, backed up drainage systems and choked exhaust pipes. Pneumonic cars of all makes and models coughed up and down our block. Our neighbors' decks and porches, the Hess Station's awning and storefront windows on Main Street, our fence and our swimming pool were all destroyed. I was most concerned about our pool. I had pool parties every year for my birthday and didn't want that to stop. My father said there was a law: no fence, no pool.

I handed him one of the tall, smooth posts, and he dropped it into the ground with a hollow thud. The posts stood at attention like exclamation points, quietly punctuating our progress.

"Better blow up those *Little Mermaid* swimmies, boy. You'll be floatin' in no time."

My father liked to work, especially after work. In the summer, he came home from Waldbaum's supermarket in the early afternoon with a giant watermelon perched on his shoulder. Tossing his keys on the table, he gave my mother a kiss ("Hey, toots") and walked out onto the deck. I was in the pool, floating on a package of hotdogs. The supermarket often gave my father free pool floats, leftover promotional items from a Memorial Day sale. Each year, my brother and I floated on a different wheel of cheese or processed meat.

Without a word, he took a few short steps and launched the watermelon, arching it over the grass. It hit the surface like a bomb, gushing water into the air. The waves rocked my hotdog float, almost tipping me over. I rubbed the water from my eyes and watched him twirl a toothpick with his tongue.

He dragged the lawnmower from the shed and wrapped a green bungee cord around the handle, securing the safety kill switch. He liked to smoke while he cut the grass and it was a nuisance to hold the safety switch and a Winston at the same time. My mother muttered about his carelessness as she knelt in her garden, propping up sunflowers with wooden stakes.

With the roar of the mower, my father became a mime. When he passed the pool, he shot me wide-eyed, open-mouthed looks or pointed out a blue jay pecking the bird feeder. If the blade chopped a stick or hit a rock, I watched his lips form short, sharp words. He paced the grass in even strokes. Sweat began to soak through his tank top. He peeled it off in one swift movement and tucked it into his back pocket. I watched his biceps tremble each time he turned the mower. His muscles reminded me of the sacred stones in *Indiana Jones and the Temple of Doom*, the hard, tan rocks that encased precious diamonds. My father caught me staring and gripped the air with his right hand, tilted it to his mouth. I translated: *Ginger ale, boy!*

The inside of our house was freezing, quiet except for the television in the living room. It was on most of the day, even if no one was watching. In the mornings, before my mother took me to school, she turned the television on for our dog.

"Keeps him company," she said.

My father flicked his Winston into the bushes. Small blisters of sweat gathered on his shoulders. The mower roared as he drank. He had several pink spots on his back and arms. There was one on the top of his head that I couldn't see then but I knew was there; I stared at it when he fell asleep on the couch. After years of "naggin'," my mother convinced him to have some of his freckles examined. The doctor removed a few of the darker ones. The biopsies came back normal, so he figured he could stay in the sun as long as he liked. And he did.

I used to think heat made a sound—that I could hear those blurry ripples rising off a hot highway or the hood of a car. It was an electrical hum I couldn't shake from my ears. Floating in the pool, I had stared up at the oak leaves waving their final goodbyes before Hurricane Gloria, and listened to the heat.

When my father told me it was the cicadas and not the heat, I wasn't relieved. In the summer, we collected their shells and lined them on his workbench in the garage. I hunted for them in the backyard, plucked them off trees or the shingles on the house and added them to our collection. We built an army out of their brittle hollow shells. Brown, legs like needles, bulging eyes, a slit down its humpback where the larger insect had emerged. They were terrifying. I couldn't imagine what the bigger bug looked like. I took a few of them to the side of the house and crunched them beneath my sneakers like little dead light bulbs, never certain they wouldn't flicker back to life.

One day, I saw something dead in the driveway. It was a giant insect with a long plump body and black eyes. Its iridescent wings seemed baked into the asphalt. I crouched down and rolled a pebble at it, shocking it back to life—wings vibrating, slapping the asphalt. It bounced as if on a hot skillet, flipped and hovered, then darted at me and crashed into the back of my hand. I yelled, running into the house.

"Whatchu think been comin' out those shells we got in the garage?"

I didn't believe him. This thing was huge; no way it could fit inside that brittle shell. Later, as I lay in the pool on my hotdog float, I thought about the sound of heat, how there must be thousands, millions of creatures waiting in the trees.

III

BUNGLE IN
THE JUNGLE

I don't want no grandkids, boy. Least not right now. Don't mean nothin', you bangin' around. Just clean up after yourself. Cable guy was here last week and the poor bastard just about needed a chisel to pry your bed off the wall. What'a'ya doin' stuffin' rubbas back there? Get rid of them things. This ain't no Easter egg hunt.

It's that one with the big hooters, ain't it? Well, glad you're bein' safe. That's important. Ain't like when I was your age. Now you catch something and that's all she wrote.

You talk to your brother 'bout all this, right? He knows. 'Less you want Mom to do it, which I doubt you do, boy. What else is there to say? It is what it is. Like I said, don't mean nothin', you havin' fun. Don't have to be worryin' 'bout pickin' out drapes or shit like that.

It was a different time back then, boy. People got married right outta high school and if you didn't have kids by the time you were twenty-three, twenty-four, older folks started lookin' at you like somethin's up.

Like with Mom. She and Haggemeyer were engaged. I was with Maddy. But by the time I got back from Vietnam, somethin' changed, you know? Lost that lovin' feelin'. All the dough I was sendin' back from Saigon, Maddy was spendin' it. Bought herself a new 'Vette. I was in love with her jugs—there was no romance there—but still, what a burn. And I guess Hag, I don't know, I never got that whole story, but Hag started screwin' things up with Mom.

Didn't bother me none. They broke up, but we all still hung out. If it bothered Mom, she never said anything.

The night I asked her out—I go over to Grandma and Grandpa's house and knock on the door and Mom answers. Musta been nervous, you know, cuz I'm on the porch doin' the friggin' Ethiopian Shim-Sham.

No, wiseguy, I didn't ask her to share a "so-dee-pop." I didn't get a chance cuz Grandma was listenin' the whole time from her bedroom, and once she heard where the conversation was headed, she yelled, "Well, it's about time!"

So, how'd we get here, boy? That's right. I was tellin' you to be safe.

18

WORD SPREAD FAST. Party hook-ups often did. One of my best friends, Joe, shunned me without a thought. The rest of my friends, guys I'd known since kindergarten, whose lives I could trace through the home movies my mother shot—the baseball and football games, Halloween parties, and Christmas plays in elementary school—turned away from me and didn't look back. Some lasted longer than others; one or two held on for a few weeks, sat with Mia and me at the back of the lunchroom, but they didn't last long. They, too, slowly left our table, like leaves falling off a tree. From the way they ignored me in the hallway, you would have thought I was dating all of their ex-girlfriends, not just Joe's. But one was bad enough.

Sorry, dude. Bros before hos.

I felt heroic in some small way—*Joe can't tell us who to love!*—plus I was part of that insignificant group in high school, the male members of which rarely got asked out on dates, let alone hooked up. It was sort of an achievement for all of us that Joe had managed to score Mia in the first place. I had dismissed notions of rising to the top of the social world long before—rich jocks and cheerleaders, brand new cars. I remember walking between the BMWs and Hummers in the student parking lot, feeling like I was wandering in a museum, searching for a tour guide.

Though I couldn't move up the social ladder, I couldn't let myself sink to the bottom, either: grow a thin, scraggly beard or wear shorts and boots all year long. I despised the limitations of my class—comfortable knock-off Polo shirts, jeans, sneakers, clean and boring haircut—not a jock, not a nerd, not a theater dork, art weirdo, or a dirtbag. But I understood that mediocrity offered a kind of camouflage. I blended in.

Overnight, I became a different breed, half of a Siamese twin. My arms grew around Mia's shoulder; her arm connected to my back. We shuffled down the hallways. I used to watch those creepy couples with my friends and had laughed when they walked by our lunch table. Now, I was one of them—attached to something stronger than myself.

Mia didn't have many friends. She was pushy, always standing up for herself and telling people what's what. If she didn't tell you off, her mother would. We would sit in Mia's room watching *Pretty Woman* as her mother, a tough Italian lady with short curly hair, argued with the principal, or a neighbor, or another parent. *Unacceptable. Absolutely unacceptable*, she would say into the phone, as if she were lecturing a child.

Since we didn't hang out with anyone else, planning the weekend was easy. Like the benefits of school uniforms: restrictive, but reliable. Mia had a hot tub in her basement. Her mother came down to check the laundry, the thermostat, asked if we wanted something eat and then sat in her robe on the recliner, the three of us gazing at the TV like a staring contest. Eventually, she gave up and went to bed. We flipped through the channels for the next fifteen minutes or so, listening to her mother brush her teeth, flush the toilet, and finally shut her bedroom door.

Mia and I stripped each other and stood kissing in the cold basement, the TV on mute. My bare feet felt the slick wooden steps leading up to the hot tub. She stood behind me with her hand on my lower back, running her nails around my waist. At the top of the steps, we stood side-by-side staring into the steaming water. I kissed her again, and slowly submerged myself to the neck.

Don had been in California for almost a year by then. I moved into his room the week he left. One of the first things I did was paint the closet door. He had painted a giant eyeball on it, red veins branching out in every direction, with glow-in-the-dark paint. The first few nights I couldn't sleep, and the neon eye glowed. Even when I pulled the sheet over my face, the glow seeped through. I smothered it with several layers of black paint.

It was fitting that I moved into my brother's room when I did. I was beginning to choose between friends and girls. A little distance was growing between me and my parents, and for some reason it was just so damn easy to sneak things or people in and out of that room. My old room was right on top of my parents' bedroom, but when I was in Don's room, I was the farthest away I could possibly be without leaving the house.

My parents took a hands-off approach with me and my brother. They allowed us to make our own decisions, to determine what was good, what was bad. So my brother drove his $75 Volare to New Paltz at a hundred miles per hour or tripped out at the golf course and pushed the carts off a cliff. I found a girlfriend with a hot tub and soaked until my fingers turned to prunes.

Perhaps my parents were stricter with my brother. Maybe they held onto him a little tighter and he struggled like some feral animal. My brother had a wild look to him: catlike eyes, sharp features. I had cheeks grandmothers were always threatening to gobble up. My brother moved too fast for that.

Mia and I began eating lunch in the library because it was more comfortable. I tried to convince myself that it was nicer in the library, quieter, and that was why we were there. We weren't hiding. We weren't social refugees huddled in the corner picking at peanut butter and jelly sandwiches, watching the silent parade of laughing students march by the windows. We were in love.

"I can *not* wait until graduation," she said.

"Me neither," I said. "Be done with all this crap."

Graduation was like an oasis, a cool paradise free of old friends and their harsh glares. It was also three years away. We ticked off the days like children preparing for Christmas.

"Are you still thinking about going to community college?" she asked.

"Yeah. I don't know. Haven't thought about it much."

She shook her head. "You're wasting your life," she said. "I'll be at NYU, then med. school, and after that, who knows where I'll be. But that's the point—I can go wherever I want."

She reached across her textbooks and held my hand.

"And I want you to come with me."

In middle school, no one seemed to care about my future; no one told me who I was supposed to be. Now everyone had an opinion. More than an opinion—aggressive advice on how I should live my life. Some kids began to talk about their "careers" and "goals." Some dressed differently as high school went on—more professionally, as if a college recruiter could spring from the hedges and interview them at any time. Even Marlon was talking about art school; he couldn't wait to be done with our town.

When I took the time to even consider college, it seemed like another elite environment, filled with people fighting for a place, an identity. I knew I'd eventually choose a community college because it was the easiest route—all I had to do was show up. I got the feeling my mother wanted me to stay home. Perhaps my brother's decision to leave had caught her off guard and she wanted more time to prepare for my departure. I wasn't going anywhere anytime soon.

"Can't we just decide what we're doing tonight first?" I asked Mia.

She shook her head, as if she were a frustrated Algebra tutor. *You're just not getting it*, her expression said.

I thought about the lunch periods when Mia had band practice or a tutoring session. Sometimes I sat in the cafeteria, alone, which was social suicide. I wolfed down my sandwich then roamed the halls, trying to vary my path enough so that no one would notice me. Other times I had my mother pick me up in the back of the faculty parking lot. I used the side entrance and walked quickly to her Ford Taurus.

"So serious," she said, as I climbed in. She took me back to our house, where she had a tuna fish sandwich waiting for me. She never asked me why I didn't want to stay in school for lunch, but she had to have known something was wrong. She didn't say anything, which was a relief. She sat with me and we talked as if we were two old girlfriends catching up. I could almost forget that I had to go back to school.

But soon I was glancing at the clock so much it seemed like the minutes changed each time I blinked. When she dropped me back at school, she waited in the parking lot until I walked inside. Sometimes I watched her from the window, not sure if she could still see me. I felt like I needed to make sure she didn't stay there for the rest of the day.

I looked across the library table at Mia. She bit into her peanut butter and jelly sandwich and quickly wiped the crumbs off her biology textbook. Then she pulled out her large three-ring binder, the one that was divided into two sections, spread it open in front of her and made notes too small for me to read.

I still had one friend left: Marlon. His mother held him back in elementary school—she might as well have locked him in the basement. So, luckily for me, our friendship operated outside of the Mia situation. He didn't hang out with my old friends; he had a whole different group. Marlon was that rare anomaly in high school—an art weirdo with thick black glasses and paint-splattered clothes who managed to transcend all social boundaries. Everyone liked him: jocks, nerds, band geeks, preppy girls and, of course, all the other art weirdos. More and more, I became known as "Marlon's friend."

Marlon's core group of friends were skaters, adrenaline junkies who seemed to know exactly who they were and didn't care if anyone had a problem with that. They had a look, an attitude, a natural confidence I hoped would rub off on me. They reminded me of my brother's friends: grungy and wild—kids who drank beer on the walk to school, got kicked out of class, started fights. Some of the high school teachers still remembered my brother and his friends, but they never seemed to make the connection between me and him. Perhaps they looked at the name, a quick flashback like a bolt of lightning, but took one glance at the quiet kid in the back row and dismissed any possible relation.

While Don was in California, we wrote each other letters. Sometimes they were four or five pages long. In each one, I found out some new detail about him that I hadn't known before. He wrote about so-and-so who lost her virginity in my bed, what nice tits she had, or how he and his friends used to score acid from a guy in Washington Square Park and bring it back to our house for parties. I thought about the secret trips my friends and I took to Stop & Shop for Jolt Cola and Doritos. He was way out of my league.

Don would also write to me about a cool new band, or the title of a movie he said I had to see, immediately. I sat in his old room listening to these strange bands—The Lemonheads, Jane's Addiction, They Might Be Giants. I watched the long, slow Jim Jarmusch movies he recommended. Often the actors in these movies—Iggy Pop, Tom Waits—were also the musicians he told me to listen to. It seemed to me that actors and musicians shared something, a mutual desire to do what the other was doing. I saw both as ways to escape, to get outside myself, to be someone else. Sometimes, late at night, I'd pull Don's old guitar out of the attic and pretend I was Gary Oldman pretending to be Sid Vicious.

I also found out from Don's letters that he worked at a porn shop in California. After that, my letters were filled with orders for me and my new friends for porno tapes and magazines, but he never sent any. Recently, I searched through an old shoe box in my mother's attic and found dozens and dozens of notes from Mia, but none of my brother's letters. At the bottom of the shoebox was a stack of blank paper, as if my brother had written his letters with invisible ink.

19

"COME OVER, DUDE. I haven't seen you in forever." Marlon inhaled sharply, then exhaled.

"I know, man. I know. I'm sorry." I stared at the letters on my phone, as if they'd spell out an excuse.

"It's that chick, isn't it? You and your fucking girlfriends."

"I've only had two."

"Two too many. Ditch her for one night."

I listened to him breathe into the phone and looked around my room. Remnants of my brother's high school life were still clearly visible, even though I had moved in several months before. The burn marks on the rug, the paint-splattered canvases in the closet, the faint smell of incense or patchouli. Marlon's words flowed out of the phone, coursed through the room, absorbing a strange power, as if saturating the dried remains of my brother's life, and finally soaked into my ears.

"Be there in ten."

I pressed the last digit of Mia's phone number and worked up some phlegm in my throat.

"Oh, poor baby, what's wrong?" Mia asked.

"I don't know," I coughed. "I just feel terrible."

She clucked, and let out a long sigh of concern. "I'll stop by with some chicken soup."

"No," I said. "Thanks, but that's okay. I just need to sleep it off."

"Okay. I'll be here if you need me."

My father was on the couch watching a Clint Eastwood marathon. I asked him if I could borrow his Monte Carlo to go to Marlon's house.

"Can't you just walk over to Brando's?"

"We were gonna go to the movies later."

My father dug through his bowl of peanut shells until he found a few that were still closed. He shook them in his hand like dice.

"Movies, huh?"

"Yeah."

"All right. Try to leave me with a little more than fumes in the tank."

I knew he'd say yes. If I had asked him to borrow his Chevy pickup, he would have looked at me like I was insane. He let me drive the Monte Carlo because it was our old family car. The first time my mother saw the Monte Carlo was when my father pulled it into our driveway. We drove it everywhere, until a different car caught my father's eye. My father couldn't completely abandon the Monte Carlo; he still washed and waxed it, scrubbed the dash and console with an old toothbrush, but it wasn't untouchable like his Chevy.

Marlon's basement was like an underground bunker, the place where he and his friends gathered to prepare for the night. The place where they got drunk before getting really drunk. The basement looked the same as when Marlon and I recorded our radio show. The walls were still lined with metal shelves crammed with hammers and screwdrivers and boxes of nails and broken telephones and skateboard wheels and a busted alarm clock. Open bags of top soil, one roller skate, piles of old keys, pieces of wood, empty cans of spray paint. In the middle of the room were stains of all kinds—oil or beer or vomit or blood (sometimes the night devolved into wrestling matches). Dozens of crushed cigarette butts sprinkled the floor. In the corner of the room, Marlon had arranged two old couches and a couple of cinderblocks for us to sit on and listen to music. Smoke rose from our mouths and hung in the basement with nowhere to go.

Two of Marlon's friends, Mike and T.J., were already there when I showed up. Mike had a reputation for drinking a lot, passing out and pissing his jeans. T.J. was the fat one of the group, but people knew better than to say that to his face. They were pouring cans of Pabst Blue Ribbon into a giant funnel. Mike had his thumb over the end of a long rubber tube. He ran his other hand through his long blonde hair. T.J. looked at him.

"Go, dude."

Mike wrapped his lips around the tube and the beer rushed into his throat.

"Yeah," Marlon whispered. "Suck it, you faggot."

Mike ignored him, swallowing three PBRs in under a minute. He collapsed onto the couch.

"Nice one," T.J. said.

Marlon sat on the other couch, carving something into the armrest with a nail file. I sat in the corner, sipping a beer, listening to their conversation.

"Is Jim coming out tonight?" Marlon asked T.J.

"I think so. Tommy and Will are supposed to pick him up."

"Cool."

Marlon's mix CD started to skip. He popped it out, spat on it, rubbed it on his shirt and dropped it back into his stereo.

"Wait. Tommy's driving?" Marlon asked.

"No. Will's got his mom's station wagon," T.J. said.

"Will's overrated," Marlon said.

"Stop with that shit," Mike said.

Marlon lit a cigarette, pushed his thick black glasses up his nose. "I just got no use for the kid, that's all. Pretty worthless if you ask me."

"Except when he's giving you a ride."

"Yeah, well, fuck you. I don't need Will's mom's station wagon. D'Aries has his dad's Monte. Anyways, I'm not even going out to-night." He nodded at me, the tip of his cigarette glowing brighter.

I had no idea who all these dudes were. Their names bounced in-side my head like ping-pong balls. Aside from nodding when Marlon introduced me to Mike and T.J., we hadn't acknowledged each other in any other way. We spoke through Marlon.

"Stop with that shit," Mike said. "You're going."

Marlon was freaking out about tonight because we were going to a party at Jamie's house in Kings Park. He claimed to have narrowly escaped a beating in Kings Park, not too far from Jamie's house, though none of us were there to witness it. Marlon didn't care; he wasn't going back.

"I'm telling you, man, those guys know me."

After a few more beers, he said he'd come but he wasn't getting out of the car. He'd stay in the car all night and drink and pass out and that was it.

We piled into the Monte. Marlon sat shotgun and told me we had to make a few quick stops. By the time we were done, the Monte was packed with people and beer. Marlon slapped me on the back.

"D'Aries, everyone. Everyone, D'Aries." Hats and hoods and brown paper bags filled the rear view mirror. We nodded at each other. I shifted into drive.

Main Street in Northport looked fake, like you could peek behind the storefronts and see a camera crew. It was lined with antique shops, flower shops, bookstores. At the end, just before the street met the harbor, there was a diner and a tackle shop. Main Street in Kings Park wasn't much different, but it didn't feel the same. There was a big used car dealership in the middle of town. Some of the stores were boarded up. There were a few more bars. The train station was visible from Main Street in Kings Park, unlike in Northport, where the train station was tucked neatly away. Kings Park High School was massive, probably double the size of ours, and as soon as we passed it, we were officially out of Northport.

T.J. shouted directions. We turned off Main Street and entered a tangle of dark side streets. Left here, left here, right, now left. Our street signs in Northport were big, green and white. These were smaller, dark blue with white letters that barely reflected our headlights. I drove slowly, hunching over the wheel to read the signs.

We came to a street lined with cars. Packs of kids, all walking in the same direction, moved up the sidewalk. In the distance, I heard a beer bottle smash against the pavement. I looped around the block twice before I gave up and parked on the next street over. We all got out except Marlon. T.J. handed me a case of PBR. As I adjusted it under my arm, I knocked on the glass. Marlon shook his head.

"Fuck him," T.J. said and walked away.

Part of me envied Marlon. I wanted to stay in the car all night with him, safely sipping warm beer and laughing. Driving to the party was one thing. Going in was another. Marlon was right, "those guys" did know him. "Those guys" knew all of us. I turned back and watched the red glow of Marlon's cigarette bloom and fade.

The Kings Park kids were mostly jocks: sharp gelled hair, square jaws, oversized hooded sweatshirts and warm-up pants. I dressed a little grungier that night, old clothes my brother had left behind, so I'd fit in with Marlon's friends. The Kings Park kids stared at us as we cut through the crowd.

We followed each other around for the first half hour or so and then we somehow split up and worked our way into the different subgroups. I thought about Jamie's parents who were out of town. They had to know that the second they left, their home would be infested with drunken teenagers, turning their potpourri palace into a hazy bar. The furniture in each room was pushed against the walls; all of the lamps, vases, and glass tables were packed into the garage. It looked like Jamie was preparing to move.

There were people in all of the bedrooms, and in every hallway. Crowds filled up the kitchen, living room, dining room, and basement. People sat on the stairs and on the counters. Groups of girls hung out in the bathroom. A crew of guys stood outside on the patio, shifting the keg and pouring in more ice. Bloated cigarette butts floated in red plastic cups; beer bottles balanced on the window sills. I watched Mike take a few sips of his beer, then pour some on the carpet, take a few more sips and pour more on the carpet, while T.J. ripped leaves off a plant and stuffed them behind the couch. Everyone and everything was fair game.

I started playing cards with one of the dudes I drove to the party and a group of girls. He seemed to be fitting in pretty well, so I figured I'd just sit down and nod and smile and be polite. He was talking to a skinny redhead. Her eyes drooped at the corners and she had lots of freckles. She was sitting very close to him, looking at his cards. He'd catch her peeking, make a show of it, and she'd laugh and hold onto his forearm. He raised his eyebrows and nodded at the group of girls in the kitchen, as if to say, *Get your own, dude.* I got up and went outside.

Somebody ordered a stack of pizzas. Mike and T.J. had already finished one.

"It's Steve's birthday." A glob of tomato sauce was stuck in the corner of Mike's mouth.

"Who the hell is Steve?" I asked.

"You know, Steve."

"D'Aries says he doesn't know Steve," T.J. said with his mouth full.

Mike scoffed. A black lab circled the table.

"Here comes Steve now," Mike said.

"Hey, Steve, what's up?" T.J. took a slice and threw it on the ground. Steve chomped on it. We started laughing. I pulled up a chair and took two slices of pizza. I ate one and tossed the other to Steve.

T.J. pointed. "I think he likes pepperoni better."

There were a dozen pizzas stacked up on the table and we were well into the third. I found out from T.J. that Jamie's brothers worked at a pizza place and the owner gave them a stack of pies to take home. No one else was out there, so we dug in.

"Here you go, Steve." Mike kicked three boxes of pizza off the table. Steve ate a hole through the middle of each one. He scratched at them until the crust buckled and then he inhaled the entire pizza. He ate nearly three whole pies in under ten minutes. We watched him slowly walk out into the grass. He collapsed and licked his paws.

T.J. walked over to Steve and started petting his belly. "Hey, boy. Hey, boy." Steve groaned and rolled onto his back. T.J. stumbled over to the pizza that Steve had been eating and bent down to pick up a slice.

"T.J., don't eat that, man," Mike said.

T.J. held the slice close to his face and sniffed it with his eyes closed. Then he walked over to the back of the house and smeared it across the sliding glass door. A group of girls in the kitchen scrunched their faces at him. T.J. spit on the glass and it dripped down, cutting clear bars through the sauce and cheese.

I grabbed a box of pizza and walked around to the front of the house. The black asphalt glistened. It was so quiet, and something like homesickness sat in my throat. I felt like I was walking on and off a stage each time I passed beneath a yellow streetlamp. Into darkness, out of darkness, into darkness. Marlon's cigarette glowed inside the car.

"Pizza, dude," I said.

"Oh, fuck yeah. Thanks."

I climbed into the Monte and sat next to him.

"How's it going in there?"

"Not bad. That kid T.J. is nuts."

"Are they in there?"

"I don't even know what those dudes look like."

"I do." Marlon chomped on his slice.

I tore off a slice and took a bite. Marlon cracked open a beer and slurped the foam.

"You going away after high school or what?" he asked.

"I don't know, man. Everyone keeps asking me that. We still got plenty of time." I stared out the window. "You still planning on moving to Baltimore?"

"Hell, yeah. Pronto."

"So weird."

"It's awesome." He took another slice and chewed with his mouth open, staring out the window. Even though Marlon had locked himself in the Monte, hiding from an enemy only he knew existed, I envied his confidence about college. I listened to him chew and thought about all the lunch periods I spent in the library with Mia or at home with my mother. I heard the party's music in the distance.

"D'Aries!"

I stood in the driveway, trying to figure out where the voice was coming from.

"D'Aries!" The dude I was playing cards with gently opened the garage door and I crawled underneath. He looked like a cornered raccoon, curled up and nervous, surrounded by boxes and old winter coats.

"That chick's got a boyfriend, man. And he's huge."

I started laughing, but he was serious. Something had happened. He told me he was flirting with the Irish girl when this big Italian told him to get the fuck away from her. He tried to get out of it, but with these guys, anything you said was an insult.

"Where's T.J.?"

"I don't know," he said.

I wanted to stay in the garage, just like I wanted to stay in the car with Marlon. I told him we'd be leaving soon and I'd come back for him.

I unlatched the wooden gate and walked into the backyard. People gathered on the patio, watching. Waiting. Mike was standing next to T.J., who was walking in small circles with his hands in his pockets. A big Italian guy with a large gap in his teeth was pointing at T.J. and yelling. He kept calling T.J. a fucking idiot. He'd point to his own head and then at T.J.

"You're a fucking idiot. You fat fucking idiot."

T.J. mumbled something. Mike tried to talk but the Italian cut him off and told him to stay out of it. People were curious about what was going on, but for the most part, the music and the party went on without us.

I turned and walked back to the front of the house, through the front door, the living room, into the kitchen. I watched the scene through the window. When I turned around, I bumped into Jamie. Her eyes were red and watery.

"Just tell them to stop." She held onto my arm. A feeling of power surged through me. For a second, I felt like a man on the cover of a romance novel, ripped chest bursting through a white silk shirt. To me, Jamie had a fearful, yet confident look on her face, as if she knew I would protect her from whatever danger lay ahead.

"Please," Jamie said.

I saw that the Italian guy had at least ten big dudes standing behind him. Even if he were by himself, we'd be screwed. T.J. was the only one who could fight. The rest of us were scrawny and scared.

"T.J., what's going on, man?"

He didn't answer me. He kept pacing and hiking up his baggy pants. I asked him again but he wouldn't answer. I wondered where his rage came from, what blew the fuse inside his head.

"They won't fight me one on one. Why won't they just fight me one on one? No, no, they won't."

I saw tears running down his face, but they weren't from sadness or fear. I didn't know where they came from.

"If they do anything, hit that piece of shit with this."

The rock was cold and heavy. He pulled another one out of his pocket and handed it to me. The crowd had thickened and the Italian and his crew couldn't see what we were doing. I kept hearing "fucking idiot" and "Northport faggots."

"T.J., are you crying? Calm down. Don't let them see that, man." Mike ran his hand through his hair and looked back and forth between me and T.J. Then T.J. started screaming, asking them why they wouldn't fight him one on one. T.J. spread his arms out wide. His voice cracked.

"This fucking pussy's crying," someone said.

"You want more pizza, you fat shit?" the Italian yelled.

T.J.'s rock cracked into the Italian's forearm. We pushed T.J. back into the house, shut and locked the doors. Jamie was yelling, spreading paper towels over Steve's puddle of red puke on the kitchen floor. We took off through the front of the house, kicking over plants, knocking miniature figurines off the mantel and stomping them into little pieces. Another big Italian dude was in the dark driveway, yelling. He chased after us and by then the people we came with were running with us, too, following us back to the Monte. Rocks spilled out of T.J.'s pants. I could have dropped my wallet, my glasses could have flown off and I wouldn't have stopped. It didn't even feel like my legs were moving. I was swept up into this parade of guys I'd just met, and I didn't want to imagine being there alone.

Marlon was passed out in the Monte and we pounded on the windows to wake him up. I fumbled with my keys in the driver seat. A guardian angel pin my mother had given to my father was stabbed into the visor above my head and sparkled in the street light.

"Start the fucking car, D'Aries!"

The keys jingled and slipped out of my hands and onto the floor. I hunched over, searching blindly with both hands. The first bottle smashed on the front bumper. The second nailed the passenger door and I could tell from the sound that it was dented. T.J. rolled down the window and started yelling. The Italian reached into the car, grabbed T.J.'s shirt and started slamming T.J.'s shoulder against the seat. The Italian slapped T.J. a few times before I finally got the car started.

We slowly rolled through the crowd of hands and feet kicking and slamming the car. I found an opening and gunned it and we took off, bottles smashing on the back, glass raining down on the street.

I blew through stop signs, screeched around corners, going nowhere. On an empty street in the next town, I pulled over. Inside the silent car, I put my head on the wheel and breathed. The door squeaked open. Someone put both feet on the street. I could hear crickets. The faint sound of water flowing into the drain. Then I turned to see Mike's back heave toward the roof. His puke came in waves, and once he was through, he spit and closed the door.

"What did I tell you?" Marlon said. "I knew it."

I drove home, slow and careful. I signaled at every turn, stopped at every yellow light, waited five seconds at every stop sign. At one of the lights, I rolled down the window and let the air cool my flushed face. I pulled the two rocks out of my pocket and weighed them in my hands. As we drove through the intersection, I tossed them out my window and heard them clack against the pavement.

Mia called me early the next morning. "How are you feeling?"

I lay in bed, trying to stop the room from spinning. I could still see part of the glow-in-the-dark eye my brother had painted on the closet door. "A little better," I said. "Still stuffed up."

"Mmm hmm."

I breathed heavily into the phone. I knew she knew about the party. She had a way of finding things out.

"I'll come over and bring soup," she said. "We'll watch a movie."

On Monday, Marlon, T.J. and some of the other guys called me over to their lunch table. Mia was waiting for me in the library, but I sat with them and talked about the party. T.J.'s face was a little swollen. We laughed. We talked about how much destruction we had caused inside Jamie's house. We could all describe in detail which plants we had knocked over, what color the figurines were that we had stomped on, or the twisted expression on the Italian's face when T.J. nailed him with the rock. For some reason, breaking stuff was the funniest thing we could talk about. We started calling ourselves Team Destructo. I looked around the cafeteria and met the gaze of my old friends, sitting on the opposite side of the room.

I said I had to get to class. Halfway there, I stopped and stood in the hallway. Each locker wore its MASTER lock like a badge. The distant sounds of the lunchroom echoed. The library, my destination, was silent.

In the next letter to my brother, I described the party in detail. I told him how many beers I had drunk, how fast I had driven the Monte, how hard I had hit the Italian with my rock. I told him that Dad never said anything about the Monte and that the morning after the party, I heard him getting ready for work. I looked out the window and watched him bend down next to the Monte's dented fender, stick his hand inside the wheel well and pop the metal back into place.

20

MEMORIAL DAY, sophomore year. Don returned home a skeleton, a ragged voodoo doll, a ghost of my brother come back to reclaim his room. The eyeball on the door must have been watching me the whole time, relaying information to my brother on the other side of the country.

But Don didn't take back his room. He dropped his duffle bag in my old room across the hall. My mother took him outside and placed a chair on the deck. She threw a black cape around him, the same one she used when she ran her beauty parlor out of our basement, where she gave volume to our neighbors' limp hair. She studied Don's unruly black locks separating in the comb's teeth and snipped them with her silver scissors. Some of his hair dropped through the deck. The rest my mother pushed back and forth with a broom, until each strand fell between the boards.

A knock on my door. Don entered with his hair damp from a shower and said, "I hope you don't think differently of me." I felt strange listening to him say this, as if he were apologizing for something he did to me, when he looked like he'd hurt himself the most. Blood rushed loud in my ears as my brother looked up at me, as if he were the last person in the audience.

I never visited Don in California. I didn't know what his room there looked like. I tried to picture him getting off the plane, hailing a cab, riding through the streets of San Francisco, pulling up outside the college, walking through the doors with a duffle bag slung over his shoulders and—then what? Or I tried to imagine my parents packing up the Explorer and driving him to California. My father would have double parked in front of the college, leaned against the side of the Explorer with his black sunglasses on, a Winston clenched in his teeth, while my mother pestered Don about the curtains that were on sale at TJ Maxx, right around the corner. My father would carry Don's mattress up three flights of stairs, pinching Don on the back of the neck once they reached the landing. After he set it down, my father would tell Don to fetch him a ginger ale.

I just couldn't see it.

For months, years, my mother spoke in code—California was the place where my brother "messed around" or "screwed up" or "started with all that crap." Then she stopped talking about it. My father said the whole thing got blown out of proportion: *Your brother took a two-year vacation and now he's paying for it. End of story.*

A couple times a week, the three of them got in Mom's Taurus and drove somewhere. Maybe I had asked to go with them; maybe I didn't. Maybe my father spoke to me the way he did when my cousin Matt died, letting me know that it was okay if I stayed home.

I do remember going with them once, but my father wasn't there. My mother drove. Don sat in the passenger seat, and I was in the backseat. We drove through Kings Park and a few other towns I recognized, but then we turned down streets I'd never seen—long, treeless roads lined with parking lots and plain buildings, like an abandoned strip mall or a modern-day ghost town.

We parked in the back. My mother told me to wait in the car. I watched them walk up to a squat brick building, Don a few steps ahead of my mother. The building had dozens of windows, but only one door. From my position in the back seat, the building looked like a big red face full of eyes, the ears lopped off. My mother and brother slowly entered the mouth.

Don and I started spending long nights together, driving around, smoking weed in parking lots. It felt the same as before he left, except now we hung out more and talked for hours. He told me stories about all the different places he and his high school friends used to party. It seemed like each patch of woods we drove by contained a secret spot I couldn't see from the main road. I wanted to ask him questions about California, but I stayed quiet.

On those long rides, he always drove. Sometimes I'd stare out the window, replaying scenes from my own childhood: that's where I jammed a stick in Marlon's spokes. That's where I used to play soccer. My father and I fished in that pond.

We drove for hours in Mom's Taurus. Our usual route: past the high school, over the train tracks, near the other side of town. We bought Taco Bell along the way and, afterwards, smoked the cigarettes we stole from our parents.

We often ended up at the garbage dump. Perhaps it was just a quiet spot to park, but we could have stopped at any of the parking lots or side streets along the way. *Why didn't the dump smell?* I wondered. A mountain of trash lay buried before us, and I could not smell one rotten egg, one container of sour milk.

Don crunched nacho after nacho, the incinerator's vaporous flame flickering from the torch at the top of the dump. I slurped my soda. All that lay beneath smoldered. Invisible gas rose up through the torch and burned blue as water.

21

SOME MEMBERS of Team Destructo and I started going to a porno shop/strip club off the Long Island Expressway called Sin-derella's. T.J. knew some older guys, and they made us all fake IDs, though we probably didn't need them. Sin-derella's didn't seem to follow many rules.

"Well, well," the skinny redheaded bouncer said, bending our IDs. "You boys are from Northport. Gotta come all the way out to Commack for some good smut."

We laughed, but the man didn't. He nodded a few times.

"Whack booths in the back, fellas."

We walked past the racks of video tapes and around the glass cases filled with dildos. We walked through the strings of beads hanging in the doorway to a large room with three wooden structures, almost like huts, painted black and edged in red neon. In the corner: an ATM with a five-dollar processing fee and a change machine, the same kind of machine I used at arcades when I was younger, except this one turned twenties into singles. The room was black save for red neon. Men circled the huts, featureless. We hesitated in the entrance.

"Fuck it," we said, with Jack Daniels on our breath, and we took out our wallets.

The huts had five entrances. One was locked from the inside. The others were covered with black curtains. Behind each curtain was a small room and a small window, shades drawn. Beneath the window was a dollar bill slot, like the kind found in a vending machine. George Washington's profile, green arrows showing how to insert the money. I stuck out my single, and the machine slurped it up.

The shade rolled open, revealing a young woman standing in a small, softly-lit room. At first, it seemed like I'd caught her backstage, an actress adjusting her costume, tightening her pink leather boots, then shifting her breasts within a black corset. I wondered if there was some sort of signal, something only she could see or hear, alerting her to my presence. Perhaps the signal was broken. She looked at me and smiled, puffed her cheeks in a long exhale. Biting a blood-red fingernail, she moved closer, each step emanating from her hips. I smelled her perfume through the glass.

We stared. She leaned against the glass, looking me up and down, then brought her eyes back to mine. I couldn't judge her expression, wasn't sure where it came from or what it meant. I almost wondered if the window was not a window at all, but a trick mirror, and she was not looking at me but seducing her reflection, attempting to surprise her image with sudden movements. Her eyes fell back in line with my own. She waited. She shrugged. She pointed down with two fingers.

I took out a wrinkled dollar from my pocket and stuffed it through the slot. The carpet at her feet was littered with crumpled green paper.

She smiled, and I understood better where her smile came from. She pressed herself against the glass. Peeled off one shoulder strap, then the other. Stuck a middle finger in her mouth, up to the first knuckle, then glided her fingernail down her chin, her neck, over her corset, her stomach—beyond the window frame.

I rose onto the tips of my toes.

A light above my window began to flash; the shade started to fall. She leaned over, lowering her head with the shade and I did the same, mimicking her movements. Lower. Lower. Her face shadowed; only her hand, fingers waving. The last face I saw was not hers, but the man's across the hut, in his room, staring through his window, dangling a dollar through the slot.

We had cased the joint for weeks. Slowly driving by after a movie, down the Expressway's dark service road. If we were feeling ballsy, maybe a loop through the gravel parking lot, hoping to glimpse a dancer strutting to her car and driving home totally naked.

"They're all fucking whores, dude," T.J. said.

We nodded, knowing that this was probably true and understanding, with utmost certainty, that conversations with T.J. were often one comment away from a fight.

Jim sat in the back, his short pants even shorter when sitting, revealing the length of his white tube socks. I was driving.

A man dressed in black save for chrome sparkling on his motorcycle boots walked out the front doors, yelling into his cell phone. He chewed a thick cigar. Waited. Reached into his pants, adjusted himself, then plucked the cigar from his teeth and resumed yelling. He looked around the parking lot.

"Let's go, guys," Jim said.

"Oh my god," T.J. said. "That guy is cool as shit."

I was in between Jim and T.J., compelled to balance the scale, appease everyone. I wasn't macho. I wasn't a geek. I was on the fence, that vast border between short pants and motorcycle boots.

I know I forced Jim to come to Sin-derella's. T.J. would've gone alone, if he hadn't lost his license for speeding. Something about Jim—his golden identity bracelet, white Nike sneakers, over-sized t-shirt exclaiming his first-drummer position in the marching band—made Sin-derella's a little less intimidating.

On the surface, I was cooler than Jim. But I knew he had more confidence than I did. He'd strut through Sin-derella's in his short pants and bright sneakers, talking like Al Bundy from *Married with Children*. "Check out the gazongas on her!" I'd turn red and walk away, while he stood there with a wide, goofy grin.

He was a spaz. We'd throw him into bushes or peg him in the head with tennis balls. No matter what we did, no matter how mad he got, he'd always come back for more. In a group, I'd pound on Jim just as hard as the rest of the guys. But when we were alone, I didn't. We'd talk. Sometimes he'd mention his father, how he took off when Jim was in elementary school. Jim told me he felt weird when his mother's boyfriend started sleeping over. I'd listen for as long as he needed, or at least until another friend came over.

Jim racked up thirty dollars in ATM processing fees. In the dark room, among the huts edged in neon, he returned again and again to the same window behind the same black curtain. T.J. and I smoked cigarettes, wondering what was so special about Jim's girl. We snuck up behind the black curtain, the music concealing our footsteps, and peeked in. We saw a woman's arched back, yellowed bruises along her spine. Jim pressed his face against the tip slot, moving his mouth. For a moment, we thought—no, they couldn't be. Jim pressed his palm against the glass. The song broke.

"...and that's kind of where I'm at these days," Jim said. The stripper nodded her head. The light above the window began to flash. Jim slipped a single through the slot. The shade came down.

"You're a fucking pussy, you know that?" T.J. said.

"Fuck you, guys! How long you been there?"

I shrugged. Neutral.

"Long enough to know you're a pussy. She's not your therapist, you idiot."

Jim held his arms out and looked around the dark room. "I don't see a sign anywhere. Do you, Anthony? Do you see a sign that says I can't talk to them?"

I laughed, but no one could hear it over the music.

"*You* need a fucking sign. No joke," T.J. said.

"Whatever. Can we just go?"

"No way. Gotta hit Club Inferno."

With this I was clearly in agreement.

"It's too bright in there," Jim said. "Feels creepy."

T.J. laughed and looked at me. "Listen to him. Creepy."

We turned and left Jim standing alone in the dark room.

New York law stated that if your dancers were totally nude, you couldn't serve alcohol. I wasn't sure what difference a G-string made but apparently the penalties for noncompliance were high. Some clubs navigated around alcohol restrictions by serving juice and allowing customers to bring their own booze. Men in lumpy coats would belly up to the stage, wave dollars in one hand, and with the other, pour nips of vodka into their cranberry juice.

A gorilla-necked bouncer encased in a white STAFF t-shirt guarded the entrance to Club Inferno. He bent and twisted my ID, waved it beneath a black light. He looked at me and smirked, then let me pass. Two drink tickets were included with the ten dollar cover charge, and the bouncer peeled them off from a giant spool; the same tickets Chuck E. Cheese used to load into Skee-Ball machines. I followed T.J. through the entrance and over to the bar, ripped off one of the tickets and redeemed it for a tall glass of orange juice. As we were about to head deeper into the club, we turned to see Jim jogging toward us, his socks glowing in black light.

The long runway, the "thrust stage," was wide at the base with a golden pole in the center. A group of Asian men in suits lined one side. A blonde woman crawled toward them, stopped, then slowly arched her back. They leaned against the stage, whispering to each other. One younger Asian man stood away from the stage. A big bronzed man with spiky blonde hair walked up to the young man and slapped him on the back. "Get your ass ringside!" he shouted. "This is your last chance!" The young man grinned like a child approaching an ice cream truck.

She slid off the pole, slinked over to the man, put his dollar between her breasts, grabbed his face and rubbed it against her. The men in suits leaned closer to the stage. The woman laughed. When she finished with the young man, she released his face, and he stepped back into his group of friends, shaking his head and fixing his messy hair with his fingers.

Once we all had our juice, we walked toward the stage and took a seat at one of the tables far away from the loud group. From there,

I saw another section of the club, a balcony overlooking the stage. A row of leather chairs faced the wall, each one containing a naked woman—Asian, black, white; big breasted, small breasted; rail-thin, pleasantly-plump. They ground themselves into their customers. Only the back of each man's head was visible: bald spots like eggs in a carton.

We sipped our juice. Whispered. Jim and I giggled. T.J. stared at the stage. The blonde was replaced by a brunette. She leaned over the railing and shouted to the DJ.

"Okay, fellas. We got Misty coming to the stage right now. Come on, give it up!"

The next song was so loud it drowned the men's cheers; their open mouths and wide eyes exclaimed nothing but the club remix of Shaggy's "It Wasn't Me," a song that begins with a man asking his friend how to hide his affair from his wife, then kicks into pulsating drum machines and synthesizers. Misty strutted down the stage, popping her hips to the bass. Her small hard nipples, visible through a white sheer bra, were like pink rocks.

"Turkey's done," T.J. whispered.

At the tip of the stage, she dropped into a spread-legged squat, slowly undulating her spine as she rose and rose. Flicked her head left, right, whipping her hair, obscuring her face. Back up the runway, strands of hair clinging to her fiery lip gloss, she kicked one leg high in the air and then rested her shoe's sharp heel on the pole. Rocked her body up, down. Her heel slid down the pole, guiding her split to the stage; then she bounced several times, head thrown back, eyes closed.

The bronzed man strutted up to the stage, reached into his hip pocket and tossed a wad of singles in the air, at least fifty dollars worth. We smirked and watched the singles rain, draping her thighs, her breasts, her forehead. The man walked back to his empty table. The Asian group went wild; the young man, like a pro, pumped his fist in the air. Misty writhed on stage, stuffing dollars into her bra, her G-string, her boots. An older black man slowly leaned over the stage, dangling a dollar above her closed eyes. She didn't take it; her chest heaved, her body spent. Then her eyes opened, and the single charmed her head up, up, up until she clenched the bill between her teeth and ripped it from his hands. He watched her, rubbing his chin. The entire room stared at Misty, everyone nodding as Shaggy told us to imagine banging her on the bathroom floor.

As the song faded, she collected the rest of her singles into a pile, scooped them up, and trotted off stage.

"Give. It. Up!"

Misty returned to the club with a red boa wrapped around her neck, draped over her bare breasts. She weaved through the cocktail tables, easing herself between chairs, leaning in to run a red fingernail down a man's cheek. Nobody paid attention to the flat Asian girl on stage.

Misty headed toward us. Our sweaty glasses of orange juice stood in tiny puddles. She motioned to an empty chair and sat beside me.

"How you fellas doin' tonight?"

T.J. reached across the table and put his hand on top of hers.

"Real good, sweetheart. Real good."

My face burned. Jim covered his mouth.

She leaned back in her chair and nodded several times, as if bopping to a tune in her head. "That's good, baby. Got plans for the evening?"

I smiled and took several quick sips. I didn't want to stare. I didn't want to be rude. I didn't want to miss a thing.

"Lookin' at it, sista."

Misty nodded again and flipped the boa around her neck. She looked older up close and smelled like baby powder. She crossed her bare legs and rubbed the top of her thighs.

"Chilly in here, right?" Jim said. T.J. shot him a look.

She laughed. "Yeah it is. Always fucking freezing."

"Need something to warm you up?" T.J. asked.

"Depends what you had in mind."

I glanced at our reflection in the mirror.

"What's the market like these days?" T.J. asked, leaning back in his chair. Misty stared at him.

"What's your friend talkin' bout?" she asked me.

I shook my head.

"You know what I'm talkin' 'bout."

Misty stared at T.J. "Twenty for twenty."

T.J. exhaled. "In this economy? That's steep, don't you think? Don't you think that's steep, fellas?"

"Seems fair," I said.

T.J. shook his head, reached into his pocket and pulled out several twenties. He peeled one off and waved it at Misty.

"Not me, darling." She flicked her boa at the bronzed man across the stage.

T.J. squinted. "Why? He gonna dance for me, too?"

Misty laughed. "House rules."

T.J. looked at her. Me. Jim.

"Well, we wouldn't want to break any rules. Heavens, no. Not here." He sipped his juice. "Not in this fine establishment."

"Shut the fuck up." Misty stood, lassoed T.J.'s neck with her boa, and guided him out of his seat and across the club. T.J. looked back and smiled.

Jim and I watched T.J. pay the bronzed man. The man nodded and pointed to the balcony. Misty led T.J. up the stairs. The last few steps she turned and walked backwards, until they reached an empty leather chair. She shoved him, and he disappeared.

My ears felt numb from the bass pumping out of the speakers. The dark red light made Club Inferno look like a giant submarine, walls covered in posters advertising new porn movies or upcoming appearances by porn stars, most of whom I knew by their first names. We traded porno movies like baseball cards. *Got 'em, got 'em, need 'em, got 'em.* Once, I found a porno in the back of my closet, one that had been passed around Team Destructo so many times that we could recite entire scenes. I must have hid it so well that I'd forgotten about it. I emptied my entire closet and was in the middle of rearranging my clothes when my father came into my room and saw the tape. He grinned.

"Hey, boy. Whatchu got there?"

"Um. You know. Just a little homework for my Film Studies class," I said.

"Yeah, I bet you been workin' at home."

I shook my head and pulled out more clothes and sneakers from the bottom of my closet.

"You tossin' all this?" he asked.

"Yeah," I lied.

"Well, then. Don't mind if I do." He bent down, picked up the tape, and walked out.

Months later, I was looking through my father's closet for a tie and saw the tape on the top shelf, hidden behind a few shoe boxes. What struck me first was that my father had hidden the tape the same way I did. He was almost fifty-five years old; who was he hiding it from? Why couldn't he just go out and buy his own? I wanted answers to these questions, but still, I was grateful. I didn't want to imagine how the situation would have been different if my mother had walked into the room.

Jim and I split a nip of vodka, mixing it into our orange juice. At first my drink gave me the chills, but I soon warmed up.

"Okay, you horny fuckers, we got fresh meat coming to the stage right now. Put yo' dicks together for the wild, the ferocious, the sexiest cat this side of the Nile—give it up, for Chee-tah!"

A club remix of Jethro Tull's "Bungle in the Jungle" blasted out of the speakers. A quick flash: my father's puzzled face listening to this mutilated version of a classic tune. But his expression, our expression, changed once Cheetah, a pale redhead in a leopard thong, crawled onto the stage.

"Holy shit," Jim said. "That's her, man."

"That's who?"

"Her. The chick from the whack booth."

Jim's eyes locked on Cheetah.

"Guess they let her out of her cage," I said, waiting for Jim to smile. He didn't.

Cheetah moved across the stage, performing a routine of sharp-nailed swipes and well-timed growls. She licked her boot. She bit singles out of the Asian men's waistbands. She crawled off the stage and roamed the audience. Jim took out a single and flapped it like a distress flag.

"What are you doing?"

"I gotta talk to her."

"Relax, man. She's not your girlfriend. She's a stripper."

"Fuck you."

He waved his dollar until it caught her eye. She grinned, and made her way to our table, scrunching her nose as she got closer, sniffing us out. When she reached Jim's feet, she put her hands on his thighs and pushed back onto her knees.

"Hey there, drummer boy." She smiled, revealing yellow and black rubber bands in her braces.

Jim leaned in and whispered to her. I had never seen Jim talk this much to a girl. I knew Jim as the kid in the basement hosting *Wrestlemania* parties in middle school, hopped up on Dr. Pepper and Ellio's Pizza, pretending to lick the screen as Jake the Snake's girlfriend bent over in jean shorts. This was different. Jim wasn't playing for laughs. He was serious.

As Cheetah whispered to Jim, I noticed the other men in the room, staring. The stage was empty, but the Auto-Tuned version of "Bungle in the Jungle" kept playing. One of the Asian guys stood up and held out his arms. The young one waved a single, trying to get Cheetah's attention. Jim leaned in closer.

"Hey buddy, this ain't a confessional." The bronzed man had a squeaky voice.

"It's okay, Chuck," Cheetah said.

Chuck looked at her. "Oh, it is? Guess I didn't get the memo." Cheetah looked back at him. "Less talkin'. More shakin'. Got me?"

Chuck stared at Cheetah. Then Jim. Jim handed Cheetah a dollar, and she tucked it into her waistband. Chuck grinned and walked away. Jim leaned back in his chair and watched Cheetah snarl and growl toward the stage. She got down on all fours, stalking around the chairs, then squatted and leapt onto the runway. A few more swipes, a few more growls, and then Cheetah crawled off stage.

"Top notch, my friends. Top fucking notch," T.J. said, settling back into his chair. I wondered when and where he had all these lap dances to compare to Misty's, but I didn't ask.

"Good shit?" I asked.

"Phenomenal. She works hard for the money," he said, snapping his fingers.

I laughed and shook my head.

"Where's Jim?"

"Said he was feeling sick. I think he's outside yacking."

T.J. laughed. "Figures."

The DJ blasted a song I'd never heard before. The blonde returned to the stage.

"Her again?" T.J. said. "Guess they don't have that many girls on tonight." He leaned back and sipped his juice. The Asian girl moved from table to table, whispering into the men's ears, but they all shook their heads.

T.J. reached into his pocket and pulled out a twenty. "Hey, sweetie!"

"Dude."

"Fuck it. Round two." T.J. stood up, hooked arms with her and led her to the bronzed man.

Alone. In a room full of muscle men and naked women, DJ blasting music, bartenders pouring juice, bouncers sweating beneath their tight shirts, I was alone. Alone in dark, shallow water. Night swimming. *I want to be here. I do. Just not right now.*

I saw the word *Adult* all over Sin-derella's. Flashing in red neon above the juice bar or printed in bold on movie and magazine posters. *Adults Only. Intended for Mature Audiences.* These words reminded me of the warning labels on cigarettes or beer: *Smoking is hazardous to your health. Pregnant women should not consume alcohol.* The labels made sense to me because they protected people. Why did I need protection against a movie or a woman?

Adults told us to act mature, that if we wanted to be treated like adults, we should behave like adults. I looked around Club Inferno. The guys laughing and shouting were around my age or a few years older. The men, the ones who I considered adults, sat alone. Some looked like they were sitting in a quiet restaurant, waiting for a meal. Others leaned over the stage and whispered in a woman's ear, tipping her again and again.

"Where's Jimmy?"

I turned to see Cheetah, slightly more clothed, hands on her hips.

"Oh, he went to the car. He should be back soon, probably. He just had to get something from his car."

She nodded. Then looked around the club and sat beside me.

"What's your story?"

"What do you mean?"

"I mean, what's your story? Got plans for the evening?"

Her eyes seemed far away, as if she were asking her questions to someone on the other side of the club. She smiled.

"I think this is the last stop for us. Probably just go home."

"Aw," she pursed her lips.

"I know. Not too exciting."

"You gotta make time for excitement. We only go around once."

"That's true," I said. "Very true."

I wondered how many times she'd done this. Our conversation so thick with clichés it was like we were yelling obscenities and speaking in code at the same time.

"Twenty for twenty?" she asked.

I looked around the club for T.J., for Jim. Then reached deep into my pocket, fished out a mess of singles and flipped through them like a gas station attendant.

"Deal."

Cheetah led me down the line of grinding bodies: bare, smooth backs; thick-knuckled hands; tangled legs. Brief eye contact with several men, their expressions a mix of confusion and pleasure. Some closer to pain: Gritted teeth. Mouths shaped to whistle.

She guided me by my wrist, stopped, turned me to face her and gently shoved me into a leather seat. She kicked her leg up, stabbing the heel of her shoe into the arm rest. The man beside me moaned; his body smothered by a gyrating black woman in pink lingerie. Cheetah touched the side of my face.

"Right here," she said, pointing to her eyes, index and middle finger forming a split.

I nodded, but I couldn't see her eyes. She was an apparition, a figure in shadow, the outline of her body bleeding into darkness. A flash of leopard print. The whiff of cheap perfume. Body glitter glinting like stars. Her fiery hair flowed over my legs, onto the leather seat. She quickly shook her head, then brought her face up below my waist. Stomach. Chest. My collarbone. My ear. Her nose brushing mine; warm minty breath. Back down. Down. A wake of baby powder, a scent I thought was Misty's. Perhaps powder is the final preparation, the last detail before the women crawl into the crowd. Perhaps most of it had rubbed off of Cheetah, but now her movements revealed another layer—chalky residue in the crook of her elbow. Her under-arms. Beneath her spotted waistband. She rubbed the length of her body against me and whimpered.

"Are you okay?"

I didn't answer. She pressed herself into me. As she moved, her thighs stuck briefly to the leather then ripped away. Stick. Rip. Stick. Rip. Until her legs began to sweat, and her skin glided slick on the cushion.

She reached down and grabbed hard, adjusting me. The top of her chest to her lower stomach—she flowed over me like warm wa-ter. Powerful, controlled movements, steady as the tide. Crashing. Crashing. Crashing. Blood ripped through my head, and I tried to stop myself—too late, too far. My body broke.

Cheetah's movements slowed. Slowed. She exhaled. The light hit her braces. A smile? She pushed back and looked down at her body.

"Thanks," I said quietly, and left.

I tied my flannel shirt around my waist before heading back down into the Inferno.

"Where you going, a fucking Pearl Jam concert?" T.J. said, leaning against the lit edge of the stage.

"Kiss off, dude."

"You missed it, man. This new black chick came out. In-sane ass. Doing that booty shake, that fuckin' ass seizure thing. I was foaming at the mouth. No joke."

"Sorry I missed it."

"Yeah, you should be." He sipped a tall glass of water.

We sat in silence. Rather, the club spoke for us, telling us to *give it up* and *show the girls some love*. New packs of guys arrived, red-faced, serious. A few men showed up alone. One man walked in clenching a twenty: right up to the bronzed man, a girl bounced down the steps, the man smiled, she smiled, disappeared into the balcony. I watched the bronzed man wrap the twenty around a thick roll of bills and tuck it into his suit pocket.

I moved in my seat, searching for a comfortable position.

"What do you say, T.J. Call it a night?"

He took a long gulp of what I now smelled to be vodka. Misty was back on stage. He gave her a two-fingered salute. She returned it with a tight-lipped smile. The Asian bachelor party was gone, perhaps off to another club: Blush or The Tender Trap further down the service road.

"Dude?"

"I heard you."

He finished his drink.

"Well?"

"Yeah. We can go. Get your shit, Pearl Jam."

We drove to Candlelight Diner—my eyes wide, hands at ten and two. The road was damp and several garbage trucks roared by en route to their morning pick-ups. I turned on the wipers.

"Let's go, Miss Daisy. I be hungry," T.J. said.

"Miss Daisy didn't drive, you dumbass. Morgan Freeman did." I shook my head. "The movie's called *Driving Miss Daisy.*"

T.J. frowned and looked out the window. "Speaking of *Driving Miss Daisy*, I wonder if this pansy in the backseat is ever gonna wake up."

"I'm up," Jim said. "I've been up."

We crashed down in the red vinyl booth and pulled the menus out from behind the mini jukebox, even though we already knew what we wanted. Jim drummed his fingers on the table, browsing the music.

"Misty was fucking amazing." T.J. pressed his nose to his sleeve and inhaled deeply. "Seriously. That girl is talented. And judging by D'Aries' outfit, Cheetah was damn good, too."

Jim turned. "Cheetah? She danced for you?"

"Yeah. I mean, she came looking for you and then, I don't know. We got to talking."

Jim nodded and flipped a page in the jukebox. I made eye contact with T.J. and shook my head.

"What?" T.J. said. "You're *supposed* to jizz your shorts. Fuck. You paid twenty bucks, right?"

I looked down at the menu.

T.J. looked at Jim. "Oh," he said. "What's the big deal, Jim? Did you think she was your fucking girlfriend?"

"No, it's not that."

"Talk to her for two minutes and she's your soul mate. You two gonna write songs together? Did you tell her you're in marching band? How you get to wear a hat with a big fucking pipe-cleaner on it?"

"Actually I did talk to her about marching band. I went to camp with her freshman year."

T.J.'s eyes widened. I looked at Jim.

"No shit," T.J. said.

"Check the yearbook."

"Oh, I will," T.J. said. "And I'll beat my shit to it all night long."

I looked at Jim and he looked right back at me. The waitress broke in and asked us what we wanted.

On the ride home, I realized it was Father's Day. Of all the holidays I could have spent drinking spiked juice and throwing singles, Father's Day was probably the best choice since my father couldn't care less about his day. But after I dropped off Jim and T.J., I stopped at 7-Eleven anyway and bought him a few scratch-offs and a gift card for a week's worth of coffee. When I pulled into the driveway, he was just leaving for work.

"Well, well," he said, grinning. "What cat drug you in, boy?"

"I didn't catch her name," I said. "Happy Father's Day, dude."

"All right. Not bad." He dug his silver dollar from his pocket and held the tickets against the hood of the Monte.

"How's everything?" he asked.

"Good."

"Good."

I watched him scratch the rest of his tickets. They were all losers, but he held up the gift card and smiled.

"Least this one's a sure thing," he said, slipping the silver dollar back into his pocket. "Gotta run. I'll probably be asleep before you wake up."

"Probably," I said.

"Tough life, boy. Tough life."

22

"HER BODY'S in good shape," my father said, "no rot." His feet crunched on the gravel as he knelt down, running his fingers along the bubbled paint like he was reading Braille.

"'68?" I asked.

"'67." He slid underneath the chassis, muttering, his voice echoing up through the rotted floor. "Shit."

I poked my head through the broken passenger-side window and saw his finger wagging through one of the rust holes in the floor. "Swiss fucking cheese." He slid out from under the Mustang and pulled a Winston from his pack, his teeth clenched. "A rotted floor is the worst. You'd have to do a ground-up restoration, which we ain't gonna do." Lighter sparked into flame. "Even then you'd probably end up like Fred Flintstone, most likely in a rain storm." Sharp inhale and long exhale, smoke pouring from his nose. I was reflected twice in his black sunglasses, two miniature versions of myself, like in cartoons when, after a small puff of smoke, a tiny, angelic version of the character appears on one shoulder, a devilish one on the other. In cartoons, the angel and devil spoke and moved independently. In my father's shades, they moved together.

"Daylight's burning," he said. I followed him down the long row of rusted cars.

I knew we'd see Billy standing next to his '72 Olds, wolfing down his second sausage sandwich, telling Greg about "what a nice fucking day" it turned out to be. Greg had a red '66 GTO convertible, smoked little black cigars, and wore a heavy set of keys that protruded from his hip like a spiny chrome tumor. Not too far off was Reggie, *The Automotologist*, setting up his sign in front of his gold Lamborghini. It was a huge white sign with a glossy finish, displaying the specs and history of the car. A lot of guys made signs, but not like Reggie's. What made Reggie's special was he had a picture of himself on there—a scrawny black man in a tan suede coat and sunglasses—and in tight, flashy script it read: *The Automotologist*. No one ever asked for an explanation. Nobody gave a shit about foreign cars anyway.

"I wonder if that peckerhead with the blue 'Vette will be there?" my father said as he bit down on his Winston and turned the wheel. I could picture Eric in his monogrammed satin jacket cleaning the rear window of his Corvette.

As we drove to the show, my father and I rattled off names of whackos we knew we'd see there. Even though we pretty much kept to ourselves, we knew a lot of names. It was either on their license plates (JOE'S 55, MIKE'S 68) or they trapped us in torturous conversation. Mark wandered over and tried to sell us a rusted center hub off a '69 Vega. Fat Ricky's shirt inched up on his white belly as he sloshed across the field to mumble about his '56 Merc. Or else it was Billy with the '72 Olds, come to breathe his sausage breath all over us. These guys were at every show. But then, so were we.

A long line of gleaming cars and trucks growled at the entrance to the fairgrounds. My father pulled in behind a black '70 El Camino. Not even two cars passed through registration before five more rumbled in behind us.

My father glanced at the side view. "Good turnout."

The thick pine trees bordering the fairgrounds and the blue cloudless sky were more than just reflected in the red and black hoods, the chrome bumpers and rims. They were absorbed into the paint, swallowed by the chrome—each car a moving landscape. The peaceful union of nature and machine tarnished only by block letter bumper stickers stating "Big Tits Save Lives" and decals of skeletons 69ing. My father had a set of flashing, magnetic boobs stuck to the dash.

We pulled into the fairgrounds and, sure enough, Billy was waiting for a sausage sandwich, Greg's keys were sparkling, and *The Automotologist* was setting up. My father grinned like he'd bet on a rigged game.

"I told ya, boy. I told ya and I told ya."

After we set up—popped the hood, unfolded the lawn chairs, took out the cooler—we walked over to the swap meet. Initially intended to be an outdoor market for used car parts, the swap meet had mutated into a god-awful yard sale. Guys dumped rusty bicycles, broken lampshades, and dusty Nintendo games onto blue tarps next to milk crates full of cracked distributor caps and grease-caked carburetors. Some didn't even sell any car parts. One guy parked his truck up against the fence so he had a spot to hang his wife's old nightgowns.

My father shook his head. "Same shit, different show."

We found the guy who sold Matchbox cars and my father stopped.

"Any '67 Chevy pickups?"

The guy thumbed through a wad of cash.

"Doubt it. Don't think they made 'em."

Guys who owned Novas or Corvettes had no trouble finding original owner manuals, tin signs, posters, calendars, hats, t-shirts, pins, buttons, stickers, or Matchbox cars. My father had to settle for generic versions: ambiguous miniature red pickups or hats that just said "Chevrolet." For all anyone knew, my father was the proud owner of a '96 Lumina.

We grabbed a couple of sausage sandwiches on our way back to the truck. By then, dozens and dozens of cars and trucks had entered the show. Parked in long rows, they stretched across three acres of patchy grass and dirt. A lot of guys would talk about the way a car "sits." They'd see a Camaro SS or a Roadrunner with over-sized rear tires and a set of air shocks lifting the tail and they'd say, "Man, that just sits nice." I stared at the cars from the edge of the swap meet. Each one of them sat nice, as if they were here first, and the world had grown around them.

The judges ticketed each car with a yellow evaluation sheet and wrote the class number on each windshield with a white marker. I didn't understand that. Here were a bunch of tough dudes, many of whom had been brown-bagging beers or something harder since breakfast, each one watching their cars and each other so closely—and then this little judge came over and scribbled on the windshield. Some guys actually winced.

My father cracked open a ginger ale. He leaned back, pushed his hat up, and tilted his head to the sun. He groaned a little as he kicked his feet up on the cooler.

"How's ol' Mama Mia doin'?"

I laughed. "She's good. She wants to hang out all the time, though."

"They all like that, boy." He sipped his ginger ale.

We watched a '67 El Camino roll through the gates, followed closely by a '56 Bel Air.

"Hey, boy, check that out." My father stood up and pointed to the Bel Air. "Mom had the same one. I mean, exact same one. Color and everything."

I tried to imagine my mother peering out through the wide windshield, but all I could see was the fat man in denim behind the wheel. A small woman sat in the passenger seat. Now and then, a few more cool cars rolled in. One of us pointed, the other said, "Yeah." Soon, "yeahs" became nods, and then silence. My father dozed off.

Sometimes I wandered the swap meet while my father was asleep. One guy set up dozens of shallow glass cases full of patches and stickers. I liked looking at them; they reminded me of the baseball cards I used to collect, and the trips my friends and I took to the store, buying pack after pack as the owner rested his belly on the glass counter. The owner would point out valuable cards and give us little plastic sheaths to protect them.

There were Camaro stickers and Nova stickers and Corvette stickers. Super Sport patches, STP patches, Valvoline patches. There was a progression to the merchandise that I was aware of but didn't understand. Like a gradient scale, the colors of the stickers and patches began to darken, until they were just white letters on a black background. THESE COLORS DON'T RUN. A silhouette of a man beneath the arcing letters POW/MIA. One patch read: SPEAK ENGLISH OR GO HOME! A man in a sleeveless denim jacket with a Rebel flag patch on his chest leaned over the case. He knocked his greasy knuckles on the glass, and the man behind the counter nodded and gave him a sticker that read: I'D RATHER BE RIDING YOUR WIFE. I watched the man walk away, dragging two young boys behind him.

I understood the stereotypical masculinity in restoring a muscle car: using your hands to rebuild a machine, the sweat, the oil, sliding underneath a chassis while "Whole Lotta Love" blasts from the garage. This seemed safe. What I didn't understand was the seamless progression from automobiles to patriotism to xenophobia to screwing someone else's wife. It wasn't clear to me what came first. What was prerequisite? What was learned on the job?

1966 Dodge Coronet 500,
360, little rust, solid floors and trunk, great interior. $2,700.

"I can't picture it exactly, but . . ." My father circled the ad in the paper, then dialed the phone. He made all the calls. He called about the black '69 Nova, the blue '67 Camaro, the orange '70 GTO, and the pea-green '76 Mustang: all of which were too expensive or too fast, the latter more my father's concern than mine. That black Nova was a beast, though. Barebones, practically stripped to the frame except for the 454 sleeping under the hood. Straight out of *Mad Max*, that car could crush the Volkswagens and BMWs that filled the high school parking lot. But my father didn't go for it.

I sat next to him at the kitchen table, listening to him talk to the guy with the Dodge. Coronet didn't sound too cool. It was too feminine, like the name of a perfume or a piece of lingerie. I looked it up in the dictionary and found a picture of a woman wearing a small crown.

I wanted a car that everyone would recognize, a car that was classically cool, like the ones caressed by models in the old car commercials. A car whose slogan made you feel unpatriotic not to drive one. Chevrolet: *The Heartbeat of America.*

"All right, so Thursday. Sounds good. Thanks, buddy."

My father scribbled something on the newspaper.

"Nice guy. I'll take half a day tomorrow and we'll check it out when you get home from school."

I agreed. I was skeptical, but curious. I was also getting impatient.

"I think it's similar to a Comet, or a Satellite," he said on his way upstairs to take a shower.

I heard the water beat down into the tub. I stared at the circled ad. While he was on the phone, my father had traced the circle so many times that it bled through the pages of the newspaper. I flipped ahead four pages and could still see the faint ring of ink.

Ron's screen door squeaked, then slammed behind him. He waved to us from the brick stoop and made his way across the lawn. He was always chomping on a piece of food you don't normally see people eating outdoors, like a handful of popcorn or a pork chop. Last week, when we first came to look at the Dodge, he introduced himself in between bites of corn bread.

"Back again, fellas?" He picked at a hunk of meatloaf wrapped in tin foil.

"Yeah, I think this is the last time, though," my father said.

I stood behind him, holding a large manila envelope containing every cent of my junior savings account.

Ron walked over to the car, popped the hood, the trunk, and opened the doors. The Dodge was a faded and bubbled cranberry color, but the original black interior gleamed like volcanic glass. Strips of chrome lined the dash. Chrome radio knobs, chrome gear shifter, chrome door handles and seat backs and ashtrays: all mirrors reflecting exactly who I wanted to be. The black leather creaked and pulled at my father's tank top as he adjusted himself in the driver's seat. He looked up. Ron poked his head in and pointed to the ceiling.

"Like I said, most headliners sag like an old broad. Not this one."

My father nodded. We got out and stood next to the car. My father and Ron talked for a little while about the car, then veered off into a conversation about upcoming shows, and soon they were talking about their first cars and spending all day and night in the garage and how sometimes they didn't know what they were doing—they just slid underneath with a wrench and poked around. My father lit a cigar and told Ron about the time he nearly burned Haggemeyer's eyebrows off.

"He looked into that carburetor like fuckin' Elmer Fudd. Backfired right in his face. Oh man, we were howling!"

I stood behind my father with the envelope. I had bent the metal clasp so many times that it had fallen off. When their laughter died down, I handed the envelope to my father.

"We'll take her."

My father passed the envelope to Ron. Ron folded it in half, and tucked it into his back pocket.

"Take care of her, son."

He gave me the keys.

"I will."

My father grinned, and walked back to his Chevy parked in the street. Ron went back in the house and closed the door. The two gold keys dangling from the ring felt foreign in my hands. Our clunky silver house key was the only key I knew. The Dodge keys were sharp, like two little swords.

The kick of the ignition—an eruption—cued the engine's beautiful rumble. Great gray puffs of smoke rose above the trunk. I checked my mirrors. Adjusted my seat. Buckled my belt. This was not Mom's Taurus. No air bags here, no padded steering wheel. No cruise control. No shoulder straps. No power brakes. I backed the Dodge into the street and followed my father to the Expressway.

At some point on the drive home, I passed him. I looked over and nodded at him sternly, as if I were a big-rig truck driver. He grinned, chewing a little piece of gum slowly. The rumble of the engine eased into a steady vibration. The wheel seemed to turn on its own, anticipating the curves in the road. I watched the slide show of sky and pine trees on the hood. The road signs I knew so well, the town names and exit numbers I'd watched from the backseat for years were different now, smaller, as if the windshield were a backward telescope. I saw my father in the rearview, his bald head above the wheel of his Chevy. I kept looking at him, glad he was there but at the same time wishing I was alone, completely alone on the highway, driving in total silence in the car I bought with my own money, more money than I'd ever held, let alone spent. A wave of adrenaline surged through me. The asphalt world stretched out before me, and as I accelerated, the dotted lines blurred into a single white strip.

And then I broke down.

The throttle linkage had busted loose in the middle of the highway. I was giving it gas and going nowhere. I pulled over and my father quickly repaired it with some wire he had in his glove box. When we got home, he tinkered with it for the rest of the afternoon.

"No big deal," he said. "Easy fix."

We began the year-long restoration process. My father continued to shave a few hundred bucks off his paycheck. We didn't tell my mother. I started painting houses for my cousin to pay for the Dodge. I liked being outside, doing manual labor, working with tools. I liked the routine of coffee and bagels in the morning, big deli sandwiches for lunch, blasting music all day. This felt right. This was what I expected work to be: rise early, work hard, sleep well.

My father showed me how to use Bondo to fill in the rust holes. Scoop out the red goop with a putty knife and spread it evenly over the chewed metal. Sand it smooth with a piece of sandpaper wrapped around a wooden block to avoid leaving fingerprints. He repeated several tips almost every time we were in the driveway: Always check your fluids. Keep at least a quarter tank of gas. Pump your brakes.

When the car was finally ready for paint, we took off the emblems, the mirrors, the bumpers, the grille and put them on the lawn. I stopped for a second. The Dodge looked like an old man getting ready for bed, his dentures beside him on the nightstand.

"Man, wait'll she comes back," my father said. "You won't even recognize her. Remember when the Chevy was painted?"

I remembered. My father took a picture of me sitting on the step-side of the Chevy, my knees almost to my chest, the fresh red paint blazing around me like fire. My father hung the picture in the garage next to the picture of me sitting on the stepside of the truck when it was gray, my feet dangling above the driveway. Beside an old shot of my father's Triumph motorcycle—Grim Reaper airbrushed on the gas tank—there were two dim photographs of my brother's cars, the Volare and the Buick. There were no pictures of the restoration process, no images of the Volare or the Buick patched with Bondo. No shots of my father bending beside the fender, Don leaning over his shoulder, listening to my father's instructions on how to repair rusted metal. No pictures of my father and Don holding golden trophies beside their gleaming cars, validating their work. These pictures did not exist. There were only the two dim shots of Don's cars, later used to prove their original conditions to the insurance company.

"Yeah, boy," my father said in the driveway. "When she's done, she's gonna look mint."

I couldn't wait to see Billy with the '72 Olds look up from his sausage sandwich and see me rolling in behind my father. Greg with the '66 GTO would be right behind him, standing up on his toes to get a look at the Dodge. I'd tell *The Automotologist* he'd better print a sign up for me. It felt a little weird not driving to the show with my father. I saw him in the rearview, chewing gum, his wrist resting on top of the wheel. Sometimes it felt like he was close enough to see my eyes move and that he knew when I was looking back. Other times he seemed too far away.

We registered and rolled through the rows of cars and trucks. I saw Billy with the '72 Olds and a few other guys check us out. My father and I parked next to each other in the shade.

"I thought Billy was gonna shit when he saw you roll in."

The Dodge did look good. We picked an aggressive red, somewhere between fire and blood. It complemented the black interior, made the new bumpers and mirrors pop. I borrowed some of my father's spray-on wax to clean the dirt and pollen off the hood. He did the same, then took out the chairs. I unloaded the cooler from my trunk.

"Let's do it," I said. We headed over to the swap meet.

Around four, they started announcing the winners. Even though my father took first once, he'd be the first to tell you it was only because the competition was light that day. The guys who took first were rich and retired. Their cars were full restorations, right down to the last washer. We did what we could.

My father took second. He stood with his arms crossed, waiting for the judge to announce my class. The judge called out a two-way tie for third—a ratty orange El Camino and an ugly silver Mustang. I knew I had them beat. My father looked over and nodded.

"Okay. In second place," he shuffled through some papers; the microphone squealed, "we got Anthony's '66 Do-"

"Yeah, boy!" My father yelled out and squeezed my neck. I started laughing, and walked up to get my trophy. When I turned around, my father was waiting for me, halfway between the crowd and the trophy table. Billy's Olds took first. My father and I heard them announce it as we compared trophies at the back of the crowd.

We hung around for a while, listening to the engines start up and then fade away. The sausage guy climbed down from his truck and dumped out a stainless steel bin full of grease. He got back in and drove out through the front gates.

My father had been talking about taking pictures of my car and his truck, parked next to each other, on the opposite side of the fairgrounds. The grass was fuller on that side, and the pine trees formed a natural wall, blocking out the highway. We hopped in and drove over.

My father made a wide turn, pulling in at an angle. I did the same on the opposite side, angling the front end of the Dodge toward the truck. We got out and my father snapped a few pictures.

"That looks good, right?" He snapped a few more.

"Yeah, it looks awesome."

We wanted to take one with both of us standing in front, but everyone else had already left. We'd stayed so long we'd lost track of time.

On the way home, thick clouds of steam billowed from the front of the Dodge. It smelled horrible, like there was a bonfire of plastic trapped under the hood. My face flushed. I lifted my foot off the gas but didn't brake. I just coasted, letting the road pull a little, slowing me down. My father blew the Chevy's air horn, and I saw him stabbing his finger toward the shoulder. I pulled over.

"You fuck. You motherfucker." My father stuck a rag in the radiator to stop the antifreeze from gushing out.

"What happened?" I stood behind him, rubbing my palm with my thumb.

"The fuckin' radiator cap blew."

The inside of the hood was dripping with antifreeze. It left ugly green streaks on the valve covers and boiled in little puddles on each manifold bolt. The distributor cap was pock marked, the battery cables soaked.

"Get another rag, huh?"

I ran to the trunk and grabbed all the rags.

He wiped down all the cables and bolts. He let some rags sit and soak up the puddles.

I stood next to him for a while, watching him clean off the engine and then I walked back to his Chevy and climbed in. When the tow truck came, my father flicked his Winston and lit another. He watched the driver place the long steel supports behind the tires. When the driver was ready to go, my father slowly walked back to the truck. It took about a half hour to get home and we spent it in silence, the Dodge dragging in front of us.

After my father paid the tow truck driver, he pulled the Dodge into the driveway. He got out and popped the hood. With his white hand-kerchief, he polished the valve covers, the carburetor, each manifold bolt. I stood behind him, watching him work. When he was finished, he closed the hood and went inside. I stood in the driveway and stared at the Dodge. The exhaust pipes ticked, a faint puff of steam seeping out from beneath the hood like breath.

I barely drove the Dodge in the winter. My father said the snow and salt would ruin the paint. It sat in the driveway, underneath a dark blue cover, and the snow piled up in three thick squares—one on the hood, one on the roof, and one on the trunk. After a storm, I'd go out and clean off the snow.

On bright, dry winter days, I drove the Dodge and listened to the engine. When I accelerated, I heard a noise like a bomb ticking. Once, I tried to yield to a tractor-trailer on the Expressway and the brake pedal dropped to the floor. I swerved onto the shoulder, coast-ing over the rumble strip, until the dirt and gravel slowed me down enough to shift into park with a loud bang. I popped the hood. The brake lines were bone dry.

I didn't tell my father. I kept the Dodge's flaws to myself, unless they were impossible to hide. If I could top off the fluids or fix a flat without him knowing, I would. I wanted all the internal parts to seem as perfect as the external—the bright chrome, the blood-red paint as bold and powerful as each piston pumping inside the engine. To take the whole car apart, to bring each piece into daylight, would be like staring at the anti-smoking poster hanging in health class, the one where a woman's face is covered in black, sticky tar. The caption asked us if we'd still smoke if what happened on the inside, happened on the outside. Full car restoration starts inside and moves outward, but my father and I didn't have the money. Instead, we patched the body and gave the surface a glossy coat.

23

MIA MOVED AWAY to school. For the first couple of months, she tried to convince me to come visit. I did a few times, but eventually, we stopped returning each other's calls. It was harder than I thought. I remember sitting in the kitchen, crying to my mother about not being able to see Mia. Perhaps I still missed my old friends, or perhaps my crying was a desperate attempt to get out of my busboy job that night, or maybe I really did miss Mia. Wherever my tears came from, they were uncontrollable. As my mother tried to comfort me, my father walked into the kitchen.

"What's the scoop?"

"Nothing," my mother said. "I think he misses his girlfriend."

I looked up at my father. He was confused. Another round of tears poured out of me.

"God damn, boy. You gotta toughen up."

"Donny," my mother said, but my father shook his head. He refilled his bowl of peanuts and walked back into the living room. I told my mother to get away—that I was fine. She backed off. I grabbed my coat and went to work.

Most of my new friends moved away that year, too. Marlon went to art school in Baltimore, just like he said he would, and he'd call me every now and then and tell me details about dorm rooms and beer pong and late-night pizza binges. I could tell by the way he was breathing that he was smoking weed or a cigarette or a mix of both. He seemed to linger in each exhale, as if giving me time to wrap my head around how different his life was from mine.

"Nobody knows me here, dude. You can be whoever you want."

I took the bus to visit him because I wasn't sure the Dodge would make it. My father preferred that I drive the Dodge only short distances.

Most days, I took my mother's Taurus to class and left the Dodge in the driveway beneath its blue cover. I didn't mind that much. It was better on gas, and I didn't have to worry about getting it dirty. I held the wheel with one hand, ate gooey egg sandwiches from the other. I wiped my hands on my jeans and tossed the wrappers in the back. I didn't have to check the weather or think about where to park. I could just go.

I sat in the parking lot before class, watching my English professor shuffle through the dead leaves on his way to the low brick buildings. Except for a single row of dorms painted hospital green, it was a commuter college. No one I talked to was entirely sure why they were there, as if they got into their cars wearing their high school graduation gowns and coasted into the parking lot. Stepping out, they scratched their heads, bought their books and went to class.

The few times I drove the Dodge to school, I parked at the back of the lot, far away from the other cars. On my lunch break, I sat in my car, the smell of greasy hamburgers and French fries overpowering the naked lady air freshener that dangled from my emergency brake pedal. I wiped my hands on my pants and watched the granules of salt tumble between the seats.

When I finished eating, I rolled down the window and lit a cigarette. There were a few other students who drove classic cars and parked as far away as I did, but we also parked far away from each other. We pretended we didn't see the other pull up or eat his lunch or light his cigarette. Our exhales rose like smoke signals, vanishing in the air.

I began spending my afternoons at my cousin Shannon's house. She was an English teacher, and she helped me prepare my applications. I wanted to transfer, to leave community college and go to Boston. I focused on that word: transfer. Transference. I saw my life as a decal, a sticker peeled off one bumper and placed onto another. Would it be possible to take all of me with me, to scrape off every piece of glue that once held me and transfer it to another place?

I thought about that as I drove my car around potholes or walked to its distant spot in the parking lot. One rainy day, the Dodge sat in the driveway beneath its blue cover. My brother asked me for a ride to the train station.

"I can't," I said, "it's raining."

He looked at me. "It's a car, dude. You drive the fucking thing. That's what it's there for."

I was compelled to argue, but out of habit. He was right. I peeled the cover off the car and drove him to the station.

After a full day of classes, I parked the Taurus and sat in the dark driveway. Our neighbor's cat crept out of the bushes, tripping the sensor on the flood light above the garage. The bright light bounced off her eyes before she darted back into the bush. I sat in the light for a few minutes, then it shut off. When I opened the door, the dome light flicked on. I walked up to my house and turned back toward the Taurus. Through the lit interior, I glimpsed the blue cover of the Dodge parked next to it. Then the dome light shut off and the driveway was dark again.

My father was on the couch watching *Easy Rider*. My mother sat in her chair, flipping through *Better Homes and Gardens*.

"Guys, I need to talk to you."

My mother tucked her legs underneath herself. My father gripped the top of the couch and pulled himself up.

Internal combustion—the words shot out of my mouth: "I'm selling the car and moving to Boston."

My father clicked off the TV. He scratched the sandpaper stubble on his neck.

"When did you decide this?" he asked.

"I don't know. I sent in my applications and I figure I'll need some cash to get me started and..." My voice trailed off. I turned up my palms and shrugged. I thought about my brother filling out his college applications by himself, without the help of a cousin or friend or our parents. Even though he left and came back, I felt he had changed, experienced something that didn't exist in arrivals or departures, but somewhere in between.

My father made a sound in his throat. "Just like that, huh?"

I didn't say anything.

He scratched his stubble again and raised his eyebrows.

"Hey, if that's what you want. I'll bring home For Sale signs tomorrow." He flicked on the TV and lay back down. My mother smiled and flipped a page in her magazine.

That was easy, I thought.

The summer before I left, we drove the Dodge to a show, the For Sale sign taped to the back window. The guys at the show looked at the car differently now that it was available. They licked their lips, moseyed over like cowboys sizing up a burlesque dancer, cupped their faces and peered into the smooth black interior. My father and I got out, walked through the crowd, wandered over to the swap meet. Behind us the crowd of leather and denim—patches and buttons and pins proclaiming their positions in the world—inched closer to the Dodge, its irresistible candy-red paint.

I never talked to the woman who bought it. I wasn't there when my father sold it to her: I was finishing up my final exams. He told me that she brought a small white envelope filled with seventy-two hundred dollar bills. She didn't ask any questions. She didn't try to negotiate. She didn't even test-drive it. She told my father that her father had the same car years ago, but her brother had crashed it. She was buying it for her father for Christmas.

"Not bad," my father later said to me. "I think we broke even."

24

I HAD BEEN working as a busboy at a restaurant in Northport for a few years. One of the waitresses, Alba, was a tough old biker chick who didn't mind when I hid in the kitchen, pretending to refill the salad dressings. She used to pinch my ass and call me nicknames like "Chubby" or "Scooter." Sometimes she'd ask me if I wanted to play "kiss and touch," then she'd laugh and smack me lightly on the cheek. She was the female-version of my father, and I looked forward to when we shared shifts.

One day, she called me over to the hostess stand.

"Chubby, what's your story? You got an old lady or what?" Alba shook a Virginia Slim from her pack and lit it with a candle on the bar.

"No," I said.

She exhaled. "Why the hell not?" The way she asked her question made it seem like all I had to do was get off my lazy ass and go pick up a girlfriend.

"I don't know," I said. "I haven't been thinking about it. And I'm leaving soon anyway."

"Honey, if I was twenty years younger…" She laughed, then took a long pull on her cigarette. "But you don't wanna waste your time on a wrinkled old thing like me. There's a new girl starting here tomorrow. Gorgeous. You two kinda got the same personality."

Great, I thought. If she's anything like me, we'll just sit and stare at each other all night while our minds ramble through worst-case scenarios that will never actually happen.

"I don't know," I said. "I think I should just wait."

Alba squinted, but I wasn't sure if she was blocking her eyes from the smoke or trying to get a better look at me. She stubbed out her cigarette in the glass ashtray, then took a quick sip of coffee.

"I invited her to your going-away party."

"What! No. No, you didn't."

She cackled and stood up. I asked her again and again if she was joking, but she wouldn't answer me. I stood at the hostess stand as she walked behind the bar, through the kitchen's saloon doors, into the cloud of steam rising from the dishwasher.

Word got out about my going-away party and by the end of the night, some of my old friends showed up at my parents' house. It felt like the season finale of a sitcom, when all the minor characters return to fill in the plot holes. Their voices sounded different, deeper, as if they'd gone through a second puberty. Our conversations were superficial and, after a few beers, vaguely nostalgic. I remember a part of me thinking how ridiculous the whole situation was, how our decade-long friendship had come to an end just because I had dated one of their exes for a year. I had violated a code. Whether or not the code still applied didn't matter; the violation was permanent. As the night went on, our conversations seemed to edge closer and closer to some kind of an apology. But no one mentioned it.

All night I kept an eye on the door, wondering when Vanessa would show up. After a while, I thought she wasn't going to come, and I couldn't decide if I was relieved or disappointed. Alba had been telling me details about her for the last two weeks, but I already knew Vanessa, sort of. We had gone to school together since kindergarten. She was in a lot of my home movies. While she sang in our 3rd grade production of *Horton Hears a Who!*, I played a tree. In our Halloween parade in 5th grade, she dressed as Raggedy Ann and, at five-foot-five, towered over me and the rest of the boys.

Near the end of the party, she walked through the door with a couple of her friends. I pretended not to notice. I moved from group to group, conversation to conversation. I refilled the coolers with beer, went to the bathroom several times. Eventually, the party cleared out and it was impossible to hide.

I remember our first conversation, how we talked about the restaurant. I told her that Alba was trying to play match-maker. Vanessa laughed and said Alba had been talking me up, too. At first, Alba referred to me as "Chubby," so Vanessa had no clue who she was talking about. When Alba finally said "Anthony," Vanessa remembered.

I laughed. "I'm surprised you knew who I was."

"Come on," she said. "Fifth grade. Halloween. You were the Grim Reaper. And I was gigantic. Seriously, I had boobs in third grade."

We talked the rest of the night, but what I remember most is the way her face looked when she listened. She turned her head a little to one side. She smiled and nodded, even when I took long pauses, trying to find the right words. Though she later told me she was nervous, she didn't seem that way. She didn't finish my sentences or repeat what I said in her own words. When she spoke, her voice was soft and quiet. I leaned close.

She laughed.

"What?" I said.

"Nothing," she said. "It's just that most people can never hear me."

Vanessa was already going to school in Worcester, about an hour from Boston. After the party, we made a plan to drive up together. I asked if she wanted me to write down the directions, but she said she knew how to get there.

A month later, she accepted an internship in Namibia. She would be gone for six months. As her departure date approached, we took long, aimless drives through unfamiliar suburbs between Boston and Worcester, sometimes talking about what our plan was, other times describing our old teachers from elementary school. Neither one of us had tried a long-distance relationship before. I was under the impression, from my friends and my brother, that situations like that were doomed. We agreed to give it a shot.

A photograph. When it was taken, Vanessa was on the other side of the planet. A few members of Team Destructo and I are walking down the street in lower Manhattan. It's raining, and I'm not wearing a shirt. My hair is long and my beard is full. I am in my Jim Morrison phase, which means I am binge drinking and writing bad poetry. In my hand is a wet, beer-can-shaped paper bag.

I don't remember who took the picture, but I remember clearly what happened after. We stepped down into a subway station and in the middle of the staircase, I threw my fist through the fluorescent light above our heads. Bits of powdery glass fell on our heads, sprinkled the steps. A girl we had just met asked me what the hell was wrong with me. My friends laughed. We high-fived at the bottom of the steps as a K-9 cop adjusted his rifle. His German Shepherd bared its teeth. I was no longer drunk, but I pretended I could barely stand.

"You gotta be shittin' me," the cop said. "Up against the wall."

He patted each of us down, then told us to turn around. His dog sniffed my kneecap.

"Which one of you did it?" He looked at each one of us. "I bet it was you," he said to one of my friends. "You skinny punk." The cop turned to the girls standing behind him. "Keep moving, ladies. G'head." I listened to the turnstiles click as each of them walked away.

The cop shook his head and told the attendant in the glass booth to get us a broom. As we swept up the broken glass, I heard the cop's leather belt creak as he shifted his weight.

"Pullin' this, now? With all this terrorist shit going on?"

I didn't know what 9/11 had to do with me breaking a light bulb, but the cop, and the dog, seemed convinced that our actions were particularly shameful. For some reason, he let us leave, and we met up with the girls waiting for us on the platform.

I wrote to Vanessa in Africa about my performance in the subway. I described it in detail, leaving out the parts about me being scared or acting drunker than I was. To my guy friends, in our little part of the world, I was a hero. In their eyes, I had achieved something.

Team Destructo had dispersed to different colleges across New England. Even though we were far apart, our objectives remained clear: #1—Drink. #2—Break Stuff. With enough alcohol, even our own stuff was vulnerable. When a group of us visited T.J. at college, we spent the better part of the night kicking out the wooden spindles on his banister. He got me back, though, when he came to my place and chucked two-by-fours off the roof and dropped 40-ounce beer bottles onto the cars behind my building.

We often tried to combine destruction with self-inflicted pain. Breaking beer bottles over our heads, lighting our chest hair on fire, punching ourselves in the face. We subscribed to the anger and adrenaline of punk rock and skate boarding. Though I was never much of a skater, I enjoyed watching my friends fall down.

The fact that we didn't know where our anger came from made us all the more mad—not that we questioned it or anything else at the time. "Mad" was a word we used constantly, but to us, the term meant "a lot," as in "I drank mad beers yesterday," or "I got mad homework." "Mad" was our way of saying *beaucoup*.

Public urination was a popular activity for Team Destructo. Like a pack of wild dogs, we wandered the streets, marking our territory. Once we arrived at so-and-so's party or dorm room, it was only a matter of time before we pissed in the washing machine or on one of the beds. The riskier the place, the better. We kept an unspoken tally, and we were always trying to outdo each other. It wasn't rare to wake up to the rain tapping on the roof and realize it was actually one of us staking our claim on your beanbag chair.

We didn't think, we just *did*, and our impulsiveness was invigorating. Up until Team Destructo, I lived inside my head, or vicariously through actors or musicians. Then, simply by consuming a lot of Southern Comfort and punching out a window, I could make people remember my name.

We humped each other. Humping was hilarious, a sure-fire way of getting all the guys in the room to crack up. We'd sit on the couch, watching a movie, drinking beer and without warning, I'd roll over and straddle Marlon or T.J. and pump my hips into their chest until they gasped.

"C-c-cut it out, D-D-D'Aries."

But I wouldn't stop because the other guys were laughing, plus whoever I was humping had most likely humped me earlier that day and it was payback time.

Sometimes we snuck up behind each other and humped so hard we dropped our drinks, but that didn't matter; we kept humping. We held each other down on the ground and humped until we were both out of breath. Sometimes the other guy got pissed off and tried to punch his way out of the hump, but once the humping started, it was near impossible to stop.

At a beach party one night, Team Destructo stood around a large bonfire. A few high school kids showed up. One was the younger brother of a Team Destructo member, but they didn't acknowledge each other. After a few beers, one of the guys from our group threw the younger brother on the ground beside the fire and humped his face. He humped him so hard his glasses fell off. The kid cursed and screamed, but the humper didn't stop until he faked orgasm and rolled over on his back. His chest heaved. The kid lifted his head, his lips and cheek coated in sand. We had tears in our eyes from laughter.

When we got tired of humping, we punched each other in the balls.

Sometimes when I watched war movies, the narrator talked about soldiers "humping" up a mountain or across a rice paddy. A part of me laughed each time I heard the word because all I could think of was the freshman's face slamming into the sand. But the soldiers on screen weren't holding each other down and thrusting their hips; they were hunched over beneath the weight on their backs. They took slow, even steps. They marched.

The meaning of the word "hump" was confusing. Did it mean what my friends and I thought it meant? Or did it mean to carry a weight?

How could something we did in our parents' basements or on the beach have anything to do with men in green stomping through the mud?

Near the end of my first semester of college in Boston, I took a bus to Don's apartment for a party. He had recently moved to Brooklyn. Sometimes before I visited Don, my mother would tell me to keep any eye on him. I told her not to worry. I'd been watching my brother my whole life.

As the bus idled at a rest stop, my phone vibrated in my pocket and shocked me out of sleep.

"Hey, Ant, it's Mom." She always identified herself on the phone.

"I know, Mom, who else—"

"Your father had a stroke. He's okay. He's good and eating and talking, but the man had a stroke and I think you should come home."

My body felt like it was sliding down the seat, but I wasn't moving. She kept talking, but I only heard her each time she said "the man." She had started referring to her own father as "the man" when he went into the hospital. "The man is sick, doesn't anyone get that?" or "The man has cancer, okay?" or "The man's been through a lot." He used to bum Winstons off my father in between chemo treatments. I watched my father hand him one, filter-end first. My grandfather—who my father called "Duke" because he walked and talked like John Wayne—broke off the filter, squeezed the cigarette between his teeth. My father gave him his lighter. Within the smoke of his first exhale, I saw my grandfather transported out of his wheelchair and back to his home in New Jersey, my father helping him tie his boat to the dock. In hindsight, I judge them both, and myself, but in those moments, the ends far outweighed the means.

My mother said my father was doing well but I sensed she was convincing herself. She told me to go to the party, have a good time, and come see him in the morning.

"Did you tell Don?" I asked.

"No. Not yet." She paused. "Can you?"

"Sure," I said, surprised at how quickly I agreed.

I told her we'd be home early the next morning. I closed my phone and shifted in my seat, searching for a comfortable position that did not exist. I felt guilty for not saying more to my mother, not offering anything but a few prescribed words of encouragement. *I'm sure he'll be fine. At least they caught it early. He's a fighter.* I didn't really know any of this, could not be certain that my words were true or if I was conveying an accurate description of my father in the hospital. Though I had spent little time in either place, hospitals always reminded me of churches. The echoing halls, the scent of disinfectant, the equal capacity for life and death. Priests in their robes, doctors in their long coats. Hospitals were only a step closer to the grave. A rosary. A stethoscope. No guarantee.

The strangers on the bus crumpled their hamburger wrappers, slurped their sodas. I still had three hours before we reached New York.

When I arrived at my brother's apartment in the early evening, we went out for dinner. I could have mentioned it at any time but I didn't. I kept quiet. I was in possession of privileged information, and a part of me lingered in the moment.

In his kitchen, after everyone had stumbled home, I told him.

"Are you serious? What the hell, dude, why didn't you tell me earlier?"

"I don't know." I said. "There just wasn't a good time."

He walked into his room and dragged a pillow and a sheet down from the cabinet above his closet. I took them from him. I made up my bed and he stood in the doorway, staring at the floor, asking silent questions for which I had no answer.

The double-sided elevator chimed, revealing two frail doctors in oversized white coats. When we reached their floor, the doctors nodded as Don and I stepped aside. Alone, we rode up to the sixth floor.

For some reason, it stopped on every floor and each time both sides opened to empty halls. By the time we made it to our floor, my mouth was sour with motion sickness.

Don bit his nails as we walked down the hall. I felt like we should be talking, but all I heard was the sound of our sneakers on the tile, screeching like school kids on their way to the principal's office. The sound drew stern looks from doctors, squinty glances from patients in their dimly-lit rooms.

First I saw my mother, sitting in a chair, rolling the back of her hand against her palm, talking to a shadow behind a curtain. She stood and smiled when we walked in. On the other side of the curtain was my father, sitting on the edge of the bed, twirling his silver dollar on the dinner tray.

"Yo! What up?" He stood and gave me a strong hug. I felt the bare skin of his back, exposed by the opening in his gown. I stepped aside so he could reach Don, and I couldn't remember the last time I saw them hug for that long. Maybe they had and I just never saw it. I gave my mother a kiss and walked around to the other side of the bed and leaned against the windows. He looked at me. Then at Don. Then back to me.

"So," I started, "how are you feeling?"

"I feel good. You know, a little tired but not too bad." He told us about the previous day, waking up, looking at his lip in the mirror, going to work. I detected a lisp in his speech, as if he were speaking with an ice cube in his mouth.

"But uh, the doc says I'm lucky. Just gotta take a pill, lay off the smokes."

"That's right," my mother said. "He's quitting; we both are."

"Yeah, I'm done." He looked out the window; my mother nodded at the floor.

"So how was that bus ride, boy?"

"Fine," I said. "Long."

"Oh, yeah? Any traffic?"

"No. Not really. A little when we hit the city but other than that—"

"Good, good."

197

"So why didn't you go to the hospital right away? What were you waiting for?" Don asked.

Sometimes my brother speaks over me, through me. Occasionally, his words ring at that common octave, the familiar twist and blend of our parents' vocal cords, and I hear his speech expressing my thoughts. At the time, I didn't like the accusatory tone of his questions, but I was thinking the same thing. Why didn't you go to the hospital right away? What were you waiting for? Is work more important than your life?

My father tapped his upper lip with his middle finger. "I don't know. Never dawned on me. Tell ya, though, my lip feels friggin' weird." He poked at it. "Doc says all the feeling will come back over time. Same with my tongue."

"You sound much better now than you did before," my mother said.

He moved his jaw like a horse. "Just feels awkward, you know. But it's coming back."

We talked about blood tests and CT scans and hospital food. Then we watched a little bit of *King Kong* on my father's bedside television. The scene where Kong is captured, strapped to a massive wooden gurney.

"Holy shit," I said. "That's Jeff Bridges?"

"I know, right?" my father said. "He's young in this."

"Was this before or after *Starman?*"

My brother looked at me. "Dude. Way before. Are you kidding?"

I glanced at my mother beside me, and she smiled as if waiting to be called on. She rubbed my knee and asked me about college. In the middle of my response, a woman holding a big basket of fruit wrapped in orange cellophane entered the room.

"Oh, poor baby! How are you?" She gasped and leaned over to kiss my father's cheek. I looked at my brother. He was still watching *King Kong.*

"Hey, Rosie, what's shakin'?"

"Nothing, Don, nothing. Can you believe him?" she said, turning to us. "Can you believe this man? In the hospital and he's asking about me."

My mother smiled. I smiled, too.

"I just wanted to stop by and see you and let you know we're all thinking about you. When I saw you, pale as a frickin' ghost, my god." She held her breast.

My father grinned. "Then you two-timed me and called the fuzz."

"Oh, please," Rosie said. She shook her head at my mother. My mother shook her head, too.

"They saved your life," my mother said.

"How'd you guys make out today? Jesus bang in sick again?"

"We're fine, Don. We're fine. Don't worry about Jesus."

Rosie sounded like she smoked unfiltered cigarettes. She was decorated in large, plastic jewelry, each piece a different primary color. Her bracelets clacked together as she talked. I couldn't tell if my mother had met this woman before. She didn't know me or my brother, but somehow she scooted into my father's room as if she were continuing an old conversation.

"I'll let you get back to your family now. But you get better soon, you hear me?" She laughed and leaned in to kiss him goodbye. "He loves the way I smell. Remember you said you could always know when I was coming in the store?"

I stood there watching as if this were a soap opera, a corny hospital scene where the romantic lead is on his death bed. My mother smiled so wide her eyes disappeared. My brother glanced at the basket, then returned to *King Kong*.

"Bye-bye," she said. "Enjoy the fruit!" I heard her clack down the hall.

"Well," my mother said. "That was nice of her." She looked at me, then at Don.

My father picked up the fruit basket, peeling off a sticker that read *Edible Arrangements*. He slid out a slice of honeydew melon. "Gimme a little volume on this, Don."

The nurse came in to tell us visiting hours were over. We thanked her.

"Shit," my father said. "Hey, I'll walk you guys out. My ass is getting flat." He hopped off the bed and untangled his wires. I let him go ahead of me. He held the IV stand like a pitch fork. His gown was too big for him, and as he stepped, I glimpsed the pale skin of his ass.

In the hallway, our sneakers screeched; my father's bare, callused feet shuffled over the floor as if his soles were made of sandpaper. I put my arm on his shoulder, felt his bones move beneath the gown. When we reached the elevators, we hugged and said goodbye. My mother wanted to stay over, so she kissed us and gave us money for a pizza. As we waited for the elevator, we watched my mother and my father walk down the white hallway, the bottom of my father's gown dragging behind him, the shoulder pads of my mother's blazer shifting with each step. Several elevators arrived and a succession of chimes echoed down the hall. My mother leaned close to my father's ear and whispered. He nodded. A doctor waited for them at the end of the hall holding a clipboard against his chest. He smiled, and guided them back to my father's dimly-lit room.

The cold wind screamed in my ear. I felt like I had just woken up from a long, unexpected nap. Yellow street lamps spotlighted the near-empty parking lot. Don and I walked to the car in silence. I lifted the handle of the locked passenger door, triggering the interior light.

"Hang on," Don said.

He unlocked it and we both got in. We sat there, the pressure of the quiet car swirling in our ears. I tried to coax a yawn, but nothing worked. The pressure would not go away.

"You think he'll be okay?" Don asked.

"Yeah I think so. The speech thing was a little noticeable but they said it should go away."

"It was totally noticeable. I told Mom. I told her months ago Dad wasn't looking so good, that he should get checked out."

"You were right."

"I know I was right. Fucking lucky he's not a vegetable. How many chances does he think he's got?"

He lit a Camel Ultra Light and rolled down the window. I lit one, too. The cold air pushed the smoke in, then quickly sucked it out.

"What was up with that woman?" I asked.

"What? What about her?"

"I don't know," I said. "Seemed kinda weird."

Don exhaled. "Whatever. Dad's a flirty dude, you know that."

We stopped at Taco Bell and ate it when we got home, while we watched the rest of *King Kong*.

Months went by, the snow melted, the sun shone longer. My father came home from the hospital, took his pill, laid off the smokes. His tongue began to thaw and his warm, throaty voice returned.

I wrote to Vanessa and told her what had happened. There was an unspoken competition between us to see who could write the longest e-mail. We saved all of them and while many of our lines were sentimental pillow talk, there were dozens and dozens of questions. Sometimes we made lists of questions that covered all kinds of topics, from favorite foods and colors to whether or not she'd still date me if I always wore pants filled with cottage cheese. We asked each other when we had lost our virginity, how many people we'd slept with, what our fantasies were—all the things we would have avoided in our first month of dating. Perhaps longer.

She wrote about her father—his drinking, his temper, his death. She wrote about the winter night he locked her and her mother out of the house. They stood in the street, watching his shadow move from room to room. She told me she remembered things that her sister didn't, and how odd it felt to hear conflicting stories about the same man. But what bothered her most was that their last conversation was a fight, and she'd hung up the phone without telling him she loved him.

She was glad my father was doing okay, but more importantly, that I didn't wait too long to see him.

In July, my father and I fished off the coast of Montauk on Bobby Haggemeyer's boat, one of the lucky vessels to survive Hurricane Gloria. My father told Bobby he should change the name of his boat from "Reelin' in the Years," a Steely Dan song, to Van Morrison's "Gloria."

"He even spells it out for you, Hag," my father said, popping a piece of gum into his mouth.

"Smart guy, right. That's not his, though. Who did it?"

"Shit, a lot of people covered that tune. The Doors did. Animals?"

"Nope," Bobby said, patting his pockets for a cigarette.

"Wait. Hold the phone, Hag. It *is* Van Morrison."

Bobby clenched the brown filter between his teeth, eyes widening.

"Fuckin' kiddin' me, right?"

"I'm tellin' ya. Wasn't a solo thing. It was when he was with Them. Think it was a B-side."

Bobby sparked his lighter several times, but couldn't get a flame. They often went back and forth over who did what, what song was a cover, what was original. Bobby started to talk around his unlit cigarette, then got impatient and ripped it from his mouth.

"Fuck it. Either way, I ain't changin' the name."

My father grinned.

A red sun pulsated above us. My father peeled off his tank top and let the rays bake him back to his true tone. He kicked his feet up on the edge of the boat and leaned against the cabin. The waves rocked the boat hard but he leaned further, the butt of his pole pressed against his thigh. Bobby passed him a Winston and offered him his lighter. My father took the cigarette, shaking his head, and dug deep into his pocket. He turned toward the sky, smoke swirling around his face, eyes hidden behind black sunglasses.

A fluke jarred the rod in my hands and I hooked him, the sudden weight pulling, dragging me toward the water.

IV

THE MOVING WALL

*My old man used to race pigeons. Him and his buddies. Kept a lil'
coop on the side of our house. The old man would load those nasty
squawkin' things into crates and take 'em out east and let 'em go.
They'd bet on which pigeon would make it home first. I don't know
how the hell those things knew where our house was. But wherever
the old man let 'em go, they'd find their way back.*

*First thing I ever worked on was a pigeon. My brother and I stole
one of the old man's birds, stuffed it in a paper bag, and held it over
the tailpipe of my Roadrunner. Birds are tough to mount. Gotta get
'em dead in the best shape you can. The old man didn't care cuz here
and there a bird would get loose on its own and fly away. He didn't
exactly keep a close count.*

*The old man's timing was always off. I don't think things worked
out the way he planned. After the airport closed, he was bouncin'
around for a while, doin' this or that. Had a bait shop for a little bit,
then he got into aluminum siding. I worked with him the summer I
got back from Vietnam. Puttin' up sheetrock, paintin', stuff like that.
I think he had a chance to buy into some contracting business, but
he never did. Then he was out of work for a long time and started
drinkin'.*

*He loved the farm, though. That was the best gig in the world for
him and my mother. But somethin' stupid happened with the owner
and the old man got pissed off and that was that. Like I say, things
just didn't work out for him.*

*He wasn't much older than I am now. I don't know, after my stroke,
who knows. I never thought I was in it for the long haul anyway.*

25

THREE P.M. MY TIME. The time I've been thinking about since breakfast, since yesterday, since the last time. I can smell Vanessa's shampoo, the steam from her shower lingers in the hallway, but she's gone and I'm glad. I want to be alone. I need to be alone.

I lock our front door and attach the chain. I walk into our bedroom, shut the door. Our cat tries to scratch her way in, but if I ignore her long enough, she'll stop. I pull the blinds, draw the curtains. My finger finds the *Power* button in the dark. Windows loads on screen, and the room hums in blue light. The wait gives me time to think, to consider doing something else for two hours. But that goes away. Like the cat.

I hear voices in the apartment above me. Footsteps. Someone in the parking lot slams a door. I check the drapes, the blinds, turn the volume down a little lower. I wear my gym shorts because that's where I'm supposed to be, plus they're easier to pull on and off, in case Vanessa forgot her apron. But that's why the door is chained and our bedroom door is shut. Buys me time.

Because there is never enough. I start clicking through image after image and minutes become seconds, hours become minutes. Everything is suspended—I am not in our room or out of our room. I am not here or there; I'm somewhere else and that's exactly where I want to be. But time knows—tethers me to now, and no matter how quickly I click from image to image, video to video—no matter how short or long I stare at the women on screen—the tiny digits in the corner of my screen tick away.

A woman speaks with her mouth full. A man's skin burns Viagra-red, so much blood forced to the surface. Some men struggle, clamp themselves at the base, force the blood to flow. The woman asks for more, begs for more. She isn't satisfied. The man pushes harder, faster, grows redder and the woman's expression flicks from pleasure to pain to confusion to some mixture of the three. She says she wants everything the man has, but when he gives it to her, she seems disappointed. I click away.

I sink my fingers into a jar of Vanessa's body cream. The scent does not remind me of her, but of myself, of my own scent, my own routine. I'll smell it on her later that day or week and will not be drawn to her, but to myself. When she is in the kitchen, making us dinner, I am in the bedroom. I have another purpose. My grip on here, on now, slips.

I'll click away if I hear the hallway floor creak beneath her feet. I'll pull my hand from my waist and add a sentence to my cover letter. I'll clear our computer's history. But she knows. And she knows that I know. So when I'm done, we'll sit in the living room and I'll try to think of questions to ask her, but I'm empty.

Vanessa and I were twenty-two and had been living together for six months. I was attempting to mesh my high school and college habits with our new life, and I was failing. Each time we fought, I talked about other couples, other friends who probably watched just as much porn as I did. They didn't have anyone nagging at them. They didn't have all these stupid hang-ups. Why do we?

I cut her off. I got defensive, angry, but couldn't say why. Perhaps part of me was frustrated because I didn't have a solid reason for why I watched so much porn. I said other guys did, too, but I had no real proof. And if I thought it was normal, natural—why did I feel guilty? Why did I have to hide in a dark room, behind locked doors?

I talked to my brother and my guy friends. I knew they'd understand, and they did. They said Vanessa just needs to chill out and lay off me. *All guys do it*, they said. *It's not a big deal.* I didn't tell them that I watched at least an hour a day, that I was pretending to look for work while Vanessa supported us by waiting tables, that I often skipped meals or canceled plans to fit in my routine. I was the one in college who remembered all the porn stars' names, even the men, and could say them on cue whenever my friends wanted. I was the one with the most extensive sexual vocabulary. And I was the one who forwarded images of women on their knees, their faces like melted candles. *Sick, dude,* my friends wrote back. Then they'd ask me where I found it.

Once, Vanessa came home early from work. I pulled up my pants, screwed the top back on her body cream, and ran to the bathroom. I turned the shower on, finished myself off, and cursed her for disturbing my privacy. When I came out she was sitting on our bed, staring at the image I'd left on screen. I stood in the doorway with a towel around my waist, dripping water on the hardwood floor.

Vanessa undid her apron. "Is this what you do all day?"

I didn't say anything. I shook my head.

"Say something!" she yelled. I didn't recognize her voice.

"No. Not all day."

"I don't know what else to do," she said. "This whole thing, all of this, is totally out of balance. *We* are out of balance."

"Babe, you're acting like—"

She stood up. "I'm not acting like anything. We haven't had sex in five months. But you've had plenty of time and energy to spend on this shit."

I tightened the towel around my waist, walked over to the computer and turned it off. "I wish you'd just chill out. Everybody watches it! It doesn't have to be such a big deal."

"Who's everyone?" she said. "Who? And you're right, it doesn't have to be such a big deal. But *you* made it a big deal. "

"You're the one freaking out about this. I don't know what the hell you want to hear. I do this. All my friends do this. So what?"

She walked to the door, her sneakers squeaking on the wet floor.

"You think I hate porn. You think I'm just some crazy repressed chick. But what bothers me is how you've handled this. We can't do this together. We've *never* done this together. And now it's tainted with all your bullshit."

She slammed our bedroom door, then our front door. I listened to her walk down the hallway and heard her finger jab the elevator button several times before she gave up and took the stairs.

I want to say her words—*out of balance*—pierced through my fog, that her wake-up call made me bolt upright instead of sink deeper into my dream. I had a choice. Listen to the woman who slept beside me, whose books were mixed with mine on the shelf, who worked double-shifts to keep us warm, who tolerated months and months and months of me, me, me. I could listen to her or I could turn my back and face the screen. I could search for another image. I could slip off my towel, listen to a woman moan and interpret her sounds however I pleased.

I pressed *Power.*

26

I AM PAID to listen to strangers. I temp for a company that provides speech-recognition software to health insurance companies. So if you receive an automated call from Blue Cross or Harvard Pilgrim and your reply to "Do you have any comments or suggestions on how to improve this call?" is "Piss off" or "Suck my dick," I am listening. I am rewinding. I am typing out your comments, word for word.

For some technical reason I never question, my hours are five a.m. to noon, which means I wake up at three and leave Boston by three forty-five. I don't mind. I feel like my father, waking up before sunrise, drinking coffee. I can even smell him because I am borrowing his Explorer to drive to work. When I met with the hiring manager last week, she'd said she had a position I might be over-qualified for, that it required me to sit in an empty office before dawn, wear headphones and listen to other people speak to a recording. I said I could start immediately.

Each day, I come in and sit down, put on my headphones, and listen to angry people, crazy people, happy people, funny people, sad people, and people who don't understand a word because they don't speak English. I hear strangers curse and yell and tell a machine to go fuck itself. I hear potato chips crunching and a television on full blast. I hear a lonely voice thank a phone for listening. I type out all of their comments, hit spell check, and send a status update to my boss in Seattle, a woman I've never met.

Some laugh. Some cry. Some simply let the call run its course. The violent and angry calls are disturbing. After a few misrecognized answers—the chipper automated voice repeating "I'm sorry I missed that. Could you please repeat?"—a young man or old woman could become hysterical. Screams and shouts, racial and sexual slurs will erupt from their mouths and make the red equalizer levels boil on my computer until they finally slam the phone down. I stare at the screen, black as the five-a.m. sky, reflecting my headphoned image.

I listen to a call from an old woman. Her voice is unsteady. Each time the software delivers a question, the woman asks if the nice young lady could slow down and repeat the question again. Each time she thanks the young lady for her patience. *You know something, darling, you sure sound an awful lot like my daughter. Are you from Phoenix? Well, now, if you keep asking me the same questions, how we gonna talk? Yes, I believe you are from Phoenix. I'm headed out there this afternoon for my grandson's baseball game. Pardon me? Yes, I do have high blood pressure. Thank you for asking.*

The job only lasts a few months. I am unemployed, again. Vanessa is worried and not only for financial reasons. I am scared, too. I don't trust myself. While I was a transcriber, I didn't have time for pornography. Vanessa and I had more sex. We got along better. But that in itself frightened me. If a job didn't dictate my schedule, if I was left to my own free will, would I always position myself in front of a screen and search for something else?

I talk to my mother on the phone a few times a week. At first, I think she is pleased to hear from me, but after months and months of listening to me, she changes her tone.

"You know, Grandpa, Dad's dad, was out of work for years."

"Really?" I asked. "What happened?"

"He turned into a bitter bastard. It was a very unhealthy situation."

A few months later, the temp agency gives me another position. This time I'm working in the basement of a large office building, organizing files. The filing cabinets are massive black towers on wheels controlled by switches on the wall, like a giant puzzle.

I'm the only one there, so after I put away all the files, I mess around with the controls, seeing what shapes and designs I can make out of the towers. Once, a wheel popped off and one of the towers almost toppled over. It banged into the wall so loudly that I waited a few minutes to see if anyone would come down and check on me. No one did.

As in many of the temp jobs, I am assigned to 8-hour days, but the work takes no more than four. I start making up stories on scraps of paper, creating characters out of the odd yet pleasant people I sometimes temp with. One co-temp also works as a blackjack dealer at Mohegan Sun. He tells me he once dealt to Bruce Willis.

"He's an asshole. Vince Vaughn is pretty nice, though."

Another guy I observe is an old man who seems to be the head honcho in the rolling-filing-cabinet industry. He knows everything about them. He trains me on how to gently turn the dials, how to position certain cabinets so I can access the files against the wall. His eyebrows look like the heads of old toothbrushes. Each instruction whistles from his mouth. I make up a story about him flipping one of the cabinets over and making a bed out of it and how he sleeps there for years without anyone noticing. One night, he dies in his sleep and all the company does is readjust the cabinets so that the one that contains him is hidden against the wall.

But no matter how much I try to capture the man's voice, he always sounds like my father. In my stories, the old man uses words like *bennies* and calls his lazy supervisor a *putz*. His wife doesn't know much about him, except that his favorite meal is pork chops. She often has it on the table waiting for him, after a long day of filing.

Eventually the old man I write about no longer works in the basement but at a supermarket. The man is a little younger, smokes a lot of cigarettes, likes to work on cars. He is a taxidermist and a Vietnam Veteran. More and more, a little boy appears in my stories.

I send some of my writing to an old professor of mine that I admired, along with a note explaining who I am and understanding ahead of time if he doesn't remember me. He remembers. He remembers which class I was in. He even references some of my old scenes and characters. I'm amazed, since I had sat in the back of his class and hardly said a word.

He encourages me to apply to a graduate writing program, but I'm skeptical. I had started telling people I'm a writer who temps to make ends meet. Instead of the truth, which is that I temp because I don't know what else to do. I feel I should have a more important reason for filling out the application, but only one seems honest: *It'll give me a purpose.*

All of the nonfiction writers in my class are women. I figure I'll eventually switch over to fiction because that's *real* writing. I admire writers like Tobias Wolff or Raymond Carver, tough men whose stories make me feel like I'm spying on a suburban family through their living room window. I read their characters' dialogue over and over and wonder how "Could you please pass the salt?" became such a loaded question.

The fiction writers and even some of the faculty are surprised that I write nonfiction. "You'd make a great fiction writer," they say. Even my brother questions my genre. I wonder why, but at the same time, I have my own doubts. Why do I feel that fictionalized events are somehow more real? Is a self-portrait not as creative as an invented landscape? And why do many of the male fiction students roll their eyes at nonfiction, while the female nonfiction students seem relieved to have me in class? Often during a heated discussion, they'll lean over their manuscripts and say: "Let's have Anthony's opinion."

By the end of the first semester, all of my closest friends are women. They introduce me to writers like Joan Didion, Dorianne Laux, Lorrie Moore. Like these women, many of my classmates write about abuse. Verbal, physical, sexual. Sometimes all three. They write about silence. Their words on the page whisper like a secret.

Sometimes I feel like the male representative for our genre, some kind of expert on my gender, but I don't have any answers.

Before summer break, I have to choose a mentor. I meet with a man named David Mura. In one of his essays, there is a description of a place like Sin-derella's—plywood video booths painted black, a quarter for five minutes. The perfect image is always a quarter away. He buys a stack of magazines, but as soon as he opens them, they are not enough. While Carver or Wolff's work made me feel like a voyeur, David's writing seemed to turn the camera on me.

David is in his mid-fifties, a member of my father's generation. I tell him that Vanessa and I are getting ready to leave for Vietnam, that the trip is part honeymoon, part research. He speaks with a faint Japanese accent and though he looks nothing like Mr. Miyagi, I can't help but draw reference to the only other wise Japanese man I know.

"So what are your plans for this semester?" he asks.

"I want to write about my family."

He nods. "That's a good place to start."

27

A FEW MONTHS after we return from Vietnam, Vanessa writes her thesis: Relationship Power Dynamics and Condom Use Among Female Sex Partners of Injecting Drug Users. I stare at a blinking cursor and decide if, in this scene, my father would say "bearded clam" or "snatch." Perhaps Vanessa knows not to ask for details because she has already seen me frustrated, pacing in front of my laptop.

"I have no idea what I'm trying to say."

"Sure, you do," she says.

She sits across from me in our living room, outlining her paper, gathering the data and figures from her work at the clinic. Vanessa is organized, focused, her work packed snugly into color-coded, three-ring binders. Her planner is a work of art, written with the patient hand of a pointillist painter.

Since we've been back, I've tried to piece together my father's stories with my own. A part of me wishes I could go back to the time before our trip, before I interviewed my father. There are too many voices in my head, too many conflicting sounds and images. I don't know where to start, and even if I did, I wouldn't know where to go from there.

Later that night, I replay my interview with my father. I remember driving from Boston to my parents' house on Long Island, my notebook filled with questions: *Where were you when you found out you were drafted? What was the last thing Grandma and Grandpa said to you? What was it like over there?* As my tires hummed along the road, I felt like I was traveling toward my father's story—our story—a feeling so tangible I imagined its own exit off the Expressway.

After dinner, my father and I went upstairs. I shut the door on the canned laughter of my mother's *I Love Lucy* reruns in the living room. In the quiet bedroom, I heard my father breathing through his mustache. He took off his flannel shirt and draped it over the desk chair. For a moment, it seemed like he didn't know where to sit. Finally, he lay down on the rug, folded a pillow between his neck and the wall, and propped his feet up on the edge of the bed.

"So is this gonna be like, '*In the beginning...*'?" he asked, searching for a comfortable position.

I laughed. "Maybe."

I fumbled with my new recorder, trying to place it in the perfect spot. As he waited for my first question, my father dug his silver dollar from his pocket and slowly spun it in his fingertips.

"So what were you doing around the time you were drafted?"

"The usual. Just hangin' out. Havin' a good time." His tone implied that this answer contained everything I needed to know.

"But what exactly were you doing? Where were you living? What were your plans for the future?" The red light on the recorder burned brighter with each word.

"Didn't have any." He shrugged. "I was working in the supermarket, hangin' out with my friends, and then I got drafted. Just one of those things, you know?"

I watched the seconds tick away as the recorder captured our silence. The excitement and purpose I had felt in the car faded. *What exactly was I searching for?* Did I want a bloody war tale, something my father had never told anyone—not my Grandmother, not my mother, no one? A story that would validate my work, infuse my sentimental scenes with violence, tragedy? Maybe my questions would conjure up forgotten images of napalm-scorched children screaming in my father's arms, or help him remember the soothing words he whispered around the grenade pin in his teeth. I had encouraged such images in the minds of those who asked what I was writing about with my purposefully vague response: *My father's experiences in Vietnam?* You've seen *Apocalypse Now*, you've heard the horror—yeah, that's my Dad.

As he sat on the floor beside me, my father tossed his silver dollar in the air and let it slap back into his palm. Then he looked at me.

"How far is all this gonna go, boy?"

"No further than it needs to."

"Boy's grillin' me like a two-dollar burger," my father said to my mother. He went into the kitchen to get a glass of ginger ale. Don had just walked in and was sitting on the couch, still wearing his coat.

"What are you guys doing up there?" he asked.

"Just a little research," I said.

Don nodded without looking away from the television. I heard the ice in my father's ginger ale knock against the side of his glass as he walked up the stairs, taking two steps at a time.

"Hey, boy, get that thing rollin' again. I just thought of somethin' else."

28

"WHY DO YOU gotta ask this shit?" my brother says across a table of empty wine bottles. We have just finished an expensive dinner for my father's 60th birthday. I had asked my father if he was satisfied with his life. He shrugged. The question ricocheted off him and landed in front of my mother. She didn't answer.

My brother once told me that he respected my "quest for truth" but sometimes it was a bit much. My quest had been going on for years, as if my interviews would never end. It didn't matter that I didn't have my recorder; I asked questions all the time, whenever they popped into my head. I wanted to know everything. *Mom, what was your first car? Dad, where did you and Mom go on your first date? How old were you guys when you lost your virginity? Was it to each other? What was your wedding song? What was the first movie you saw together?* I didn't know what I planned to do with this information, but I thought: I lived with these people for almost twenty years and there is so much I still don't know.

Perhaps I felt comfortable asking these questions because I had listened to so many conversations between Vanessa and her family—how instead of talking about traffic or re-runs, they grilled each other, in a light-hearted way. With the television on mute, Vanessa asked her Mom about sex and drugs, what her life was like before Vanessa was born, what she wanted to do with her life, and if she felt satisfied with the way things turned out. Sometimes these conversations moved from laughter to tears in seconds, and I'd suddenly become very interested in the food on my plate. But after they cried together, they seemed closer.

I didn't understand why my question at dinner derailed the conversation. Vanessa and I asked each other questions like that all the time. "Checking in," we called it. It was our way of making sure we were living the lives we wanted, that we weren't coasting through year after year. But my question seems too direct for my family, as if I've thrown them on stage and watched them burn in the spotlight. My father looks away. My mother stirs the melting ice in her glass. Don shakes his head.

"Just let it go, man." Don says. "Move on."

I used to think all I had to do was let go. So you were a shy kid, let it go. So you spent most of your life listening, let it go. So you never felt connected with yourself, with others, let it go.

My brother moved on at a hundred miles per hour. He seemed to not only have the ability to let go, but crumple the past into a ball and toss it over his shoulder. Sometimes our phone conversations sound as if I'm tapping into his audio diary. The fast-forward button is stuck and his tape is racing, racing, racing, telling me about all the "justs" standing in his way: If he could *just* leave his job, *just* find a new apartment, *just* get his brain out of this damn fog. Once he said to me, "I sometimes wish I'd die before I'm thirty, *just* so I wouldn't have to think anymore." He just turned thirty-four.

I wanted to shout: I feel the same way! All I do is listen and think. This should have been a moment for us to connect. But we didn't. I wasn't there. I was on the phone and I was listening, but I was in a bar years earlier, trying to find the words to express my disconnection from everything in my life, my own fog that descended on me or that I put myself in, obscuring my vision, muffling my heartbeat. I had spent months searching for the words but found nothing. In the corner of the bar, I turned my empty palms up as if they were the only place I hadn't looked. Don sipped his beer and stared at me.

"You know, your depression is really starting to bring me down, dude."

I want to play this tape in reverse, scratch the needle back across the record and hear a secret message. There must be another sound, a faint instrument I haven't heard. There must be.

I had planned to interview my brother. Drive down from Boston to his apartment, set the digital recorder on his coffee table, and start asking questions. *Did you consider yourself a rebellious kid? Do you live more in the past or present? List from earliest to latest the cars you've crashed.* I was set to do it, even told him why I was coming, but I chickened out. I was almost twenty-six, but I felt like the chubby little kid sitting on the hood of Don's Volare, watching him and the other characters in his world. I wanted to ask him about his life in California. Sometimes I'd bring it up and he'd sigh and ask me why I wanted to know about that. I'd shrug and say, "I don't know. Just curious."

As I dug through my backpack in his living room, preparing to change into shorts and go to sleep, I felt my recorder rubber-banded to my black notebook full of questions. My brother was in his room, opening and closing dresser drawers. He came out into the living room, to the kitchen, then back to his room. He forgot something, returned to the kitchen, then back to his room once more. He came back out and stood in the doorway.

"Goodnight, bro," I said, rolling over.

I felt him linger in the room. The floor creaked beneath his feet. "Okay."

Instead of talking to him, I sent him an e-mail. It felt like when I used to write him letters in high school, especially since I still had many of the same questions. But I could articulate them better now, and my e-mail wasn't bogged down with my, and my friends', orders for *Hustler*.

He wrote back a long e-mail that I read over and over. He told me he did consider himself a rebellious kid: "Ever notice how many 'troubled teen' books Mom has around the house?" But he also thought that in order to rebel, one had to spit in the face of a controlling element, and he didn't have that. It was my parents' "hands-off" approach that allowed him to run wild. Only when the conflict was unavoidable, when my parents could not ignore the damage my brother did to himself or his cars did they respond—my father's once-a-year blowouts, an Old Faithful of *fucks* letting my brother and anyone else in the room know what was going on inside him.

At the end of Don's e-mail, he wrote about his cars:

'78 Plymouth Volare. Cherry red with a white soft top. Slant 6 engine that wouldn't die. I think I changed the oil once in two years. Slammed that one into a cement divider on the Expressway when it hydroplaned out of control. I stepped on the brakes too hard at the last minute. Car had a habit of sliding a lot anyways and I still get nervous taking sharp turns or hitting the brakes too hard, especially in the rain.

'79 Buick Regal. Matte black with red velvet interior and faux-wood dash. So sweet. Had a Buzz Lightyear super-glued to the hood as an ornament. Coming off the Expressway, a woman in a Volvo station wagon ran a light at a three-way stop (she had no license, and no insurance) and I slammed into her on the driver's side. No stopping time. Almost broke my nose. Blood gushed out like a fountain. Totaled.

'98 Jeep Wrangler. White. Sweet. Crashed across a few lawns one night. I was pretty messed up and no sleep, and should not have been driving. Just a few minutes before I had been pulled over by a cop for swerving on the road. I did the sobriety/walk the line/touch your nose test and told him I was just tired. Got out of the car and walked home. Mom and Dad were asleep. Came back the next morning and saw the path of destruction across a Japanese garden and the cars and trees I scraped, but just barely missed smacking into and either destroying or being destroyed by.

Yup, crashed 'em all. Can't wait to own a motorcycle.

When my father and Don fought in the living room, the backyard, the driveway, I listened. *Fuck you* and *fuck you, too*, and *get out of my house*, and *I am*, and *good, start walking*. And when it was over, the house hummed with silence and the air around my face felt close and thick. Don would be gone for a few days and then he'd return and the house became calm. Eventually, Don quit or got fired from the gas station or department store, and the weather within our home would begin to change again. A shift in temperature. Each morning my father woke up, each morning my brother went to sleep, they crossed paths like jet streams flowing in opposite directions.

Most fights rumbled like dormant volcanoes. No explosions, no fire. No clear winner or loser. A latent heat spread across our landscape, and I searched for clues within the ripples steaming at the surface.

When I think about my brother, I see a boy holding his breath. In the summers, when I was in elementary school and Don was in high school, we spent afternoons in the pool. He dove to the bottom, air bubbling from his lungs, and sank like an egg in a pot of boiling water. I followed him down, forcing air out of my body, but I couldn't quite sit on the bottom. I didn't realize that if I remained still, if I tucked in my arms and feet like Don, I would sink quicker. I struggled to get my knees down. I felt the roots beneath the pool pushing up through the blue liner.

Don sat across from me, eyes wide. I stared back at him, slowly flapping my arms, trying to keep my body submerged. Our voices sounded like the adults in Charlie Brown. We pretended we were at a fancy Hollywood party. Don pressed his hand to his ear and I repeated my question; he raised his pointer finger, complimenting my astute observations of his latest script. When he spoke, I rubbed my chin and nodded, as if yes, I agree, he would be perfect for my next film. I wanted to stay down there forever, but my eyes burned and the water felt heavy against my chest. I tapped the top of my wrist as if I were late for an appointment, then pushed myself to the top. Before I reached the air, I looked back at Don on the floor. He gazed from left to right as if chatting with other guests at the party. Each word bubbled from his mouth—small, clear balloons on a turbulent path to the surface.

Don never wanted to live a stalled life: Suburbs, mortgage, kids, television. So he moved on. Moved on to high school graduation and gas stations and community college. Moved on to art school. Moved from class to class, party to party, drug to drug. Moving and moving and moving. Moving at the speed of sound: waves crashing beneath the Golden Gate Bridge. The speed of light: neon throbbing in the window as he rang up films of people feigning pleasure. Moved back home, then back out. Plowed through college a second time, won awards for his paintings and photographs, steady job, steady girlfriend, but there was always something. Something pulling him. Something else.

I feel like my brother and I have been sitting on opposite ends of the same see-saw. We listen to the same music, watch the same movies, but often at different times: He'll be in his Rolling Stones and Scorsese phase, while I'm headlong into The Coen Brothers and Bob Dylan. We read nonfiction, but he'll loan me books about larger-than-life explorers navigating through the Amazon or high-profile serial killers at the turn of the century. I'll offer memoirs about domestic issues or father-son relationships, books by Tobias and Geoffrey Wolff—two brothers writing about the same man.

Don tries to introduce me to new music, bands that are still making the rounds at small bars and clubs in Brooklyn. He makes me mixes of this unfamiliar music and FedEx's them to Boston. I open the CDs and check the playlists for bands I recognize, songs I know by heart. I put the CD in my desk drawer where it will remain, for days, months, sometimes years, unheard.

Until one day I decide to clean. I pop in one of Don's CDs for background music, songs that won't distract me. As I scrub around the bathroom floor, sponging up renegade bobby pins and strands of my hair and Vanessa's, I pause. I hear a song I recognize. Not a tune I know by heart, but it's familiar. I walk over to the computer and check the artist, the title, and try to place the song. But it can't be placed. It's new. Something I've never heard before.

29

BEFORE MY first interview with my father, my mother took me to Radio Shack and helped me pick out a new recorder. As we approached the register, she reached into her purse.

"No, Mom."

"I want to," she said, smiling. "I think it's a good idea."

That afternoon, her smile faded when I took out the recorder and sat with her in her garden. Hands caked in soil, she knelt on a thick foam pad beside a small metal sign: *Gardeners Have the Best Dirt.* She said she had nothing to say, that it was my father who should be talking. I knew that wasn't true. I knew from the hours and hours we spent on the phone over the years, as she talked about this sister or that brother, often the same family events again and again. These jumbled characters and plots seemed to have no origin or destination, like pollen in the breeze. At the end of these conversations, she'd apologize for "talking my ear off." She brushed the dirt from her hands and stretched her back. Then she began a story she'd told me before, but this time slower, and in detail.

But first, like my father's mother, she would interrupt herself and talk about her jobs, the ones she worked from home. Selling arts and crafts or Mary Kay beauty products. For a while, she sold weight-loss pills called Herbalife. I remembered the giant green pill box sitting on our kitchen table. Sometimes I'd lie awake in bed and listen to her drop each pill into its proper place.

She told me about nursing school and the public speaking course that scared her off. She used to tell me this story when I was worried about giving a presentation in school. I thought this was the only reason she dropped out but, in her garden, she told me about the months she worked at a state hospital, scrubbing bed pans and drawing blood. There was one man who liked to talk to her. He told her war stories, heroic sea tales from his time in the Navy during World War I. When she'd lean over to adjust his IV, he'd slip his hand up her skirt. She told him to stop. He'd cut it out for a day or two and then start up again. Eventually, she turned in her uniform and quit.

Then she told me about her father. I could see my grandfather shuffle across his living room rug in pin-striped pajamas, sleeves cut off just above his anchor tattoo. The anchor was the color of a vein, a red heart stabbed on the anchor's fluke. In the summer, the mercury in the red ink made the heart swell like a blood blister. Sometimes I had to fight the urge to reach out and pop it. He made his way across the rug and paused in front of the china cabinet. His knees cracked and popped as he bent down and retrieved a bottle of amber liquid and a small silver cup. He filled the cup once, knocked it back. Again, slower this time, sipping. He sucked air through his teeth, then looked at me and grinned. I grinned back as if we had just shared a secret. Though I'm sure my mother and father were watching, at the time I thought my grandfather and I were playing our own private game of charades.

My mother stuck her shovel in the dirt and began the story she intended to tell me from the beginning. Her twin brothers, Richard and Robert. Robert was wild, rebellious, liked to cut school and smoke cigarettes behind the supermarket. Richard, a quiet boy, ran track—a sprinter. He sat in the front of the classroom. Excellent penmanship. The steady hand of a calligrapher.

When Robert was fifteen, he cut class to hang out at a friend's house. Maybe Richard told him not to, maybe he didn't. "Depends who's telling the story," my mother said. "Richard always blames himself."

Robert and his friend played cops and robbers, stalking around the couch, beneath the dining room table, down the hallway, into the bedroom. Pow. Bang, bang. Pow. I got you. No you didn't. Yes I did.

The boy's sister had a boyfriend. He was a real cop, fought real crime with a real gun. The gun went off and hit Robert in the stomach.

My grandparents received a call, from whom my mother couldn't remember. An ambulance took Robert to the hospital. He died an hour later. That night my grandfather stood in the living room, still wearing his postman's uniform. A ship unmoored, swaying with the tide. My mother pressed her ear to her bedroom door, listening to her father, to the man she said always had an answer, repeat over and over: *I don't know.*

The next day, my mother's sister got married. Robert's wake was the following day, and it lasted for two days and two nights. My mother's sister announced she was pregnant. My grandmother passed out tranquilizers. Robert was buried.

"Busy weekend, wouldn't you say?" my mother said, shaking her head. "After that, I don't know. Things were hard for grandma and grandpa. He was at the bar all the time and grandma kinda checked out. I think she was scared to get close to us, to let anyone get close to her. Richard had a very hard time."

Richard stopped sprinting. He trained for long distances. He took a scholarship and ran away. Headed south: Arizona, North Carolina, Kentucky, Georgia. Years later, my parents traveled down from Long Island to visit him. They spent the night at his house. His land was overgrown, and there was a rusty oil tank beside the shed. My father found a piece of PVC piping and attached it to the top of the oil tank to make it look like a beached submarine. They posed in front as my mother took their picture. On the back of the photograph, my father wrote *S.S. Redneck.*

My mother stood up and stretched her knees. She grabbed a packet of seeds off the deck and sprinkled them into the holes in the ground. I raised my recorder to her lips.

"I think Richard sort of absorbed Robert's personality."

I nodded and thought about the water displacement experiments I used to do in science class. Drop in a cube made of wood, then aluminum, then lead. Measure the volume until the beaker overflows.

My mother bent down and pressed a seed into the dirt. "All of Robert's stuff was boxed up and we never talked about him. Not until grandma got sick. I hardly knew the woman, Anthony. I talked to her more in her last week alive than I had my whole life."

Robert died while my father was in Vietnam. I imagine my father in his hooch: crew cut, dark green sunglasses, toned body pressing against his green uniform. Hands in his pockets, twirling Eisenhower's profile, the coin he'd rub as his "freedom bird" lifted off from Saigon six months later. The coin he held as medics rushed bodies across Long Binh to the hospital. The coin he flipped as non-compliant American soldiers were escorted to the prison on the other side of the base.

Between the sick and the damned, he twirled a coin and prayed for luck.

One night, the red-alert sirens shocked him out of sleep. He left the coin in his hooch, rushed to the perimeter, gripping his M-16. Dropped to the dirt and took aim at no one, everyone. Squeezed his trigger and emptied a magazine of bullets into the dark.

My mother squinted into the sun. "I never wanted to limit you or your brother." She seemed like she was about to cry. Her tears snuck up on her. She breathed deeply. "Who am I to tell you guys what to do?"

30

NOT LONG AFTER my father's stroke, Don starts talking about getting him a tattoo for Christmas. I drive down from Boston and pick up Don at the train station. He tells me what assholes tattoo artists are and how they're elitists and you walk in there and before you even ask a question, before they even know anything about you, they assume you're some jerk-off who wants barbed-wire around your bicep or Yosemite Sam on your calf.

"What the fuck do you have to be stressed about, dude?" Don says to the windshield. "You're a tattoo artist. You got the coolest job in the world. Relax. And without customers, you wouldn't have shit."

"I know," I say. "I hate that. It's like you owe–"

"Owe them something! Exactly! Owe them something just for coming in."

Don used to talk about being a tattoo artist, and I think he may have been an apprentice for a little while, if not in New York, then maybe in San Francisco. But he hasn't mentioned it in years.

Don takes out a newspaper clipping of an eagle, the feathers red, white and blue.

"I can't believe this is what Dad wants," he says.

"Are you sure he really wants a tattoo?" I ask.

"He will after I get him a gift certificate."

"All right. Just asking."

"I know, dude. You already asked me."

I park beside the snow bank in front of Vintage Tattoo. Before my Honda rolls to a stop, Don pulls on the handle, but the door is locked. He pulls harder, swearing under his breath. I unlock it, but the door doesn't open because he's still pulling on the handle. I hit the button again and this time the door pops open.

"All right." He exhales. "Game face." He checks himself in the mirror and steps out.

My little silver Honda trembles as Hummers and Escalades zoom by, splashing the windshield with dirty water. I step out and Don is on the sidewalk with his arms spread like he doesn't know where to put them.

"What are you doing?" he asks.

"Walking. What are you doing?"

"Waiting."

"I can see that." I step into the deep footprints Don made in the snow bank, steadying myself as I cross over yellow pock marks and brown craters. I make it to the sidewalk and stomp my boots. Don watches me through the fogged glass. I follow his trail of melting snow inside.

We flip through the big black portfolio books full of basic tattoo designs. Don finds a page of Yosemite Sams, taps the plastic and nods. I smile and point to the wall of tribal tattoos and Chinese letters behind him. He shakes his head.

Don looks at the woman behind the counter.

"Are we gonna get some service here or what?" he says, not to me, not to her. His question seeps out of his mouth and disappears, like the incense burning on the coffee table.

"Did you ask?"

"No, I sat here like an asshole. Yes, I asked. She said she'd be right over."

I flip a page. "Well, then, she'll be right over."

"Yeah, well, when?"

A big bald guy with earlobes like janitor's keys jingles into the tattoo parlor and points at us.

"You my one o'clock septum?"

Don and I look at each other. "No, man" Don says. "We're waiting on some information about tattoos."

"Oh," the man says. "My bad. Sylvia'll be right with you."

"Thanks," I say.

All I can see of Sylvia is the back of her head. She's hunched over a shirtless young man. The girl who appears to be his girlfriend leans in the doorway, watching Sylvia cut into his chest.

Don holds up a page full of hearts that say *Mom* and *Dad*.

"Let's get 'em."

I laugh and shake my head.

"What? Come on, let's get matching tattoos."

"Yeah, right."

Sylvia's needle buzzes. Stops. Buzzes.

"Fuck it, I'd do it right now," Don says.

"Let's start with Dad's, okay?"

"Why?" he says, looking straight at me. "You said you wanted another one."

"I do." I flip another page and stare at each design. "But I'm not gonna just pick out something random."

The buzzing stops. "Okay, what can I do for you boys?"

Don closes the portfolio, tells Sylvia he's looking to get a tattoo for his father. He unfolds the paper.

"This is what he wants. I don't know if you can do it or not. If it's too detailed or whatever."

Sylvia scrunches her face. "No, I can do this."

"Okay, cool," Don says. "Just that another place said they couldn't so that's why I said that."

"Is this your father's first tattoo?"

"Yes, it is." Don's voice goes up an octave and he drums a quick beat on the counter.

"When do you want to do it?" Sylvia asks, opening her planner.

Don grins. "Day after Christmas?"

Sylvia looks up. "I'm booked through February."

I turn toward the window and grin. Nearly an inch of fresh snow covers my car. A parade of plows and salt trucks roll by, their flashing yellow lights momentarily filling the tattoo parlor.

"February 3rd is my first available. It's a Wednesday."

"Oh, perfect," Don says. "He's off on Wednesdays."

"I'm supposed to start teaching in January," I say to Sylvia.

"What?" Don asks.

"That job I told you about."

Sylvia looks at me, then Don.

"Well, this is from both of us, dude," Don says.

Sylvia turns to me.

"I know that. But I'm saying if you want me there, it might have to wait a little while."

Sylvia turns to Don.

"I understand that. And I'm saying we should both be there." Don turns back to Sylvia. "Got anything the first week in March?"

Sylvia looks at her book. "I could do March 3rd, it's a Wednesday."

"Not sure I can take off that soon," I say.

Don sighs. "Okay, fuck it, February 3rd."

Sylvia looks back at me for the last time and writes in her book.

"Guess you'll just have to see it when it's done," Don says.

I nod and give Sylvia a tight-lipped smile, though I want to scream, stand up on the counter and look down at Don and tell him that Dad's waited sixty years to get a tattoo. What's another couple of months? But I can't slow him down. I'm used to Don moving away from my father. That's the role he established, the one he played so well. Lately, Don is trying to get close, and I don't know how to act.

Aren't I the one who lingers in the past, digs through old photographs and watches videos of our summer vacations? The Don I grew up with barreled through the present, drove headlong into the future, leaving the past coated in dust. Since my father's stroke, I've seen a different side of Don—a desire, desperate at times, to create something tangible, something he can point to as evidence, proof that he and my father existed.

We don't talk again until we step outside. The dog piss and shit at the side of the road is covered with a fresh layer of snow, and the foot holes that helped me cross have slowly begun to refill.

"All right," Don says. "She turned out to be pretty cool. Man, I shoulda scheduled this earlier."

I pretend I can't hear him over the trucks roaring by, but it doesn't seem to matter because he continues to talk about how there are still some nice people left in the world and it all depends on our attitudes as customers and if everyone could just relax and be patient with each other, the world would be a much calmer place.

I had recently left the temp agency. They offered me a "marketing position," which really meant handing out free newspapers on the corner. A friend of mine told me about a teaching position at a prison in Boston. As part of my graduate program, I had taught a few creative writing classes in a correctional facility, so I applied.

Today is casual Friday, which means I can wear a t-shirt and jeans. "Civilian" clothes, my students say. They wear the same uniforms as yesterday, unless they've changed units. Drug recovery is blue, kitchen is brown, re-entry is maroon. Green and beige do not have specific requirements, and guys who live in these units can sit in their cells all day watching TV. When I say I don't own a television, one of my students, Tito, looks at me.

"Get ya'self a Blu-Ray, man. Shit. They ain't gonna break ya' wallet."

I smile and shake my head. "It's not about the money, Tito. I just don't like it. It's a distraction."

Terrance, one of my larger students who used to frighten the hell out of me, speaks up.

"Man, I remember when I'd come home from a job. Kick off my boots, pour myself a tall glass of Wild Irish Rose, mix that shit up with some Hennessy, splash'a ginger ale–"

"That sounds awful, Terrance," I say. Tito laughs.

"What!" Terrance says, "You out ya mind, man. Let me finish my story. I mix the Wild Irish Rose with the Hennessey and the ginger ale, throw in a can of fruit cocktail, mix it all up and suck it down." He holds the drink to his lips and slurps.

"Shiiit. We all know where it's headed," Tito says. "You start pimpin' ya nasty-ass hoes, drinkin' that shit, passin' out to *The Jeffersons*."

The class erupts with laughter, even Terrance. Terrance is a big bald guy, mid-sixties, calluses and scars shaped like hands. On his first day in class, I asked him if he'd like some help with his reading. He looked at me, then picked up the excerpt from *One Flew Over the Cuckoo's Nest* on my desk.

"This the one with Jack Nicholson?"

"Yeah," I said. "Sort of."

"Either it is or it ain't."

"No, yeah. It is."

He held the paper as if weighing it in his hands. "All right, sign me up."

Terrance sits back in his seat, drumming his fingers on his book.

"Are we still talking about television, Terrance?"

"Yeah we are, if you let me finish. God damn. He musta got some last night, Tito. He's all feisty today. In his jeans and t-shirt."

"You and the ol' lady start the weekend early?" Tito asks.

"So I mix it all up, walk into my living room and take a seat in my nice leather chair. Flip on the tube and just relax. Now you tell me. You tell me what's so wrong with that?"

"Nothing, Terrance. Nothing at all."

"Well, then why don't you have a TV, man? Sometimes it's nice to zone out."

I shake my head. "I grew up in a house where the TV was always on. I go home now and it's still on. Dad comes home from work, watches TV. Mom comes home from work, watches TV. Is that living?"

The class is quiet for a rare second, but it doesn't last.

"They all lived out," Tito says. "Ya ol' man's tired. Ain't no thing."

"Hey, ain't we supposed to watch *Cuckoo's Nest*, today?" Terrance asks. "You been promisin' us a movie for months, man."

"I got it, I got it. And it hasn't been months, Terrance. It's been two weeks."

"Yeah, right. Sure feels like months."

I walk to the back of the room. The set is a TV/VCR combination, but there is a DVD player plugged in beside it. I feel old looking at this outdated equipment, like my parents must feel looking at a box of reel-to-reels. I pop in the DVD and press *Play*.

"1975," Terrance says. "The year this came out. Swept the Oscars, man. Took my girl to see it down at the Paramount. She was lookin' good, too."

I smile. "That's great, Terrance. Did she like it?"

"I don't remember and I don't give a shit. I liked it."

I skip through the coming attractions. "Well, as long as you enjoyed yourself. That's all that counts."

Terrance looks at Tito. "Finally, man. Finally he's making some sense."

"Rest yo' neck, killa. Movie's on."

I step back from the TV and take a seat next to Terrance, trying not to stare into the new camera in the corner of my classroom. The room must never be dark, so we watch the movie beneath fluorescent light, our faces glaring back at us on screen. Jack Nicholson walks into the dayroom in a leather jacket, jeans, and wool hat. He speaks to the giant Indian for the first time.

"Shiiit. Ain't he supposed to have red sideburns?" Tito asks, flipping through his book.

"You're right, Tito. In the book he does."

Tito shrugs and turns back to the screen and laughs as Jack Nicholson jokes with the patients. The Big Nurse begins the day's therapy session. Many of my students receive a steady dose of group therapy: AA, NA, Anger Management. Jack Nicholson and the patients sit in a semi-circle around the Big Nurse.

Terrance's belly laugh fills the room. "He look a bit like Ant, don't he, Tito?"

"Terrance, remember when we played the silent game?"

He looks at me. "Gettin' cute, now."

We return our attention to the movie, but my mind wanders. I remember how I used to bring in material I thought the students would relate to—hip-hop lyrics or articles on affordable housing and CORI reform. These lessons often drew blank stares. They had heard it all before. Listening is their full-time job: to officers, caseworkers, lawyers, teachers, guest speakers, parents, wives, girlfriends, children. I encourage them to talk.

Once, I was alone in the classroom with Terrance. He spoke more quietly than when he was around the other guys. I stared at his big, cracked hands as he gripped a pencil. We were reviewing long vowel sounds.

"After this bid, Ant, I'm gonna need a job."

"I thought you were retired."

"I am. But I still gotta earn." He asked me if I could show him how to fill out a job application. He also wanted to know what kind of words he should use in an interview. I pulled a blank application out of my filing cabinet and put it on the table. Terrance stared at it.

"Where do I start?"

I pointed to the blank line at the top of the page. "Start with your name."

"Well, who'd a'thunk it? Shy guy ends up teaching in the joint," my father says when I tell him I got the job. He wants to know if my students wear shackles in class or if any of them can make a knife out of a bar of soap. My mother asks if there are officers in the room with me at all times. I lie and say yes.

Some students are intimidating, guys who look the way movies tell you prisoners should look, like they spend all their time lifting weights and ticking time with chalk on their cell wall. But more often than not, the tough façade falls, and they pull me aside after class one day and whisper, "I can't read shit. You gotta help me."

Even now, after teaching there for three years, I'm still struck by how well-versed my students are in their different slangs, the languages they employ as pimps, drug dealers, arsonists, bank robbers. But when I call them up to the board for the first time, they don't say a word, their eyes locked on the blurry symbols inked into their hands.

The picture my brother took with his cell phone is small, but I can see my father's lips pressed tight, his eyes slightly closed. He wears a sleeveless shirt, tiny skeleton printed above his heart, as Sylvia, the tattoo artist, bends over his right shoulder. He leans against a black leather recliner, but I know that on the back of his shirt are two skeletons, one bending the other over a tombstone. The male skeleton wears a black bandana, the female a pink bikini. Above them, in white block letters: *The Boneyard*.

Sylvia holds the blurry silver needle, etching the eagle head into the tan skin of my father's shoulder. An hour later, Don sends another picture, a close-up of the eagle's eye and beak. An hour later, another picture, the feathers red, white and blue. The last picture arrives and the eagle is finished. Above and below the eagle are black letters and numbers that did not appear in the newspaper where my father first saw the eagle. The bottom characters arc in a smile, the top in a frown: *Vietnam / 1970–1971*.

In high school, Don gave himself a tattoo. He used a sewing needle and the ink from one of his sketch pens. A small star with a long, looping tail, just below his ankle bone. I glimpsed it in the mornings before school, as he shuffled to the bathroom like a zombie. If my parents noticed, I never heard them say anything.

A shooting star didn't seem to fit my brother's personality. A middle finger, sure. The cover of Pink Floyd's *The Wall* across his back, fine. But a shooting star?

It wasn't until years later that he told me the tattoo wasn't finished. He had plans to make a whole galaxy on his foot, turn the pale skin of his heel black with stars and comets and moons. He wanted it to curl up the side of his ankle, and his girlfriend at the time would get the same thing on her ankle, but it would be a little different, a few unique details since they were doing it freehand. I asked him why he didn't finish it. He shrugged. Perhaps it was too painful. Perhaps they ran out of ink. Perhaps the star got infected.

To me, the tattoo is a clue to my brother's secret life, the one set inside his smoky bedroom, in the woods behind the high school, within the four doors of his hydroplaning Volare. It hints at his unknown universe beyond our town, his life in San Francisco, a city that developed a mythic lore in my family. The shooting star is evidence of an unseen world, the dark landscape my brother moved through that my parents did not understand and of which I was too afraid.

Recently, I've gotten a better look at Don's tattoo, while we sit barefoot on the deck in the summer or rest our feet on the ottoman while we open Christmas presents. It's hard to tell which direction the star is shooting.

My father's tattoo was something he and Don could talk about. Don was knowledgeable on the subject and could speak at length about the healing process, which ointments were the best, which sunblocks to use.

"Whatever you do, man, don't pick the scab. Or you'll fuck it up."

My father sat on the couch with his elbows resting on his knees, leaning in to Don's advice. I sat on the opposite side of the room watching *Die Hard* with the sound off, the closed caption scrolling across the screen. I often did this with movies I knew by heart. Sometimes there were discrepancies between the spoken and printed dialogue, and each time I caught one of these errors, I felt I had righted a wrong.

"So when are we going back for your next one?" Don said, re-tying the laces on his sneakers.

I laughed. My father shrugged. Then he rolled up his sleeve.

"Always thought it'd be cool to have a tiger over here." He outlined the image on his arm. "Like on a tree branch. Have'm stalkin' a rabbit or some shit."

I imagined my father covered in animal tattoos, like an illustrated map of the Brooklyn Zoo. Each animal posed exactly the way he wanted. I pictured his forearm lined with the profiles of all the animals he preserved in the basement. A visual showcase of his work.

Don and I looked at each other. "Really?" Don asked.

"Yeah. Think that'd come out pretty good." I watched him draw the image again, circling the location of the unsuspecting rabbit. He stopped, and the white outline stood out on his tan skin, then quickly refilled with blood.

"What about matching tats?" Don asked.

My father looked up from his arm. "Matching to what?"

"You and me. What if we get matching tattoos?"

Bruce Willis was about to jump off the roof of Nakatomi Plaza with a fire hose wrapped around his waist, but at the last second, the movie cut to a commercial.

"I hate it when they do that shit," my father said.

Don finished tying his shoes, stood up and went to the kitchen. He came back with a beer and leaned in the doorway to the living room. He stood the way he had when I was supposed to interview him. A controlled, eager expression that made him look like a little boy.

"So, what do you think?" Don asked.

"'Bout what?"

Don sighed. "What do you mean 'about what?' About getting matching tattoos."

My father laughed. "Think I'll let this one heal first."

31

MY CELL PHONE lights up with my brother's name. I don't answer. He sends me a text.

Call me right now.

"What's up?" I ask.

"Dad had a heart attack."

I sigh and ask when. My body feels as if it's sliding off the chair, just like it did on the bus six years ago, but I am not surprised. Each Winston between my father's lips burned like a fuse.

Vanessa offers to come with me, but I tell her I want to go alone. I'm more angry than sad. Don and I had recently talked to my father about smoking, a sort of impromptu intervention that went surprisingly well. Don didn't cut me off and attack my father, and I was direct and didn't back down. I told him I knew about denial and escapism, how we conform our lives around seemingly essential habits. He thought I was talking about how I quit smoking. As I gave him my speech, I thought back five years ago, of Vanessa waiting tables while I sat in the bedroom of our first apartment, searching for another image.

I grab my iPod, an extra shirt, and as I squeeze my feet into my boots, I lift my keys off the hook. The silver dollar that I bought in Vietnam sits in an old ashtray by the door. I haven't mentioned it to my father yet because I always seem to be waiting for the perfect moment. I slip the coin into my shirt pocket.

It's almost midnight on a Wednesday, and the Massachusetts Turnpike is dark, nearly empty. How quickly the night can change: one minute I'm watching an episode of *Arrested Development*, the next I'm in a cold car a half hour out of town. My iPod plays Bruce

Springsteen's *Nebraska*, the album he released the year I was born. He recorded the songs on a four-track tape deck in his bedroom, alone. I let the full album play, something I haven't done for a long time.

Each lyric flows heavily through my body, settles in my right foot. Eighty. Ninety. A man dreams he is a child, walking to his father's house. Through the forest, trying to make it home before darkness falls. On the hill, his father's house shines like a beacon, ghostly voices rising from the fields. The path to the house is broken, unsteady, and the guitar is nearly silent. Just an echo of a voice—the boy running until the front door opens and he falls shaking into his father's arms. The man wakes from his dream, puts on his clothes and rushes out into the night. He walks the broken path to his father's house, but a strange woman answers and tells him no one by that name lives there.

Slow fade to a man standing over a dead dog on the side of the highway, poking it with a stick, as if the dog might get back up and run, but I don't see a dog, I see my father stopping on the way to work, scraping a raccoon off the pavement. Another droning guitar, but stronger, like an idling Mack truck. The quick harmonica like a head nodding; Bruce telling me we all have a "Reason to Believe." But as on every track, the guitar, the harmonica, the vocals fade, and by the time I drive past the turnpike's final exit and pull into a tollbooth, the car is quiet.

I hear what I want to hear. I extract lyrics—*father, mother, brother, son, quiet*—fish them like pyrite from a rushing river and sell them to myself as gold. All these stories, all these different perspectives talking to themselves, their questions answered only by their own echoes, their words unable to jump the track and speak to one another.

I'm not even out of Massachusetts before *Nebraska* restarts.

In neutral outside my brother's apartment in Brooklyn, I tap my horn. His kitchen light shuts off. He comes out the front door holding his iPod and an extra shirt.

"Damn, dude," he says. "You got here fast."

I smile. "When The Boss says drive, you drive."

He glances down at my iPod and sees the *Nebraska* album cover.

"Oh, nice," he says. "That's one of those albums you gotta listen to the whole way through."

Not long before my father had his heart attack, Don invited us all to view his paintings at a gallery in Brooklyn. "Art" is not a word my father uses often and when he does, it's usually laced with skepticism. My father walked closely behind Don and pointed at photographs of plain brick walls or canvases splattered with paint.

"That's art?" my father said. "Shit, I could do that."

I watched him walk with my brother around the gallery. My father wore a black and white flannel shirt tucked into jeans, his razor-sharp goatee splashed in Afta's Arctic Breeze. He had recently bleached his white Reebok sneakers, and they squeaked when he stopped in front of a painting, sometimes drawing stares from the tan, thin couples wrapped in leather or fur.

He paused in front of my brother's painting of a half-erect penis.

"Nice johnson."

Don looked over his shoulder and shook his head.

"What?" my father said. "That's what it is, ain't it?"

"Just look at it, dude. No comments."

My father laughed and turned to my mother. "Am I missing something here?"

She smiled and shrugged. "It's very...realistic."

"So what's it supposed to mean, Don?" my father asked.

"Nothing. I don't know. Whatever you want it to mean."

My father pressed his lips together and nodded. A woman holding a tray of hors d'oeuvres walked by.

"Hey, honey, what does this mean to you?"

"Oh, Christ," Don said and walked away.

My father laughed and popped a stuffed mushroom in his mouth.

"Art or no art. That's a dick."

As Don and I pull onto the Expressway, I start laughing.

"What?" he says, pausing my iPod.

"Nothing."

"No, what? What's so funny?"

"I was thinking about Dad at the art gallery. You know, when he saw your paintings."

Don shakes his head. "Like he'd never seen a dick before. Kept trying to figure out the hidden meaning." Don laughs. The car is quiet for a moment, except for the tires humming over the bridge. Then Don hits *Play*.

We walk into the same hospital where my father was treated for his stroke, his varicose veins. Same elevators, same corridor, same Cardiovascular Unit. A re-run.

We walk into my father's room and he's alone, sitting up in his bed, reading Cormac McCarthy's *No Country for Old Men*.

"Yo! What's shakin', fellas?" He goes to stand up, but tubes and wires keep him in his bed. "Shit."

"Easy, dude," I say. "I'll come to you." I walk around the rolling dinner tray, bend beneath the wires and stand up beside him. I don't so much hug him as press my body against his. Don does the same. As they try to hug, I stare at the book's bright red cover.

"Don't be eyeballin' my readin' material, boy."

"No, no, I'm not. That's a great book," I say.

"Just like the movie," he says, nodding. "Mom got me a few of 'em." He points to the stack of books on a chair beside his bed: *The Five People You Meet in Heaven, Feelin' Lucky: The Life and Times of Clint Eastwood*, and a thick colorful book titled, simply, *Trucks*.

"Those should keep you busy," Don says.

My father nods. "Don't know how long she thinks I'm gonna be here. Plannin' on rollin' out in a day or two."

"What's the rush?" Don asks.

My father looks at him. Me. Then pans the room, the skin around his eyes delicate without his glasses. "I ain't staying here a second too long."

The door swings open and my mother walks quickly into the room, holding a paper bag and a tray of 7-Eleven coffees, a dark stain in the bag's corner. She kisses us and leans over to kiss my father. Before she takes off her coat, she mixes my father's coffee and places the steaming cup on the tray in front of him. He sips. She places two scratch-off tickets beside his cup.

"Now you're talkin'," he says, digging through the pockets of his jeans, which hang in a clear plastic bag beside his bed with the rest of his clothes.

"When did you boys get here?"

"Couple minutes ago," I say. My eyes fall again on the book's red cover.

My mother smiles. "I know; I was shocked, too. Guess it just took a heart attack to pull him away from the television."

My father takes another sip of his coffee. He stops scratching his ticket and looks up at my mother. "It's good. Just like the movie."

I look at the silver dollar in his hand. "Oh, dude, check this out." I reach into my shirt pocket and pull out the silver dollar. "Found this in Hanoi. Crazy, huh? Same year."

My father presses his lips together and nods. "No shit?" He takes the coin from me and flips it over. He holds it up against his coin. "Is it real?"

"I hope so," I say. "It cost four bucks."

He shakes his head. "Shit never changes."

"But I did do some research on it. They didn't release the Eisenhower dollar until the middle of '71, so there's no way you could have had it with you before you left."

He bites his lip. "Hmm." I don't know why I tell him that. Maybe the wires and tubes and beeping machines make me want to talk about something else. Or perhaps I want the coin to mean more than it does, to give some new value to my father, to me, to our story. But what I said doesn't seem to throw him off or make him question his version of the truth. He shrugs and takes a sip of coffee. He looks up at me, grinning.

"Guess you better delete chapter one, boy."

"You need to know this," my mother tells my father as they lean over bills and paystubs and direct deposit forms scattered on the dining room table. He nods, sucks his cheek between his teeth. She pushes aside coasters shaped like Rudolph so she has room to write—a lefty in a house of righties. She's always written in that lefty manner, as if she were trying to twist her left hand into a right. At the dinner table, she sat at the end so she could use her fork without disturbing me or my father or my brother. We kept her spot open until she placed the food on the table and took her seat. Robert De Niro shouts, *I'm not an animal!* in the empty living room. My mother forges my father's signature as he jumps up and trots toward the television with a grin on his face, passing my brother and me in the kitchen.

"Great fuckin' part, guys."

My brother follows my father into the living room. I go to the kitchen to get more iced tea. I hear De Niro bash his head against a stone wall over and over and over, grunting and snarling like a trapped dog. "I'll do it myself," my mother says, sighing. "But you need to know this." She stacks my father's paystubs, gathering crinkled receipts into a pile. If she still smoked in the house instead of sneaking them in the bathroom or on the ride to work, she'd drop her match into the pile, let it burn and see if anyone could interpret her signals. Leaning over the flaming receipts, she'd toss in my father's paystubs, glance at the file cabinet, and decide simply to breathe. Deep inhalations, soft whispers. Her words turn to ash.

Sometimes I feel like I'm the only one who hears her off-camera comments. Under-her-breath, out-of-earshot. It's possible, with my father's hearing getting worse each year, evident by the television's volume creeping louder and louder each time I visit. But my father can also name the brand of exhaust system on a '68 Camaro cruising up the block or tell you who originally wrote George Thorogood's "Move It On Over," even though the song played at a barely audible volume on the garage radio and all of Thorogood's songs sound the same. Selective hearing.

Perhaps he chooses not to hear my mother's side comment, opts instead to watch De Niro bash his head into a wall. After the scene is over, he chuckles, walks past my mother in the dining room, through the kitchen, grabs a bag of peanuts and returns to the living room. As he crashes down beside me and my brother, he mutters, "I don't need to know shit."

"I guess I'll show *you*," my mother says to me later that evening. My father and brother are still in the living room, flipping through channels.

She pulls out her address book, the one covered with baby-blue perennials, from beneath the phone. "They're all in here," she says.

Flipping each page with a licked index finger, she passes by the numbers and addresses of relatives. *K* is a long section, her maiden name *Kall*, or *Call* as the telemarketers sometimes say.

"I can't blame him," she says to herself. "I can't. I never let him do anything on his own."

She passes Vanessa and my address in Boston, my brother's in Brooklyn. Any changes have been updated in pencil.

"Here," she says, pointing to a list of usernames and passwords.

"What's all this?" I ask. "Do you want tea?"

"Yes, milk, no—"

"No sugar."

They drew first blood. Not me.

"What are they watching?" my mother asks.

"*Rambo.*"

She shakes her head. "Haven't seen that one enough."

I don't say anything because I am completing the dialogue in my head. I love this part, when Stallone unsheathes his giant knife and presses the blade against his cheek. My father and brother laugh and I can see their expressions; their faces paused in my mind.

"These are all the passwords to the online accounts. They're all here. Chase. The mortgage, the oil company, my 401K, which I believe is this one here. Yes. Fidelity."

She stirs her tea.

"Because someday somebody's gonna need to know all this stuff."

I nod and sip even though I know I'll burn my tongue.

"Ow," I say, breathing in sharply.

"Oh, honey. Careful. You have to let it cool first."

The doctors told my father to refrain from physical activity. A few weeks later, I come home and see him mowing the lawn, a cigar cupped behind his back.

That night, I set my digital recorder on the table beside him.

"Would you mind reading the letter?"

He nods and grabs the crinkled yellow paper from my hand. Before he begins, he stuffs three small chocolate chip cookies in his mouth.

"*Dear Kathy,*" he mumbles.

"Wait. Hold on." I reposition the recorder. "Okay, go."

"*Dear Kathy,*"

"*Hey, baby, how's my little girl? I got two letters from you recently and figured it was about time I got my backfield in motion and wrote you one. So . . . the hell that say? I'm big daddy over here?*"

We start laughing.

"*Well, I guess that makes you my little momma. Gotta work out that way. It sounds like Ernie and Patty really got their shit together. I hope he just stays stateside long enough for Patty to have the baby. I had a buddy over here who had kids while they were...* wait a minute...*I had two buddies...*Jesus Christ, I can't read my own fuckin' writin'...*who had kids while they were away. They really happy but not the same if they were there wit' the old lady. Can you dig that?*"

We laugh.

"*Wow, mommy, you comin' on pretty heavy with the mush-mush rap.* Man, are you taping this?"

"Aw, yeah, brotha."

"Jesus. All right. *Let's not get rational now and go spoiling it by telling Maddy. You gonna have to control yo' emotions 'til I get home. I got a hundred twenty five days to go. I hope you can't wait, but try. If my mustache tickles, I'll shave it off.*"

I'm laughing, but he doesn't stop reading.

"*I think I'll keep it though, as I'm so used to it. I heard it through the vine that The Carrot got his walkin' papers.*"

"Wait, who's The Carrot?"

"Oh, that must be Red."

"Who's Red?"

"Yeah, that's right. Kevin joined the Air Force and got thrown out."

I stop asking who he's talking about, though I'm insatiably curious about these mysterious people. Maddy and The Carrot—they sounded like characters in a comic strip.

"*What a bummer. He'll regret it later. 'Specially that GI loan. I'm takin' every penny I can squeeze outta Uncle Sam's asshole. I'd like to get a promotion, for the bread, not the rank. I might go before the Spec Board this month. I was scratched off last month 'cause I didn't have enough time in grade as Spec 4. A General? You gotta be kiddin' me. I'm only gonna be in the Army for 19 months not 19 years.*"

The letter rustles in his fingertips as he flips it over.

"*I asked my buddies about the class that Bob runs his 'Vette in and they never heard of it. Guess it's a new class. Can you get me a little more info on it? Is it the same as B-gas or B-modified or what? We're really in—*"

"Yeah, what's that all about?"

"Well, your Uncle Bob, you never met him, but he used to race his Corvette at the race track. So, uh, let's see. Where was I?"

"Oh, so you were asking what class he was racing in?"

"Right."

"You're right, I didn't know who you meant when you said 'sexy handsome guys in the pictures.' I . . . ah, I can't read that shit. *The closing of your letter cracked me up. It said, and I quote 'well, I guess I'll be going now before I fall asleep on you.' I dig that! If youse was ever that close you wouldn't be sleepin', I guarantee it! I better cut that out. I'm gettin' outta control."*

"Rainy season is startin' now. Everyday at 3:25 it starts to rain. Rains so heavy you couldn't see from your front window to the fence around your house. I'm gonna try to get a few pictures of it and send 'em to ya."

"Well, babe, I'm just about outta shit to talk about. Nothing much happenin'. Same old shit day after day. Take good care and I'll see you real soon. Bye for now. Love, Donny."

The letter crinkles in his hands as he passes it back to me.

"Well, that's that."

"Nah, that was good."

"Old letter, boy," he says, still working a cookie out from his back teeth.

Later that evening, I play the recording for my mother and Don. I mute the television and place the recorder on the coffee table. Even at maximum volume, the recording is faint. We lean in close to listen. Don laughs at the part about Dad's mustache. My mother blushes. As I watch her turn her head and listen, I wonder what happened to her letter. Perhaps it was lost when my father returned from Vietnam, or maybe the monsoon soaked the pages, turning her words to water.

"I can't believe he read that to you," Don says.

"I can't believe he wrote that," my mother says. "I had forgotten all about it."

32

THE YEAR AFTER his heart attack, a couple of weeks before Halloween, I get a call from my father. There's a noise in the background, as if while he is mowing the lawn or cleaning the pool filter, the telephone suddenly appears in his free hand and I'm on the other end.

"Yo, boy. What's shakin'?"

"Not much. What are you doing?"

"Just putzin' around the garage. Didn't wake ya, did I?"

I laugh. "Nah, dude. I get up early now."

"That so?"

"I'm almost thirty, man. A real, live adult."

"'Scuse me."

"What's up?"

"The Moving Wall's coming to Northport. To the VA."

A pause.

"Ain't you supposed to be readin' up on this shit?" he asks. "The Moving Wall, boy. You know the one in DC, right?"

"Sure."

"Same thing. Just smaller."

"And moving."

"Yeah. Moving. Anyways, it's comin' to Northport for the first time. Big shindig. They're gonna get this Billy Joel cover band to do "Goodnight Saigon." Me and a buddy are gonna work the grounds."

I wonder if he's talking about Haggemeyer. But he would have said "Hag," not "buddy." Did my father make a new friend?

"So, I was thinkin' youse could come down."

This is the first time my father has ever invited me to anything. We did plenty of stuff together, but I can't remember him asking me flat out to spend time with him. Sometimes my brother would ask me how Dad and I hung out so much—at car shows or camping trips or fishing on Hag's boat. "He never asked me," Don would say. I'd shrug. He didn't ask me either. I just went.

"Bring Van Halen, too," my father said. "She'll like it. Donny's bringing L-O-L-A."

Vanessa lies next to me in bed. I point at the phone and mouth the word "Dad." She nods and smiles. "Sure," I say. "I'll tell her."

When I get home, my father's in the garage blasting "Roll Me Away" by Bob Seger and sewing brand-new patches onto his Army jacket. On the back of the jacket is a giant peace sign. Within the sign are the dates of his tour. I stand in the doorway, staring at his gleaming Chevy. He taps his foot to the music. I watch him work a needle and thread through the camouflage material. After a few stitches, he stops and holds the jacket up to the light.

"Lookin' sharp," I say.

He whips his head around, wide-eyed. "Damn, boy. Don't be sneakin' up on me."

"Sorry." I glance down at the patches. "Where'd you get all these?"

"Mom dug 'em up on the Web," he says, grinning and shaking his head. "Can't believe she found all this stuff."

I don't know what all these symbols and insignias mean, but a couple of the patches are printed in the same thick, bold lettering used on the hats and pins Vietnamese children sold outside the bars in Saigon. My father's patches shout phrases like "VIETNAM VET AND DAMN PROUD OF IT!" and "ONCE STRANGERS, FOREVER BROTHERS."

"What time does this shindig start?" I ask.

"Well, you guys don't have to be there until later. I gotta boogie early and start settin' up."

I smile. It feels strange, but good, to hear my father talk about work that doesn't involve bologna or gasoline. He's on the verge of retiring, which for him means "career change." I've never seen him as excited as he is when he talks about trading in his bloody deli apron and becoming a school bus driver or working in the kitchen at the VA. It's as if something has held him back all these years, some invisible barrier between his life and his desire, something other than the deli or bills standing in his way.

Perhaps I am assuming too much, shoehorning my father's words into restrictive definitions. But lately, he uses the phrase *I've earned it*. I'm not sure what "it" is or what exactly he had to do to achieve "it," but wherever "it" is, he's glad to be there.

The Fox switches from Seger to Otis Redding's "(Sittin' On) The Dock of the Bay."

"Yeah, boy," my father says. "You know they released this tune after Redding kicked the bucket?" He turns up the volume, whistling, and continues sewing his patches. I step out of the garage, and he doesn't look up when I leave.

"Fuck me. Pull over," Don says after I pick him up from the train station. He and Lola are in the back. Vanessa sits in the passenger seat. I pull into the parking lot of CVS.

"I told you to get them before we left," Don says to Lola.

She shrugs and uses her fingernail to dig the dead batteries out of her hearing aids.

"Every time," he says. "Seriously. Every time we're home."

I can't tell if he's still talking to Lola or if I should respond. Lola gets out of the car.

"So Dad's really into this, huh?" I say.

"Big time. Did he tell you what happened with the tattoo?"

"What?"

"He goes to the heart doctor and the nurse sees it. She says, 'Oh, you were in Vietnam?' and he says, 'Yeah.' So she tells him that the

VA is doing a study on the link between Agent Orange and heart disease. All he's gotta do is sign up and he gets *beaucoup* bennies."

"Wow," I say. "That's amazing."

My brother nods. "Told ya the tattoo was a good idea."

While everyone else is getting ready to go to the VA, I snoop around the garage. Hammers and hacksaws hang perfectly straight. Screwdrivers holstered in my father's leather tool belt. I sit down on the stool, a scene of vintage cars at a hamburger stand printed on the black vinyl. The edge of the workbench is just below my knees. There are a few new tools on the wall in front of me that I've never seen before. They hang beside the old ones. The vice screwed into the workbench is the same one I used to crush the insides of the trash I took apart when I was little, the pieces that couldn't be broken down any further. My father had recently given the vice a fresh coat of paint. In its teeth, I see bits of rusty metal and old plastic.

I lean over and stare at the workbench. I see the faint outlines of *shit* and *kisser*, can almost make out the word *ass* or *mother*. I'm tempted to pick up the pen stuck into an old piston head at the back of the workbench and finish each word, but I don't. I suppose I had more guts when I was ten, when I didn't edit my language and wrote in plain sight.

The Fox kicks on and the fluorescent light flickers above me. I turn around and Don is standing in the doorway, his hand still on the switch.

"Ready?"

We pull into the VA parking lot, next to a long row of Harleys decked out with frilled leather saddlebags and tall radio antennas. American flags and Vietnam Veteran stickers cover nearly every inch of metal. There are a few classic cars in the parking lot—a couple of Novas, a Chevelle—as well as aisle after aisle of beat-up Hondas and Toyotas from New York, Connecticut, Massachusetts, a few from

Maine and DC I see my father's Chevy, a brand-new American flag spread out on the dash.

Don and Lola are in the backseat. Vanessa and I get out of the car, hoping they'll follow. Through the window, I see their lips move, but I can't hear what they're saying. My brother holds up the package of tiny batteries, squinting at the small print. He takes Lola's hearing aid and opens the back. Once he snaps the battery into place, Don holds back her hair and gently places the little beige device into her ear.

"All right," Don says, stepping out of the car. "Locked and loaded."

Vanessa and Don walk ahead of me and Lola. Lola's camera hangs from her neck and, as we make our way across the parking lot, she snaps pictures of the cars, then shoots a couple of bikers leaning against a short stone wall sipping 7-Eleven coffees.

The crowd reminds me of the guys at the swap meets my father and I used to go to: packs of denim and leather and black sunglasses. Lola takes another picture, then looks at me.

"There's like thousands of your Dad here."

"I know, right? He's everywhere."

"Oh, I wanted to tell you," Lola says, making sure Don and Vanessa are far ahead of us. "I got your Dad and Don flying lessons for Christmas. Think they'll like that?"

"That sounds awesome," I say.

She smiles. "Yeah, I thought it'd be cool. They'll fly over the whole island."

Some kids holding small American flags run across the parking lot and Lola quickly snaps a few more pictures. I imagine Don and my father in the cockpit of a small airplane, their wake scarring the sky. They climb above the clouds, above the weather, keeping an eye on their speed, their altitude. I think of the miles my father and I traveled to and from car shows in the Dodge. My father and Don need to move faster. They have more ground to cover.

"Yo! What up!" My father shouts from across the parking lot. He looks like the human incarnation of Peter Fonda's motorcycle in *Easy Rider*. His American flag bandana is wrapped so tight it looks like his bald head is painted red, white and blue. His keys jingle on his hip as he walks over. His sunglasses' silver frames gleam in the sun. Did he polish them?

He struts across the grass the same way he did at my wedding: chest puffed, arms swinging, big grin on his face. He nods at a couple of guys holding cardboard boxes. "Set it down right there, fellas." He turns and gives me a strong hug and a slap on the back. He gives my brother the same hug. Then he holds Vanessa and Lola by the wrist and gives them each a kiss.

"Good to see ya, ladies. Some rough-lookin' broads 'round here. God damn."

"Where's Mom?" I ask.

"She's down by the tent, holding seats. You guys ain't gonna believe this fuckin' thing. It's so cool. Wait'll you see it."

He turns and starts walking quickly. We all look at each other, then follow him. Lola takes a few pictures. We almost lose him in a crowd of camouflage and denim, but once we make our way through, we see him on the other side, standing in front of the long black wall.

"Check it out!"

The wall is much bigger than I expected. My father and the other volunteers constructed the long ramp that runs the length of the wall, where visitors walk and search for names. The ground in front is covered with fresh mulch and newly-planted flowers and trees. In the middle of a small pond is a flagpole waving several flags: American, POW/MIA, and a third one I don't recognize, but can make out the words flapping in the breeze—*The Moving Dignity Wall*.

"Man," I say to my father. "That looks great."

"Right? Like it's always been there. You wouldn't think lookin' at it that it all came in pieces."

I want to walk over and get a closer look, but my mother is waving to us beside the big white tent. Men in uniform march up to the stage and take their seats beside the podium. A tall, broad man who appears to be in his early sixties walks like a statue up to the microphone. Short strands of yellow, braided rope hang from his shoulders; the white brim of his dark-blue hat rests low on his forehead. His chest is covered in medals that look like miniature versions of the tools hanging on my father's garage wall. He clinks as he walks. We take our seats next to my mother. She smiles and rubs my back as the man on stage waits for the audience's full attention.

My father leans over and juts his chin at the stage. "The big kahuna."

"Good evening!" The man's voice blasts through the tent. "I want to welcome all of you here tonight!" His voice is so loud I can feel it in my lungs. I look at Don; he winces at each word. Lola rubs her ear. My mother and Vanessa adjust themselves in their seats. I glance over at my father. He sits up straight, clapping.

The man tells us that the Vietnam War was the first televised war, and because of that, many people have misconceptions about what really happened. He talks about the media's skewed representation of our troops and what they were trying to accomplish. He asks us to recall a photograph: a naked Vietnamese girl standing in the middle of a napalmed street, her face a silent scream. The man describes how this image spread across magazines and the evening news like wild fire. It became an iconic photograph, illustrating the brutal and savage force America used in Vietnam.

"But what many people do not realize," the man shouts, "is that the destruction caused in this photograph was not done by American forces! This is actually a photograph of a South Vietnamese napalm attack!"

My father leans back in his seat and nods. I feel the word "attack" vibrating between my ears. I know the image he's talking about. I know that the little girl is screaming, *nong qua, nong qua:* "too hot, too hot." I know that the photograph was taken a year after my father returned from Vietnam and now the little girl, Kim Phuc, is a middle-aged woman and motivational speaker. The man on stage isn't talking about the present, but rather telling us whom to blame for the past.

After the opening ceremony, we walk back to the wall.

"Something else, huh?" my mother says.

"Sure is," I say.

"Dad's been talking about this for months. I've never seen him so excited."

My father stands at the entrance to the ramp and waves us over. He leads us down the long black marble. Don and Lola stop and stare at one section of the wall.

"Even got eight women on here, Vanessa," my father says. "Amazing."

Vanessa smiles. "Recognize any of them?"

My father looks at me and grins. "I think your main squeeze is gettin' fresh, boy."

He turns and puts his arm around my mother, stretching the peace symbol on his back. She rests her head on his shoulder. They walk down the wall alone. I watch my father point out names to my mother. She nods and looks up at him, as he tells her a story I can't hear. Vanessa takes my hand. We turn to face the wall, and see our reflections behind the wide list of names.

Acknowledgments

My editor, Bill Patrick, took me under his wing, and then knew when to push me out of the nest. Bill, my man, I didn't think anyone else could care about this book as much as I could, but you proved me wrong. Thanks to Sue Petrie for her care and patience. Thank you to the entire editorial team at Hudson Whitman for their insightful critique of this book in its early stages.

Thank you to my mentors at Stonecoast—David Mura, Joan Connor, Leila Philip, and Baron Wormser. Thank you to Suzanne Strempek Shea for her enthusiasm and encouragement. I'm grateful for Richard Hoffman's wisdom and support. Without him, this book would still be a Word document. Richard, I can't thank you enough for everything you've done for me these past nine years.

Thank you, thank you, thank you to Adrienne, Beth, Gina, Kayni, Meghan, and Michelle for reading draft after draft, offering helpful feedback, and for listening to me babble about Vietnam and Bruce Springsteen. You are my dear friends and I am extremely lucky to have you in my life. Thanks to Bunny Goodjohn and the English Department at Randolph College for being such remarkable hosts. Thanks to Michael Steinberg for our long chats about writing. Thank you to Dottie Dunford and all the teachers at SCHOC. Shout out to my Lit. 1 students from around the way.

I'd like to thank my family for their love and support, even when I ventured into, as my father said, "no man's land." Don, thanks for teaching me how to drive, when to yield and when to floor it. Mom, thank you for talking to me in your garden, for sharing a place where life comes back year after year. Thank you, Dad, for inspiring me to write. You taught me how to preserve the past. You encouraged me to stand tall. Can I take my seat now?

Vanessa, my love, without you this book would have a much darker ending. Thank you for reminding me that it's always daytime somewhere in the world. Thank you for understanding why I needed to write about us. My story is our story and will shape our children's stories. Thank you for sticking with me as I figured out what kind of man I wanted to be.

ANTHONY D'ARIES received the 2010 PEN/New England Discovery Award in Nonfiction. He is a graduate of the Stonecoast MFA program and currently teaches literacy and creative writing in correctional facilities in Massachusetts.

Anthony's website:
anthonydaries.com

About Hudson Whitman

Hudson Whitman is a new, small press affiliated with Excelsior College in upstate New York.

Our tagline is "Books That Make a Difference" and we aim to publish high quality nonfiction books and multi-media projects in areas that complement Excelsior's academic strengths: education, nursing, health care, military interests, business & technology, with one "open" category, American culture & society.

If you would like to submit a manuscript or proposal, please review the guidelines on our website, hudsonwhitman.com. Feel free to send a note with any questions. We endeavor to respond as soon as possible.

OTHER TITLES BY HUDSON WHITMAN

Courageous Learning:
Finding a New Path through Higher Education
John Ebersole and William Patrick (print and e-book)

Saving Troy:
A Year with Firefighters and Paramedics in a Battered City
William Patrick (e-book only)

CPSIA information can be obtained at www.ICGtesting.com
Printed in the USA
BVOW031734301012

304257BV00003B/7/P